Python GUI Programming Cookbook

Second Edition

Use recipes to develop responsive and powerful
GUIs using Tkinter

Burkhard A. Meier

BIRMINGHAM - MUMBAI

Python GUI Programming Cookbook

Second Edition

First published: November 2015

Second edition: May 2017

Production reference: 1190517

Published by Packt Publishing Ltd.
Livery Place
35 Livery Street
Birmingham
B3 2PB, UK.
ISBN 978-1-78712-945-0

www.packtpub.com

Credits

Author
Burkhard A. Meier

Reviewer
Mohit

Commissioning Editor
Kunal Parikh

Acquisition Editor
Denim Pinto

Content Development Editor
Anurag Ghogre

Technical Editor
Prashant Mishra

Copy Editor
Muktikant Garimella

Project Coordinator
Ulhas Kambali

Proofreader
Safis Editing

Indexer
Aishwarya Gangawane

Graphics
Abhinash Sahu

Production Coordinator
Nilesh Mohite

About the Author

Burkhard A. Meier has more than 17 years of professional experience working in the software industry as a software tester and developer, specializing in software test automation development, execution, and analysis. He has a very strong background in Python 3 software test automation development, as well as in SQL relational database administration, the development of stored procedures, and debugging code.

While experienced in Visual Studio .NET C#, Visual Test, TestComplete, and other testing languages (such as C/C++), the main focus of the author over the past five years has been developing test automation written in Python 3 to test the leading edge of FLIR ONE (now in its third generation) infrared cameras for iPhone and Android smart phones and handheld tablets, as well as assuring the quality of FLIR bolometer IR camera platforms.

Being highly appreciative of art, beauty, and programming, the author developed GUIs in C# and Python to streamline everyday test automation tasks, enabling these automated tests to run unattended for weeks, collecting very useful data to be analyzed, automatically plotted in graphs, and e-mailed to upper management upon completion of nightly automated test runs.

His previous jobs include working as a senior test automation engineer and designer for InfoGenesis (now Agilysys), QAD, InTouch Health, and FLIR Systems.

You can get in touch with him through his LinkedIn account, `https://www.linkedin.com/pub/burkhard-meier/5/246/296`.

I would like to thank all truly great artists, such as Leonardo da Vinci, Charles Baudelaire, Edgar Allan Poe, and so many more for bringing the presence of beauty into our human lives. This book is about creating very beautiful GUIs written in the Python programming language, and it was inspired by these truly great artists.
I would like to thank all of the great people that made this book possible. Without any of you, this book would only exist in my mind. I would like to especially thank all of my editors at Packt Publishing: Sonali, Anurag, Prashant, Vivek, Arwa, Sumeet, Saurabh, Pramod, Nikhil, and so many more. I would also like to thank all of the reviewers of the code of this book. Without them, this book would be harder to read and apply to real-world problems. Last but not least, I'd like to thank my wife, our daughter, and our parents for the emotional support they provided so successfully during the writing of the second edition of this book. I'd also like to give thanks to the creator of the very beautiful and powerful programming language that Python truly is. Thank you Guido.

About the Reviewer

Mohit (mohitraj.cs@gmail.com) is a Python programmer with a keen interest in the field of information security. He completed his bachelor's in technology in computer science from Kurukshetra University, Kurukshetra, and master's in engineering (2012) in computer science from Thapar University, Patiala. He is a C I EH, ECSA from EC-Council USA and former IBMer. He has published several articles in national and international magazines. He is the author of Python Penetration Testing Essentials and Python Penetration Testing for Developers, also by Packt Publishing.

www.PacktPub.com

For support files and downloads related to your book, please visit `www.PacktPub.com`.

Did you know that Packt offers eBook versions of every book published, with PDF and ePub files available? You can upgrade to the eBook version at `www.PacktPub.com` and as a print book customer, you are entitled to a discount on the eBook copy. Get in touch with us at `service@packtpub.com` for more details.

At `www.PacktPub.com`, you can also read a collection of free technical articles, sign up for a range of free newsletters and receive exclusive discounts and offers on Packt books and eBooks.

`https://www.packtpub.com/mapt`

Get the most in-demand software skills with Mapt. Mapt gives you full access to all Packt books and video courses, as well as industry-leading tools to help you plan your personal development and advance your career.

Why subscribe?

- Fully searchable across every book published by Packt
- Copy and paste, print, and bookmark content
- On demand and accessible via a web browser

Customer Feedback

Thanks for purchasing this Packt book. At Packt, quality is at the heart of our editorial process. To help us improve, please leave us an honest review on this book's Amazon page at https://www.amazon.com/dp/1787129454.

If you'd like to join our team of regular reviewers, you can e-mail us at customerreviews@packtpub.com. We award our regular reviewers with free eBooks and videos in exchange for their valuable feedback. Help us be relentless in improving our products!

Table of Contents

Preface

In the second edition of this book, we will explore the beautiful world of graphical user interfaces (GUIs) using the Python programming language. We will be using the latest version of Python 3. All of the recipes from the First Edition are included in this edition. We have added a few new recipes to the Second Edition, which you might not easily find via a Google search. I think these new recipes will be useful and interesting to the reader.

This is a programming cookbook. Every chapter is self-contained and explains a certain programming solution. We will start very simply, yet throughout this book we will build a working application written in Python 3. Each recipe will extend building this application. Along the way, we will talk to networks, queues, databases, the OpenGL graphical library, and many more technologies. We will apply design patterns and use best practices.

The book assumes that the reader has some experience using the Python programming language, but that is not really required to successfully use this book. This book can also be used as an introduction to the Python programming language, if, and only if, you are dedicated in your desire to become a Pythonic programmer.

If you are an experienced developer in any other language, you will have a fun time extending your professional toolbox by adding writing GUIs using Python to your toolbox. Are you ready?

Let's start on our journey…

What this book covers

Chapter 1, *Creating the GUI Form and Adding Widgets*, explains how to develop our first GUI in Python. We will start with the minimum code required to build a running GUI application. Each recipe then adds different widgets to the GUI form.

Chapter 2, *Layout Management*, explores how to arrange widgets to create our Python GUI. The grid layout manager is one of the most important layout tools built into tkinter that we will be using.

Chapter 3, *Look and Feel Customization*, shows several examples of how to create a good look and feel GUI. On a practical level, we will add functionality to the Help | About menu item we created in one of the recipes.

Chapter 4, *Data and Classes*, discusses saving the data our GUI displays. We will start using object-oriented programming (OOP) in order to extend Python's built-in functionality.

Chapter 5, *Matplotlib Charts*, explains how to create beautiful charts that visually represent data. Depending upon the format of the data source, we can plot one or several columns of data within the same chart.

Chapter 6, *Threads and Networking*, explains how to extend the functionality of our Python GUI using threads, queues, and network connections. This will show us that our GUI is not limited at all to the local scope of our PC.

Chapter 7, *Storing Data in Our MySQL Database via Our GUI*, shows us how to connect to a MySQL database server. The first recipe in this chapter will show how to install the free MySQL Server Community Edition, and in the following recipes we will create databases, tables, and then load data into those tables as well as modify these data. We will also read the data back out from the MySQL server into our GUI.

Chapter 8, *Internationalization and Testing*, shows how to internationalize our GUI by displaying text on labels, buttons, tabs, and other widgets in different languages. We will start simple and then explore how we can prepare our GUI for internationalization at the design level. We will also explore several ways to automatically test our GUI using Python's built-in unit testing framework.

Chapter 9, *Extending Our GUI with the wxPython Library*, introduces another Python GUI toolkit that currently does not ship with Python. It is called wxPython, and we will be using the Phoenix version of wxPython, which was designed to work well with Python 3.

Chapter 10, *Creating Amazing 3D GUIs with PyOpenGL and PyGLet*, shows how to transform our GUI by giving it true three-dimensional capabilities. We will use two Python third-party packages. PyOpenGL is a Python binding to the OpenGL standard, which is a graphics library that comes built-in with all major operating systems. This gives the resulting widgets a native look and feel. PyGLet is another such binding that we will explore in this chapter. We will also show some code that directly uses the PyOpenGL library. This is a low-level approach that might open some doors for the interested reader.

Chapter 11, *Best Practices*, explores different best practices that can help us to build our GUI in an efficient way and keep it both maintainable and extendible. Best practices are applicable to any good code, and our GUI is no exception to designing and implementing good software practices.

What you need for this book

All required software for this book is available online and is free of charge. This starts with Python 3 itself, and then extends to Python's add-on modules. In order to download any required software, you will need a working Internet connection.

Who this book is for

This book is for programmers who wish to create a GUI. You might be surprised by what we can achieve by creating beautiful, functional, and powerful GUIs using the Python programming language. Python is a wonderful, intuitive programming language, and is very easy to learn.

I invite you to start on this journey now. It will be a lot of fun!

Conventions

In this book, you will find a number of styles of text that distinguish between different kinds of information. Here are some examples of these styles, and an explanation of their meaning.

Code words in text, database table names, folder names, filenames, file extensions, pathnames, and user input are shown as follows: "Using Python, we can create our own classes using the `class` keyword instead of the `def` keyword."

A block of code is set as follows:

```
import tkinter as tk
win = tk.Tk()
win.title("Python GUI")
win.mainloop()
```

Any command-line input or output is written as follows:

```
pip install numpy-1.9.2+mkl-cp36-none-win_amd64.whl
```

New terms and important words are shown in bold. Words that you see on the screen, in menus or dialog boxes for example, appear in the text like this: "Next, we will add functionality to the menu items, for example, closing the main window by clicking the **Exit** menu item and displaying a **Help | About** dialog."

Warnings or important notes appear in a box like this.

 Tips and tricks appear like this.

Reader feedback

Feedback from our readers is always welcome. Let us know what you think about this book-what you liked or disliked. Reader feedback is important for us as it helps us develop titles that you will really get the most out of.

To send us general feedback, simply e-mail feedback@packtpub.com, and mention the book's title in the subject of your message.

If there is a topic that you have expertise in and you are interested in either writing or contributing to a book, see our author guide at www.packtpub.com/authors.

Customer support

Now that you are the proud owner of a Packt book, we have a number of things to help you to get the most from your purchase.

Downloading the example code

You can download the example code files for this book from your account at http://www.packtpub.com. If you purchased this book elsewhere, you can visit http://www.packtpub.com/support and register to have the files e-mailed directly to you.

You can download the code files by following these steps:

1. Log in or register to our website using your e-mail address and password.
2. Hover the mouse pointer on the **SUPPORT** tab at the top.
3. Click on **Code Downloads & Errata**.
4. Enter the name of the book in the **Search** box.
5. Select the book for which you're looking to download the code files.

6. Choose from the drop-down menu where you purchased this book from.
7. Click on **Code Download**.

Once the file is downloaded, please make sure that you unzip or extract the folder using the latest version of:

- WinRAR / 7-Zip for Windows
- Zipeg / iZip / UnRarX for Mac
- 7-Zip / PeaZip for Linux

The code bundle for the book is also hosted on GitHub at `https://github.com/PacktPubl ishing/Python-GUI-Programming-Cookbook-Second-Edition`. We also have other code bundles from our rich catalog of books and videos available at `https://github.com/Packt Publishing/`. Check them out!

Downloading the color images of this book

We also provide you with a PDF file that has color images of the screenshots/diagrams used in this book. The color images will help you better understand the changes in the output. You can download this file from `https://www.packtpub.com/sites/default/files/downloads/PythonGUIProgrammingCook bookSecondEdition_ColorImages.pdf`.

Errata

Although we have taken every care to ensure the accuracy of our content, mistakes do happen. If you find a mistake in one of our books-maybe a mistake in the text or the code-we would be grateful if you could report this to us. By doing so, you can save other readers from frustration and help us improve subsequent versions of this book. If you find any errata, please report them by visiting `http://www.packtpub.com/submit-errata`, selecting your book, clicking on the **Errata Submission Form** link, and entering the details of your errata. Once your errata are verified, your submission will be accepted and the errata will be uploaded to our website or added to any list of existing errata under the Errata section of that title.

To view the previously submitted errata, go to `https://www.packtpub.com/books/conten t/support` and enter the name of the book in the search field. The required information will appear under the **Errata** section.

Piracy

Piracy of copyrighted material on the Internet is an ongoing problem across all media. At Packt, we take the protection of our copyright and licenses very seriously. If you come across any illegal copies of our works in any form on the Internet, please provide us with the location address or website name immediately so that we can pursue a remedy.

Please contact us at copyright@packtpub.com with a link to the suspected pirated material.

We appreciate your help in protecting our authors and our ability to bring you valuable content.

Questions

If you have a problem with any aspect of this book, you can contact us at questions@packtpub.com, and we will do our best to address the problem.

1

Creating the GUI Form and Adding Widgets

In this chapter, we start creating amazing GUIs using Python 3.6 and above. We will cover the following topics:

- Creating our first Python GUI
- Preventing the GUI from being resized
- Adding a label to the GUI form
- Creating buttons and changing their text property
- Text box widgets
- Setting the focus to a widget and disabling widgets
- Combo box widgets
- Creating a check button with different initial states
- Using radio button widgets
- Using scrolled text widgets
- Adding several widgets in a loop

Introduction

In this chapter, we will develop our first GUI in Python. We will start with the minimum code required to build a running GUI application. Each recipe then adds different widgets to the GUI form.

In the first two recipes, we will show the entire code, consisting of only a few lines of code. In the following recipes, we will only show the code to be added to the previous recipes.

By the end of this chapter, we will have created a working GUI application that consists of labels, buttons, text boxes, combo boxes, check buttons in various states, as well as radio buttons that change the background color of the GUI.

At the beginning of each chapter, I will show the Python modules that belong to each chapter. I will then reference the different modules that belong to the code shown, studied and run.

Here is the overview of Python modules (ending in a .py extension) for this chapter:

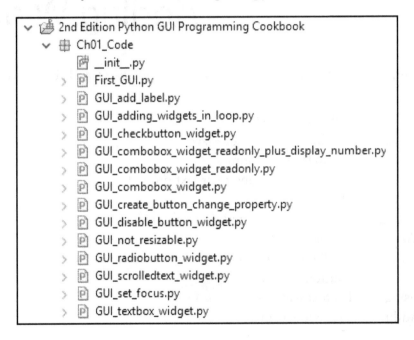

Creating our first Python GUI

Python is a very powerful programming language. It ships with the built-in `tkinter` module. In only a few lines of code (four, to be precise) we can build our first Python GUI.

Getting ready

To follow this recipe, a working Python development environment is a prerequisite. The IDLE GUI, which ships with Python, is enough to start. IDLE was built using tkinter!

- All the recipes in this book were developed using Python 3.6 on a Windows 10 64-bit OS. They have not been tested on any other configuration. As Python is a cross-platform language, the code from each recipe is expected to run everywhere.
- If you are using a Mac, it does come with built-in Python, yet it might be missing some modules such as tkinter, which we will use throughout this book.
- We are using Python 3.6, and the creator of Python intentionally chose not to make it backwards compatible with Python 2. If you are using a Mac or Python 2, you might have to install Python 3.6 from `www.python.org` in order to successfully run the recipes in this book.
- If you really wish to run the code in this book on Python 2.7, you will have to make some adjustments. For example, tkinter in Python 2.x has an uppercase *T*. The Python 2.7 print statement is a function in Python 3.6 and requires parentheses.
- While the EOL (End Of Life) for the Python 2.x branch has been extended to the year 2020, I would strongly recommend that you start using Python 3.6 and above.
- Why hold on to the past, unless you really have to?
  Here is a link to the Python Enhancement Proposal (PEP) 373 that refers to the EOL of Python 2: `https://www.python.org/dev/peps/pep-0373/`

How to do it...

Here are the four lines of `First_GUI.py` required to create the resulting GUI:

```
 6  #=======================
 7  # imports
 8  #=======================
 9  import tkinter as tk
10
11  # Create instance
12  win = tk.Tk()
13
14  # Add a title
15  win.title("Python GUI")
16
17  #=======================
18  # Start GUI
19  #=======================
20  win.mainloop()
```

Execute this code and admire the result:

How it works...

In line nine, we import the built-in `tkinter` module and alias it as `tk` to simplify our Python code. In line 12, we create an instance of the `Tk` class by calling its constructor (the parentheses appended to `Tk` turns the class into an instance). We are using the alias `tk`, so we don't have to use the longer word `tkinter`. We are assigning the class instance to a variable named `win` (short for a window). As Python is a dynamically typed language, we did not have to declare this variable before assigning to it, and we did not have to give it a specific type. Python infers the type from the assignment of this statement. Python is a strongly typed language, so every variable always has a type. We just don't have to specify its type beforehand like in other languages. This makes Python a very powerful and productive language to program in.

A little note about classes and types:

- In Python, every variable always has a type. We cannot create a variable that does not have a type. Yet, in Python, we do not have to declare the type beforehand, as we have to do in the C programming language.
- Python is smart enough to infer the type. C#, at the time of writing this book, also has this capability.
  Using Python, we can create our own classes using the `class` keyword instead of the `def` keyword.
- In order to assign the class to a variable, we first have to create an instance of our class. We create the instance and assign this instance to our variable, for example:
  ```
  class AClass(object):
      print('Hello from AClass')
  class_instance = AClass()
  ```
  Now, the variable, `class_instance`, is of the `AClass` type.
  If this sounds confusing, do not worry. We will cover OOP in the coming chapters.

In line 15, we use the instance variable (`win`) of the class to give our window a title via the `title` property. In line 20, we start the window's event loop by calling the `mainloop` method on the class instance, `win`. Up to this point in our code, we created an instance and set one property, but the GUI will not be displayed until we start the main event loop.

- An event loop is a mechanism that makes our GUI work. We can think of it as an endless loop where our GUI is waiting for events to be sent to it. A button click creates an event within our GUI, or our GUI being resized also creates an event.
- We can write all of our GUI code in advance and nothing will be displayed on the user's screen until we call this endless loop (`win.mainloop()` in the preceding code).
  The event loop ends when the user clicks the red **X** button or a widget that we have programmed to end our GUI. When the event loop ends, our GUI also ends.

There's more...

This recipe used a minimum amount of Python code to create our first GUI program. However, throughout this book we will use OOP when it makes sense.

Preventing the GUI from being resized

By default, a GUI created using tkinter can be resized. This is not always ideal. The widgets we place onto our GUI forms might end up being resized in an improper way, so in this recipe, we will learn how to prevent our GUI from being resized by the user of our GUI application.

Getting ready

This recipe extends the previous one, *Creating our first Python GUI*, so one requirement is to have typed the first recipe yourself into a project of your own, or download the code from h
ttps://github.com/PacktPublishing/Python-GUI-Programming-Cookbook-Second-Edi
tion/.

How to do it...

We are preventing the GUI from being resized, look at:
GUI_not_resizable.py

```
6  #=======================
7  # imports
8  #=======================
9  import tkinter as tk
10
11 # Create instance
12 win = tk.Tk()
13
14 # Add a title
15 win.title("Python GUI")
16
17 # Disable resizing the GUI by passing in False/False
18 win.resizable(False, False)
19
20 # Enable resizing x-dimension, disable y-dimension
21 # win.resizable(True, False)
22
23 #=======================
24 # Start GUI
25 #=======================
26 win.mainloop()
```

Running the code creates this GUI:

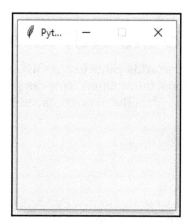

How it works...

Line 18 prevents the Python GUI from being resized.

Running this code will result in a GUI similar to the one we created in the first recipe. However, the user can no longer resize it. Also, note how the maximize button in the toolbar of the window is grayed out.

Why is this important? Because once we add widgets to our form, resizing can make our GUI look not as good as we want it to be. We will add widgets to our GUI in the next recipes.

The `resizable()` method is of the `Tk()` class, and by passing in `(False, False)`, we prevent the GUI from being resized. We can disable both the x and y dimensions of the GUI from being resized, or we can enable one or both dimensions by passing in `True` or any number other than zero. `(True, False)` would enable the x-dimension but prevent the y-dimension from being resized.

We also added comments to our code in preparation for the recipes contained in this book.

 In visual programming IDEs such as Visual Studio .NET, C# programmers often do not think of preventing the user from resizing the GUI they developed in this language. This creates inferior GUIs. Adding this one line of Python code can make our users appreciate our GUI.

Adding a label to the GUI form

A label is a very simple widget that adds value to our GUI. It explains the purpose of the other widgets, providing additional information. This can guide the user to the meaning of an Entry widget, and it can also explain the data displayed by widgets without the user having to enter data into it.

Getting ready

We are extending the first recipe, *Creating our first Python GUI*. We will leave the GUI resizable, so don't use the code from the second recipe (or comment the `win.resizable` line out).

How to do it…

In order to add a Label widget to our GUI, we will import the ttk module from tkinter. Please note the two import statements. Add the following code just above win.mainloop(), which is located at the bottom of the first and second recipes:

GUI_add_label.py

```
 6  #========================
 7  # imports
 8  #========================
 9  import tkinter as tk
10  from tkinter import ttk
11
12  # Create instance
13  win = tk.Tk()
14
15  # Add a title
16  win.title("Python GUI")
17
18  # Adding a Label
19  ttk.Label(win, text="A Label").grid(column=0, row=0)
20
21  #========================
22  # Start GUI
23  #========================
24  win.mainloop()
```

Running the code adds a label to our GUI:

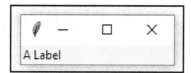

How it works…

In line 10 of the preceding code, we import a separate module from the tkinter package. The ttk module has some advanced widgets that make our GUI look great. In a sense, ttk is an extension within the tkinter package.

We still need to import the `tkinter` package itself, but we have to specify that we now want to also use `ttk` from the `tkinter` package.

 `ttk` stands for *themed tk*. It improves our GUI's look and feel.

Line 19 adds the label to the GUI, just before we call `mainloop`.

We pass our window instance into the `ttk.Label` constructor and set the text property. This becomes the text our `Label` will display.

We also make use of the grid layout manager, which we'll explore in much more depth in `Chapter 2`, *Layout Management*.

Note how our GUI suddenly got much smaller than in the previous recipes.

The reason why it became so small is that we added a widget to our form. Without a widget, the `tkinter` package uses a default size. Adding a widget causes optimization, which generally means using as little space as necessary to display the widget(s).

If we make the text of the label longer, the GUI will expand automatically. We will cover this automatic form size adjustment in a later recipe in `Chapter 2`, *Layout Management*.

There's more...

Try resizing and maximizing this GUI with a label and watch what happens.

Creating buttons and changing their text property

In this recipe, we will add a button widget, and we will use this button to change a property of another widget that is a part of our GUI. This introduces us to callback functions and event handling in a Python GUI environment.

Getting ready

This recipe extends the previous one, *Adding a label to the GUI form.* You can download the entire code from `https://github.com/PacktPublishing/Python-GUI-Programming-Cook book-Second-Edition/`.

How to do it...

We add a button that, when clicked, performs an action. In this recipe, we will update the label we added in the previous recipe as well as the text property of the button:

GUI_create_button_change_property.py

```
18  # Adding a Label that will get modified
19  a_label = ttk.Label(win, text="A Label")
20  a_label.grid(column=0, row=0)
21
22  # Button Click Event Function
23  def click_me():
24      action.configure(text="** I have been Clicked! **")
25      a_label.configure(foreground='red')
26      a_label.configure(text='A Red Label')
27
28  # Adding a Button
29  action = ttk.Button(win, text="Click Me!", command=click_me)
30  action.grid(column=1, row=0)
31
32  #=======================
33  # Start GUI
34  #=======================
35  win.mainloop()
```

The following screenshot shows how our GUI looks before clicking the button:

After clicking the button, the color of the label changed and so did the text of the button, which can be seen as follows:

How it works...

In line 19, we assign the label to a variable, and in line 20, we use this variable to position the label within the form. We need this variable in order to change its properties in the click_me() function. By default, this is a module-level variable, so we can access it inside the function, as long as we declare the variable above the function that calls it.

Line 23 is the event handler that is invoked once the button gets clicked.

In line 29, we create the button and bind the command to the click_me() function.

 GUIs are event-driven. Clicking the button creates an event. We bind what happens when this event occurs in the callback function using the command property of the ttk.Button widget. Notice how we do not use parentheses, only the name click_me.

We also change the text of the label to include red as, in the printed book, this might otherwise not be obvious. When you run the code, you can see that the color does indeed change.

Lines 20 and 30 both use the grid layout manager, which will be discussed in the following chapter. This aligns both the label and the button.

There's more...

We will continue to add more and more widgets to our GUI and we will make use of many built-in properties in the other recipes in the book.

Text box widgets

In tkinter, the typical one-line textbox widget is called Entry. In this recipe, we will add such an Entry widget to our GUI. We will make our label more useful by describing what the Entry widget is doing for the user.

Getting ready

This recipe builds upon the *Creating buttons and changing their text property* recipe.

How to do it...

Check out the following code:

GUI_textbox_widget.py

```
22  # Modified Button Click Function
23  def click_me():
24      action.configure(text='Hello ' + name.get())
25
26  # Changing our Label
27  ttk.Label(win, text="Enter a name:").grid(column=0, row=0)
28
29  # Adding a Text box Entry widget
30  name = tk.StringVar()
31  name_entered = ttk.Entry(win, width=12, textvariable=name)
32  name_entered.grid(column=0, row=1)
```

Now, our GUI looks like this:

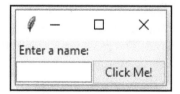

After entering some text and clicking the button, there is the following change in the GUI:

How it works...

In line 24, we get the value of the Entry widget. We have not used OOP yet, so how come we can access the value of a variable that was not even declared yet?

Without using OOP classes, in Python procedural coding, we have to physically place a name above a statement that tries to use that name. So how come this works (it does)?

The answer is that the button click event is a callback function, and by the time the button is clicked by a user, the variables referenced in this function are known and do exist.

Life is good.

Line 27 gives our label a more meaningful name; for now, it describes the text box below it. We moved the button down next to the label to visually associate the two. We are still using the grid layout manager, which will be explained in more detail in Chapter 2, *Layout Management*.

Line 30 creates a variable, name. This variable is bound to the Entry widget and, in our click_me() function, we are able to retrieve the value of the Entry widget by calling get() on this variable. This works like a charm.

Now we see that while the button displays the entire text we entered (and more), the textbox Entry widget did not expand. The reason for this is that we hardcoded it to a width of 12 in line 31.

- Python is a dynamically typed language and infers the type from the assignment. What this means is that if we assign a string to the `name` variable, it will be of the `string` type, and if we assign an integer to `name`, its type will be integer.
- Using `tkinter`, we have to declare the `name` variable as the type `tk.StringVar()` before we can use it successfully. The reason is that tkinter is not Python. We can use it from Python, but it is not the same language.

Setting the focus to a widget and disabling widgets

While our GUI is nicely improving, it would be more convenient and useful to have the cursor appear in the Entry widget as soon as the GUI appears. Here we learn how to do this.

Getting ready

This recipe extends the previous recipe, *Text box widgets*.

How to do it...

Python is truly great. All we have to do to set the focus to a specific control when the GUI appears is call the `focus()` method on an instance of a `tkinter` widget we previously created. In our current GUI example, we assigned the `ttk.Entry` class instance to a variable named, `name_entered`. Now, we can give it the focus.

Place the following code just above the code which is located at the bottom of the module and which starts the main windows event loop, like we did in the previous recipes:

GUI_set_focus.py

```
29  # Adding a Textbox Entry widget
30  name = tk.StringVar()
31  name_entered = ttk.Entry(win, width=12, textvariable=name)
32  name_entered.grid(column=0, row=1)
33
34  # Adding a Button
35  action = ttk.Button(win, text="Click Me!", command=click_me)
36  action.grid(column=1, row=1)
37
38  name_entered.focus()        # Place cursor into name Entry
39  #=======================
40  # Start GUI
41  #=======================
42  win.mainloop()
```

If you get some errors, make sure you are placing calls to variables below the code where they are declared. We are not using OOP as of yet, so this is still necessary. Later, it will no longer be necessary to do this.

 On a Mac, you might have to set the focus to the GUI window first before being able to set the focus to the Entry widget in this window.

Adding this one line (38) of Python code places the cursor in our text Entry widget, giving the text Entry widget the focus. As soon as the GUI appears, we can type into this text box without having to click it first.

Note how the cursor now defaults to residing inside the text Entry box.

We can also disable widgets. To do that, we will set a property on the widget. We can make the button disabled by adding this one line (37 below) of Python code to create the button:

```
34  # Adding a Button
35  action = ttk.Button(win, text="Click Me!", command=click_me)
36  action.grid(column=1, row=1)
37  action.configure(state='disabled')     # Disable the Button Widget
38
39  name_entered.focus()        # Place cursor into name Entry
```

After adding the preceding line of Python code, clicking the button no longer creates any action:

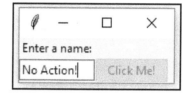

How it works...

This code is self-explanatory. We set the focus to one control and disable another widget. Good naming in programming languages helps to eliminate lengthy explanations. Later in this book, there will be some advanced tips on how to do this while programming at work or practicing our programming skills at home.

There's more...

Yes. This is only the first chapter. There is much more to come.

Combo box widgets

In this recipe, we will improve our GUI by adding drop-down combo boxes which can have initial default values. While we can restrict the user to only certain choices, we can also allow the user to type in whatever they wish.

Getting ready

This recipe extends the previous recipe, *Setting the focus to a widget and disabling widgets*.

How to do it...

We insert another column between the Entry widget and the `Button` widget using the grid layout manager. Here is the Python code:

GUI_combobox_widget.py

```
31  # Adding a Textbox Entry widget
32  name = tk.StringVar()
33  name_entered = ttk.Entry(win, width=12, textvariable=name)
34  name_entered.grid(column=0, row=1)                          # column 0
35
36  # Adding a Button
37  action = ttk.Button(win, text="Click Me!", command=click_me)
38  action.grid(column=2, row=1)                    # <= change column to 2
39
40  ttk.Label(win, text="Choose a number:").grid(column=1, row=0)
41  number = tk.StringVar()
42  number_chosen = ttk.Combobox(win, width=12, textvariable=number)
43  number_chosen['values'] = (1, 2, 4, 42, 100)
44  number_chosen.grid(column=1, row=1)             # <= Combobox in column 1
45  number_chosen.current(0)
46
47  name_entered.focus()      # Place cursor into name Entry
48  #=======================
49  # Start GUI
50  #=======================
51  win.mainloop()
```

This code, when added to the previous recipes, creates the following GUI. Note how, in line 43 in the preceding code, we assigned a tuple with default values to the combo box. These values then appear in the drop-down box. We can also change them if we like (by typing in different values when the application is running):

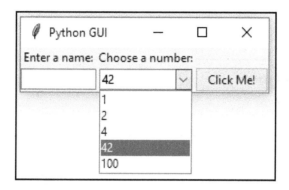

How it works...

Line 40 adds a second label to match the newly created combo box (created in line 42). Line 41 assigns the value of the box to a variable of a special tkinter type StringVar, as we did in a previous recipe.

Line 44 aligns the two new controls (label and combobox) within our previous GUI layout, and line 45 assigns a default value to be displayed when the GUI first becomes visible. This is the first value of the number_chosen['values'] tuple, the string "1". We did not place quotes around our tuple of integers in line 43, but they got casted into strings because, in line 41, we declared the values to be of the tk.StringVar type.

The preceding screenshot shows the selection made by the user as 42. This value gets assigned to the number variable.

There's more...

If we want to restrict the user to only be able to select the values we have programmed into the Combobox, we can do that by passing the state *property* into the constructor. Modify line 42 as follows:

GUI_combobox_widget_readonly_plus_display_number.py

```
40  ttk.Label(win, text="Choose a number:").grid(column=1, row=0)
41  number = tk.StringVar()
42  number_chosen = ttk.Combobox(win, width=12, textvariable=number, state='readonly')
43  number_chosen['values'] = (1, 2, 4, 42, 100)
44  number_chosen.grid(column=1, row=1)
45  number_chosen.current(0)
```

Now, users can no longer type values into the Combobox. We can display the value chosen by the user by adding the following line of code to our *Button Click Event Callback* function:

```
22  # Modified Button Click Function
23  def click_me():
24      action.configure(text='Hello ' + name.get() + ' ' +
25                       number_chosen.get())
```

After choosing a number, entering a name, and then clicking the button, we get the following GUI result, which now also displays the number selected:

Creating a check button with different initial states

In this recipe, we will add three check button widgets, each with a different initial state.

Getting ready

This recipe extends the previous recipe, *Combo box widgets*.

How to do it...

We are creating three check button widgets that differ in their states. The first is disabled and has a check mark in it. The user cannot remove this check mark as the widget is disabled.

The second check button is enabled, and by default, has no check mark in it, but the user can click it to add a check mark.

The third check button is both enabled and checked by default. The users can uncheck and recheck the widget as often as they like. Look at the following code:

GUI_checkbutton_widget.py

```
35  # Adding a Button
36  action = ttk.Button(win, text="Click Me!", command=click_me)
37  action.grid(column=2, row=1)
38
39  # Creating three checkbuttons
40  ttk.Label(win, text="Choose a number:").grid(column=1, row=0)
41  number = tk.StringVar()
42  number_chosen = ttk.Combobox(win, width=12, textvariable=number, state='readonly')
43  number_chosen['values'] = (1, 2, 4, 42, 100)
44  number_chosen.grid(column=1, row=1)
45  number_chosen.current(0)
46
47  chVarDis = tk.IntVar()
48  check1 = tk.Checkbutton(win, text="Disabled", variable=chVarDis, state='disabled')
49  check1.select()
50  check1.grid(column=0, row=4, sticky=tk.W)
51
52  chVarUn = tk.IntVar()
53  check2 = tk.Checkbutton(win, text="UnChecked", variable=chVarUn)
54  check2.deselect()
55  check2.grid(column=1, row=4, sticky=tk.W)
56
57  chVarEn = tk.IntVar()
58  check3 = tk.Checkbutton(win, text="Enabled", variable=chVarEn)
59  check3.select()
60  check3.grid(column=2, row=4, sticky=tk.W)
61
62  name_entered.focus()        # Place cursor into name Entry
63  #=======================
64  # Start GUI
65  #=======================
66  win.mainloop()
```

Running the new code results in the following GUI:

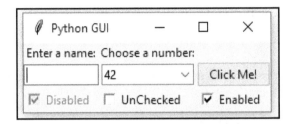

How it works...

In lines 47, 52, and 57 we create three variables of the `IntVar` type. In the line following each of these variables, we create a `Checkbutton`, passing in these variables. They will hold the state of the `Checkbutton` (unchecked or checked). By default, that is either 0 (unchecked) or 1 (checked), so the type of the variable is a `tkinter` integer.

We place these `Checkbutton` widgets in our main window, so the first argument passed into the constructor is the parent of the widget, in our case, `win`. We give each `Checkbutton` widget a different label via its `text` property.

Setting the sticky property of the grid to `tk.W` means that the widget will be aligned to the west of the grid. This is very similar to Java syntax and it means that it will be aligned to the left. When we resize our GUI, the widget will remain on the left side and not be moved towards the center of the GUI.

Lines 49 and 59 place a checkmark into the `Checkbutton` widget by calling the `select()` method on these two `Checkbutton` class instances.

We continue to arrange our widgets using the grid layout manager, which will be explained in more detail in Chapter 2, *Layout Management*.

Using radio button widgets

In this recipe, we will create three tkinter `Radiobutton` widgets. We will also add some code that changes the color of the main form, depending upon which `Radiobutton` is selected.

Getting ready

This recipe extends the previous recipe, *Creating a check button with different initial states.*

How to do it…

We add the following code to the previous recipe:

GUI_radiobutton_widget.py

```
74  # Radiobutton Globals
75  COLOR1 = "Blue"
76  COLOR2 = "Gold"
77  COLOR3 = "Red"
78
79  # Radiobutton Callback
80  def radCall():
81      radSel=radVar.get()
82      if   radSel == 1: win.configure(background=COLOR1)
83      elif radSel == 2: win.configure(background=COLOR2)
84      elif radSel == 3: win.configure(background=COLOR3)
85
86  # create three Radiobuttons using one variable
87  radVar = tk.IntVar()
88
89  rad1 = tk.Radiobutton(win, text=COLOR1, variable=radVar, value=1, command=radCall)
90  rad1.grid(column=0, row=5, sticky=tk.W, columnspan=3)
91
92  rad2 = tk.Radiobutton(win, text=COLOR2, variable=radVar, value=2, command=radCall)
93  rad2.grid(column=1, row=5, sticky=tk.W, columnspan=3)
94
95  rad3 = tk.Radiobutton(win, text=COLOR3, variable=radVar, value=3, command=radCall)
96  rad3.grid(column=2, row=5, sticky=tk.W, columnspan=3)
97
98  name_entered.focus()        # Place cursor into name Entry
99  #=======================
100 # Start GUI
101 #=======================
102 win.mainloop()
```

Running this code and selecting the Radiobutton named **Gold** creates the following window:

How it works...

In lines 75-77, we create some module-level global variables which we will use in the creation of each radio button as well as in the callback function that creates the action of changing the background color of the main form (using the instance variable win).

We are using global variables to make it easier to change the code. By assigning the name of the color to a variable and using this variable in several places, we can easily experiment with different colors. Instead of doing a global search-and-replace of a hardcoded string (which is prone to errors), we just need to change one line of code and everything else will work. This is known as the **DRY principle**, which stands for **Don't Repeat Yourself**. This is an OOP concept which we will use in the later recipes of the book.

The names of the colors we are assigning to the variables (COLOR1, COLOR2 ...) are tkinter keywords (technically, they are *symbolic names*). If we use names that are not tkinter color keywords, then the code will not work.

Line 80 is the *callback function* that changes the background of our main form (win) depending upon the user's selection.

In line 87 we create a tk.IntVar variable. What is important about this is that we create only one variable to be used by all three radio buttons. As can be seen from the screenshot, no matter which Radiobutton we select, all the others will automatically be unselected for us.

Lines 89 to 96 create the three radio buttons, assigning them to the main form, passing in the variable to be used in the callback function that creates the action of changing the background of our main window.

While this is the first recipe that changes the color of a widget, quite honestly, it looks a bit ugly. A large portion of the following recipes in this book explain how to make our GUI look truly amazing.

There's more...

Here is a small sample of the available symbolic color names that you can look up at the official **tcl** manual page at `http://www.tcl.tk/man/tcl8.5/TkCmd/colors.htm`.

Name	Red	Green	Blue
alice blue	240	248	255
AliceBlue	240	248	255
Blue	0	0	255
Gold	255	215	0
Red	255	0	0

Some of the names create the same color, so `alice blue` creates the same color as `AliceBlue`. In this recipe, we used the symbolic names `Blue`, `Gold`, and `Red`.

Using scrolled text widgets

`ScrolledText` widgets are much larger than simple `Entry` widgets and span multiple lines. They are widgets like Notepad and wrap lines, automatically enabling vertical scrollbars when the text gets larger than the height of the `ScrolledText` widget.

Getting ready

This recipe extends the previous recipe, *Using radio button widgets*. You can download the code for each chapter of this book from `https://github.com/PacktPublishing/Python-GUI-Programming-Cookbook-Second-Edition/`.

How to do it...

By adding the following lines of code, we create a ScrolledText widget:

GUI_scrolledtext_widget.py

```
 6  #========================
 7  # imports
 8  #========================
 9  import tkinter as tk
10  from tkinter import ttk
11  from tkinter import scrolledtext

99  # Using a scrolled Text control
100 scrol_w  = 30
101 scrol_h  = 3
102 scr = scrolledtext.ScrolledText(win, width=scrol_w, height=scrol_h, wrap=tk.WORD)
103 scr.grid(column=0, columnspan=3)
104
105 name_entered.focus()        # Place cursor into name Entry
106 #========================
107 # Start GUI
108 #========================
109 win.mainloop()
```

We can actually type into our widget, and if we type enough words, the lines will automatically wrap around:

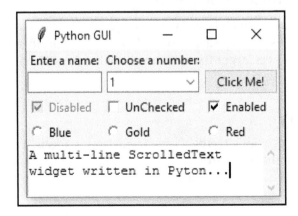

Once we type in more words than the height the widget can display, the vertical scrollbar becomes enabled. This all works out-of-the-box without us needing to write any more code to achieve this:

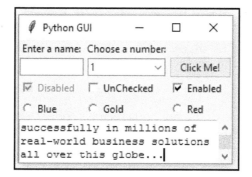

How it works...

In line 11, we import the module that contains the `ScrolledText` widget class. Add this to the top of the module, just below the other two `import` statements.

Lines 100 and 101 define the width and height of the `ScrolledText` widget we are about to create. These are hardcoded values we are passing into the `ScrolledText` widget constructor in line 102.

These values are *magic numbers* found by experimentation to work well. You might experiment by changing `scol_w` from 30 to 50 and observe the effect!

In line 102, we are also setting a property on the widget by passing in `wrap=tk.WORD`.

By setting the `wrap` property to `tk.WORD` we are telling the `ScrolledText` widget to break lines by words so that we do not wrap around within a word. The default option is `tk.CHAR`, which wraps any character regardless of whether we are in the middle of a word.

The second screenshot shows that the vertical scrollbar moved down because we are reading a longer text that does not entirely fit into the *x*, *y* dimensions of the `SrolledText` control we created.

Setting the `columnspan` property of the grid widget to 3 for the `SrolledText` widget makes this widget span all the three columns. If we do not set this property, our `SrolledText` widget would only reside in column one, which is not what we want.

Adding several widgets in a loop

So far, we have created several widgets of the same type (for example, Radiobutton) by basically copying and pasting the same code and then modifying the variations (for example, the column number). In this recipe, we start refactoring our code to make it less redundant.

Getting ready

We are refactoring some parts of the previous recipe's code, *Using scrolled text widgets*, so you need that code to apply this recipe to.

How to do it...

Here's how we refactor our code:

GUI_adding_widgets_in_loop.py

```
76  # First, we change our Radiobutton global variables into a list
77  colors = ["Blue", "Gold", "Red"]
78
79  # We have also changed the callback function to be zero-based, using the list
80  # instead of module-level global variables
81  # Radiobutton Callback
82  def radCall():
83      radSel=radVar.get()
84      if   radSel == 0: win.configure(background=colors[0])   # now zero-based
85      elif radSel == 1: win.configure(background=colors[1])   # and using list
86      elif radSel == 2: win.configure(background=colors[2])
87
88  # create three Radiobuttons using one variable
89  radVar = tk.IntVar()
90
91  # Next we are selecting a non-existing index value for radVar
92  radVar.set(99)
93
94  # Now we are creating all three Radiobutton widgets within one loop
95  for col in range(3):
96      curRad = tk.Radiobutton(win, text=colors[col], variable=radVar,
97                              value=col, command=radCall)
98      curRad.grid(column=col, row=5, sticky=tk.W)
99
```

Running this code will create the same window as before, but our code is much cleaner and easier to maintain. This will help us when we expand our GUI in the coming recipes.

How it works...

In line 77, we have turned our global variables into a list.

In line 89, we set a default value to the `tk.IntVar` variable that we named `radVar`. This is important because, while in the previous recipe we had set the value for `Radiobutton` widgets starting at 1, in our new loop it is much more convenient to use Python's zero-based indexing. If we did not set the default value to a value outside the range of our `Radiobutton` widgets, one of the radio buttons would be selected when the GUI appears. While this in itself might not be so bad, *it would not trigger the callback* and we would end up with a radio button selected that does not do its job (that is, change the color of the main win form).

In line 95, we replace the three previously hardcoded creations of the `Radiobutton` widgets with a loop that does the same. It is just more concise (fewer lines of code) and much more maintainable. For example, if we want to create 100 instead of just three `Radiobutton` widgets, all we have to change is the number inside Python's range operator. We would not have to type or copy and paste 97 sections of duplicate code, just one number.

Line 82 shows the modified callback function.

There's more...

This recipe concludes the first chapter of this book. All the following recipes in all of the next chapters will build upon the GUI we have constructed so far, greatly enhancing it.

2
Layout Management

In this chapter, we will lay out our GUI using Python 3.6 and above. We will cover the following recipes:

- Arranging several labels within a label frame widget
- Using padding to add space around widgets
- How widgets dynamically expand the GUI
- Aligning the GUI widgets by embedding frames within frames
- Creating menu bars
- Creating tabbed widgets
- Using the grid layout manager

Introduction

In this chapter, we will explore how to arrange widgets within widgets to create our Python GUI. Learning the fundamentals of GUI layout design will enable us to create great-looking GUIs. There are certain techniques that will help us in achieving this layout design.

The grid layout manager is one of the most important layout tools built into tkinter that we will be using.

We can very easily create menu bars, tabbed controls (aka Notebooks), and many more widgets using tkinter.

Here is an overview of the Python modules used in this chapter:

```
∨ 🚢 2nd Edition Python GUI Programming Cookbook
    > ⊞ Ch01_Code
    ∨ ⊞ Ch02_Code
          📄 __init__.py
        > P GUI_add_padding_loop.py
        > P GUI_add_padding.py
        > P GUI_arranging_labels_vertical.py
        > P GUI_arranging_labels.py
        > P GUI_embed_frames_align_entry_west.py
        > P GUI_embed_frames_align_west.py
        > P GUI_embed_frames_align.py
        > P GUI_embed_frames.py
        > P GUI_grid_layout.py
        > P GUI_LabelFrame_column_one.py
        > P GUI_LabelFrame_no_name.py
        > P GUI_long_label.py
        > P GUI_menubar_exit_quit.py
        > P GUI_menubar_exit.py
        > P GUI_menubar_file.py
        > P GUI_menubar_help.py
        > P GUI_menubar_separator.py
        > P GUI_menubar_tearoff.py
        > P GUI_remove_columnspan.py
        > P GUI_remove_sticky.py
        > P GUI_tabbed_all_widgets_both_tabs_radio.py
        > P GUI_tabbed_all_widgets_both_tabs.py
        > P GUI_tabbed_all_widgets.py
        > P GUI_tabbed_two_mighty_labels.py
        > P GUI_tabbed_two_mighty.py
        > P GUI_tabbed_two.py
        > P GUI_tabbed.py
```

Arranging several labels within a label frame widget

The `LabelFrame` widget allows us to design our GUI in an organized fashion. We are still using the grid layout manager as our main layout design tool, but by using `LabelFrame` widgets, we get much more control over our GUI design.

Getting ready

We will start adding more and more widgets to our GUI, and we will make the GUI fully functional in the coming recipes. Here, we will start using the `LabelFrame` widget. We will reuse the GUI from the recipe, *Adding Several Widgets in a Loop* in `Chapter 1`, *Creating the GUI Form and Adding Widgets*.

How to do it...

Add the following code just above the main event loop towards the bottom of the Python module:

GUI_LabelFrame_column_one.py

```
108  # Create a container to hold labels
109  buttons_frame = ttk.LabelFrame(win, text=' Labels in a Frame ')
110  buttons_frame.grid(column=0, row=7)
111  # buttons_frame.grid(column=1, row=7)            # now in col 1
112
113  # Place labels into the container element
114  ttk.Label(buttons_frame, text="Label1").grid(column=0, row=0, sticky=tk.W)
115  ttk.Label(buttons_frame, text="Label2").grid(column=1, row=0, sticky=tk.W)
116  ttk.Label(buttons_frame, text="Label3").grid(column=2, row=0, sticky=tk.W)
117
118  name_entered.focus()      # Place cursor into name Entry
119  #=======================
120  # Start GUI
121  #=======================
122  win.mainloop()
```

Running the code will result in the GUI looking as follows:

Uncomment line 111 and notice the different alignment of `LabelFrame`.

We can easily align the labels vertically by changing our code, as shown in the next screenshot:

```
113  # Place labels into the container element
114  ttk.Label(buttons_frame, text="Label1").grid(column=0, row=0)
115  ttk.Label(buttons_frame, text="Label2").grid(column=0, row=1)
116  ttk.Label(buttons_frame, text="Label3").grid(column=0, row=2)
117
118  for child in buttons_frame.winfo_children():
```

Note that the only change we had to make was in the column and row numbering.

Now the GUI LabelFrame looks as follows:

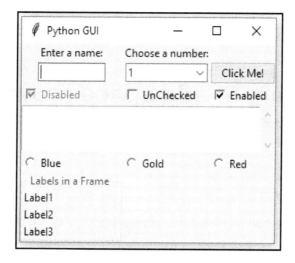

How it works...

In line 109, we create our first ttk LabelFrame widget and assign the resulting instance to the buttons_frame variable. The parent container is win, our main window.

In lines 114 to 116, we create labels and place them in LabelFrame. buttons_frame is the parent of the labels. We use the important grid layout tool to arrange the labels within the LabelFrame. The column and row properties of this layout manager give us the power to control our GUI layout.

> The parent of our labels is the buttons_frame instance variable of LabelFrame, not the win instance variable of the main window. We can see the beginning of a layout hierarchy here.

We can see how easy it is to change our layout via the column and row properties. Note how we change the column to 0, and how we layer our labels vertically by numbering the row values sequentially.

> The name ttk stands for *themed tk*. The tk-themed widget set was introduced in Tk 8.5.

There's more...

In a recipe later in this chapter, we will embed `LabelFrame` widgets within `LabelFrame` widgets, nesting them to control our GUI layout.

Using padding to add space around widgets

Our GUI is being created nicely. Next, we will improve the visual aspects of our widgets by adding a little space around them, so they can breathe.

Getting ready

While tkinter might have had a reputation for creating ugly GUIs, this has dramatically changed since version 8.5. You just have to know how to use the tools and techniques that are available. That's what we will do next.

 tkinter version 8.6 ships with Python 3.6.

How to do it...

The procedural way of adding spacing around widgets is shown first, and then we will use a loop to achieve the same thing in a much better way.

Our `LabelFrame` looks a bit tight as it blends into the main window towards the bottom. Let's fix this now.

Modify line 110 of the code snippet from `GUI_LabelFrame_column_one.py` in the previous recipe by adding `padx` and `pady`. You can also find the code in:

`GUI_add_padding.py`

```
buttons_frame.grid(column=0, row=7, padx=20, pady=40)
```

Now, our `LabelFrame` gets some breathing space:

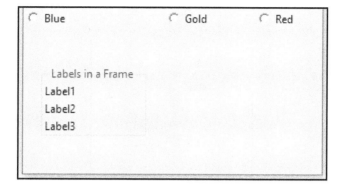

How it works...

In tkinter, adding space horizontally and vertically is done by using built-in properties named `padx` and `pady`. These can be used to add space around many widgets, improving horizontal and vertical alignments, respectively. We hardcoded 20 pixels of space to the left and right of `LabelFrame`, and we added 40 pixels to the top and bottom of the frame. Now our `LabelFrame` stands out better than it did before.

 The preceding screenshot only shows the relevant change.

We can use a loop to add space around the labels contained within `LabelFrame`:

`GUI_add_padding_loop.py`

```
113  # Place labels into the container element
114  ttk.Label(buttons_frame, text="Label1").grid(column=0, row=0)
115  ttk.Label(buttons_frame, text="Label2").grid(column=0, row=1)
116  ttk.Label(buttons_frame, text="Label3").grid(column=0, row=2)
117
118  for child in buttons_frame.winfo_children():
119      child.grid_configure(padx=8, pady=4)
120
121  name_entered.focus()        # Place cursor into name Entry
122  #=======================
123  # Start GUI
124  #=======================
125  win.mainloop()
```

Now, the labels within the `LabelFrame` widget have some space around them too:

The `grid_configure()` function enables us to modify the UI elements before the main loop displays them. So, instead of hardcoding values when we first create a widget, we can work on our layout and then arrange spacing towards the end of our file, just before the GUI is created. This is a neat technique to know.

The `winfo_children()` function returns a list of all the children belonging to the `buttons_frame` variable. This enables us to loop through them and assign the padding to each label.

 One thing to notice is that the spacing to the right of the labels is not really visible. This is because the title of `LabelFrame` is longer than the names of the labels. We can experiment with this by making the label names longer.

Consider the following changes in code as in `GUI_long_label.py`:

```
113  # Place labels into the container element - vertically with long label
114  ttk.Label(buttons_frame, text="Label1 -- sooooo much loooonger...").grid(column=0, row=0)
115  ttk.Label(buttons_frame, text="Label2").grid(column=0, row=1)
116  ttk.Label(buttons_frame, text="Label3").grid(column=0, row=2)
```

Now, our GUI looks as shown in the following screenshot. Note how there is now some space added to the right of the long label next to the dots. The last dot does not touch LabelFrame, which it otherwise would have, without the added space:

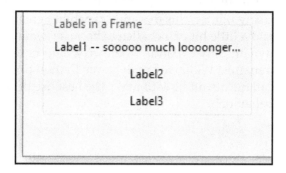

We can also remove the name of LabelFrame to see the effect padx has on the position of our labels:

GUI_LabelFrame_no_name.py

```
109  buttons_frame = ttk.LabelFrame(win, text='')        # no LabelFrame name
```

By setting the text property to an empty string, we remove the name that was previously displayed for LabelFrame:

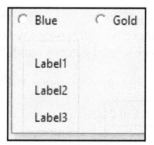

How widgets dynamically expand the GUI

You may have noticed in the previous screenshots and by running the code that the widgets have the capability of extending themselves to the space they need in order to visually display their text.

- Java introduced the concept of dynamic GUI layout management. In comparison, visual development IDEs, such as VS.NET, lay out the GUI in a visual manner, and basically hardcode the x and y coordinates of the UI elements.
- Using tkinter, this dynamic capability creates both an advantage and a little bit of a challenge because sometimes our GUI dynamically expands when we would rather it not be so dynamic! Well, we are dynamic Python programmers, so we can figure out how to make the best use of this fantastic behavior!

Getting ready

In the beginning of the previous recipe, *Using padding to add space around widgets*, we added a LabelFrame widget. This moved some of our controls to the center of column 0. We might not want this modification in our GUI layout. Next, we will explore some ways to solve this.

How to do it...

Let's first become aware of the subtle details that are going on in our GUI layout in order to understand it better.

We are using the grid layout manager widget, and it lays out our widgets in a zero-based grid. This is very similar to an Excel spreadsheet or a database table.

The following is an example of a grid layout manager with two rows and three columns:

Row 0; Col 0	Row 0; Col 1	Row 0; Col 2
Row 1; Col 0	Row 1; Col 1	Row 1; Col 2

Using the grid layout manager, what happens is that the width of any given column is determined by the longest name or widget in that column. This affects all the rows.

By adding our `LabelFrame` widget and giving it a title that is longer than some hardcoded size widget, such as the top-left label and the text entry below it, we dynamically move those widgets to the center of column 0, adding space on the left- and right-hand side of those widgets.

Incidentally, because we used the `sticky` property for the `Checkbutton` and `ScrolledText` widgets, those remain attached to the left-hand side of the frame.

Let's look in more detail at the screenshot from the first recipe of this chapter, *Arranging several labels within a label frame widget*:

We added the following code to create `LabelFrame` and then placed labels into this frame:

```
108  # Create a container to hold labels
109  buttons_frame = ttk.LabelFrame(win, text=' Labels in a Frame ')
110  buttons_frame.grid(column=0, row=7)
```

Since the text property of the `LabelFrame`, which is displayed as the title of the `LabelFrame`, is longer than both our **Enter a name:** label and the textbox entry below it, those two widgets are dynamically centered within the new width of column 0.

The `Checkbutton` and `Radiobutton` widgets in column 0 did not get centered because we used the `sticky=tk.W` property when we created those widgets.

For the `ScrolledText` widget, we used `sticky=tk.WE`, which binds the widget to both the west (aka left) and east (aka right) side of the frame.

Let's remove the `sticky` property from the `ScrolledText` widget and observe the effect this change has:

GUI_remove_sticky.py

```
# Using a scrolled Text control
scrol_w  = 30
scrol_h  =  3
scr = scrolledtext.ScrolledText(win, width=scrol_w, height=scrol_h, wrap=tk.WORD)
#### scr.grid(column=0, row=5, sticky='WE', columnspan=3)
scr.grid(column=0, row=5, columnspan=3)                # sticky property removed
```

Now, our GUI has new space around the `ScrolledText` widget, both on the left- and right-hand sides. Because we used the `columnspan=3` property, our `ScrolledText` widget still spans all three columns:

If we remove `columnspan=3`, we'll get the following GUI, which is not what we want. Now, our `ScrolledText` only occupies column 0 and, because of its size, stretches the layout:

GUI_remove_columnspan.py

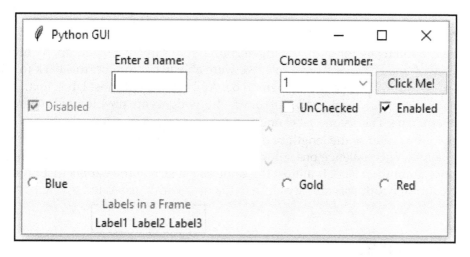

One way to get our layout back to where we were before adding LabelFrame is to adjust the grid column position. Change the column value from 0 to 1:

```
buttons_frame.grid(column=1, row=7)          # now in col 1
```

Now our GUI looks as follows:

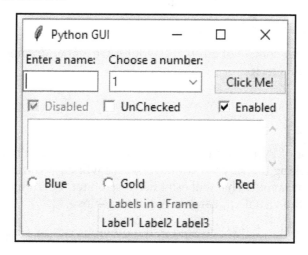

How it works...

Because we are still using individual widgets, our layout can get messed up. By moving the column value of LabelFrame from 0 to 1, we were able to get the controls back to where they used to be and where we prefer them to be. At least, the left-most label, text, Checkbutton, ScrolledText, and Radiobutton widgets are now located where we intended them to be. The second label and text Entry located in column 1 aligned themselves to the center of the length of the **Labels in a Frame** widget, so we basically moved our alignment challenge one column to the right. It is not so visible because the size of the **Choose a number:** label is almost the same as the size of the **Labels in a Frame** title, and so the column width was already close to the new width generated by LabelFrame.

There's more...

In the next recipe, *Aligning the GUI widgets by embedding frames within frames*, we will embed frames within frames to avoid the accidental misalignment of widgets we just experienced in this recipe.

Aligning the GUI widgets by embedding frames within frames

We'll have a much better control of our GUI layout if we embed frames within frames. This is what we will do in this recipe.

Getting ready

The dynamic behavior of Python and its GUI modules can create a little bit of a challenge to really get our GUI looking the way we want. Here, we will embed frames within frames to get more control of our layout. This will establish a stronger hierarchy among the different UI elements, making the visual appearance easier to achieve.

We will continue using the GUI we created in the previous recipe, *How widgets dynamically expand the GUI*.

How to do it...

Here, we will create a top-level frame that will contain other frames and widgets. This will help us get our GUI layout just the way we want.

In order to do so, we will have to embed our current controls within a central frame called `ttk.LabelFrame`. This frame `ttk.LabelFrame` is the child of the main parent window and all controls will be the children of this `ttk.LabelFrame`.

Up to this point in our recipes, we had assigned all widgets to our main GUI frame directly. Now, we will only assign `LabelFrame` to our main window and after that, we will make this `LabelFrame` the parent container for all the widgets.

This creates the following hierarchy in our GUI layout:

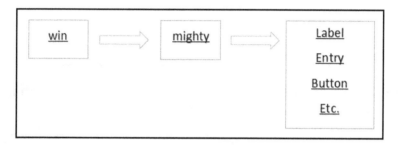

In the preceding diagram, **win** is the variable that holds a reference to our main GUI tkinter window frame, **mighty** is the variable that holds a reference to our `LabelFrame` and is a child of the main window frame (**win**), and **Label** and all other widgets are now placed into the `LabelFrame` container (**mighty**).

Add the following code towards the top of our Python module:

GUI_embed_frames.py

```
 6  #========================
 7  # imports
 8  #========================
 9  import tkinter as tk
10  from tkinter import ttk
11  from tkinter import scrolledtext
12
13  # Create instance
14  win = tk.Tk()
15
16  # Add a title
17  win.title("Python GUI")
18
19  # We are creating a container frame to hold all other widgets
20  mighty = ttk.LabelFrame(win, text=' Mighty Python ')
21  mighty.grid(column=0, row=0, padx=8, pady=4)
```

Next, we will modify the following controls to use `mighty` as the parent, replacing `win`.
Here is an example of how to do this:

```
23  # Modify adding a Label using mighty as the parent instead of win
24  a_label = ttk.Label(mighty, text="Enter a name:")
25  a_label.grid(column=0, row=0)
```

This results in the following GUI:

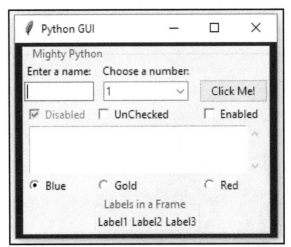

Note how all the widgets are now contained in the **Mighty Python** LabelFrame which surrounds all of them with a barely visible thin line. Next, we can reset the **Labels in a Frame** widget to the left without messing up our GUI layout:

GUI_embed_frames_align.py

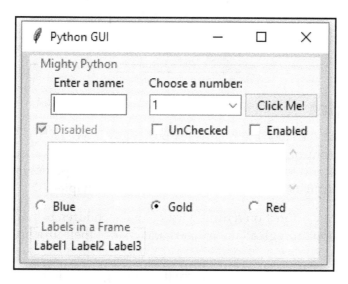

Oops - maybe not. While our frame within another frame aligned nicely to the left, it again pushed our top widgets to the center (a default).

In order to align them to the left, we have to force our GUI layout by using the sticky property. By assigning it 'W' (West), we can control the widget to be left-aligned:

GUI_embed_frames_align_west.py

```
# Modify adding a Label using mighty as the parent instead of win
a_label = ttk.Label(mighty, text="Enter a name:")
a_label.grid(column=0, row=0, sticky='W')
```

This results in the following GUI:

How it works...

Note how we aligned the label, but not the textbox below it. We have to use the `sticky` property for all the controls we want to left-align. We can do that in a loop, using the `winfo_children()` and `grid_configure(sticky='W')` properties, as we did before in the recipe, *Using padding to add space around widgets*, in this chapter.

The `winfo_children()` function returns a list of all the children belonging to the parent. This enables us to loop through all the widgets and change their properties.

- Using tkinter to force the naming to the left, right, top, or bottom is very similar to Java: West, East, North, and South, abbreviated to `'W'` and so on. We can also use the following syntax: `tk.W` instead of `'W'`. This requires having imported the `tkinter` module aliased as `tk`.

- In a previous recipe, we combined both `'W'` and `'E'` to make our `ScrolledText` widget attach itself both to the left- and right-hand sides of its container, using `'WE'`. We can add more combinations: `'NSE'` will stretch our widget to the top, bottom, and right side. If we only have one widget in our form, for example, a button, we can make it fill in the entire frame by using all options: `'NSWE'`. We can also use tuple syntax: `sticky=(tk.N, tk.S, tk.W, tk.E)`.

Let's align the entry in column 0 to the left:

```
# Adding a Textbox Entry widget
name = tk.StringVar()
name_entered = ttk.Entry(mighty, width=12, textvariable=name)
name_entered.grid(column=0, row=1, sticky=tk.W)          # align left/West
```

Now, both the label and the entry are aligned towards the West (left):

GUI_embed_frames_align_entry_west.py

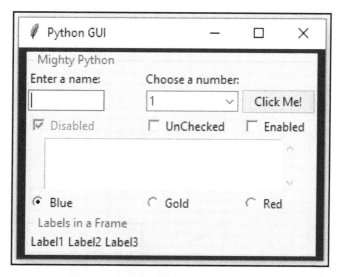

 In order to separate the influence that the length of our **Labels in a Frame** LabelFrame has on the rest of our GUI layout, we must not place this LabelFrame into the same LabelFrame as the other widgets but assign it directly to the main GUI form (win). We will do this in the later chapters.

Creating menu bars

In this recipe, we will add a menu bar to our main window, add menus to the menu bar, and then add menu items to the menus.

Getting ready

We will start by learning the techniques of how to add a menu bar, several menus, and a few menu items to show the principle of how to do it. In the beginning, clicking on a menu item will have no effect. We will then add functionality to the menu items, for example, closing the main window when clicking the **Exit** menu item and displaying a **Help** | **About** dialog.

We will continue to extend the GUI we created in the previous recipe, *Aligning the GUI widgets by embedding frames within frames.*

How to do it...

First, we'll have to import the Menu class from tkinter. Add the following line of code to the top of the Python module, where the import statements live:

```
 6  #=======================
 7  # imports
 8  #=======================
 9  import tkinter as tk
10  from tkinter import ttk
11  from tkinter import scrolledtext
12  from tkinter import Menu
13
14  # Create instance
15  win = tk.Tk()
```

Next, we will create the menu bar. Add the following code towards the bottom of the module, just above where we create the main event loop:

GUI_menubar_tearoff.py

```
118  # Creating a Menu Bar
119  menu_bar = Menu(win)
120  win.config(menu=menu_bar)
121
122  # Create menu and add menu items
123  file_menu = Menu(menu_bar)                          # create File menu
124  file_menu.add_command(label="New")                  # add File menu item
```

In line 119, we are calling the constructor of the imported `Menu` module class and pass in our main GUI instance, `win`. We save an instance of the `Menu` object in the `menu_bar` variable. In line 120, we configure our GUI to use the just created `Menu` as the `menu` for our GUI.

In order to make this work, we also have to add the menu to the menu bar and give it a label.

The menu item was already added to the menu, but we still have to add the menu to the menu bar:

GUI_menubar_file.py

```
122  # Create menu and add menu items
123  file_menu = Menu(menu_bar)                              # create File menu
124  file_menu.add_command(label="New")                      # add File menu item
125  menu_bar.add_cascade(label="File", menu=file_menu)      # add File menu to menu bar and give it a label
126
127  name_entered.focus()        # Place cursor into name Entry
128  #=======================
129  # Start GUI
130  #=======================
131  win.mainloop()
```

Running this code adds a menu bar with a menu that has a menu item:

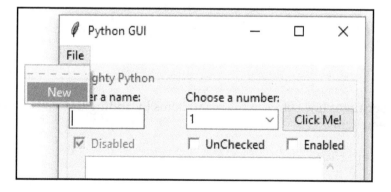

 If this tkinter `menubar` syntax seems a little bit confusing, do not worry. This is just the syntax of `tkinter` to create a `menubar`. It is not very Pythonic.

Next, we'll add a second menu item to the first menu that we added to the menu bar:

GUI_menubar_exit.py

```
122   # Add menu items
123   file_menu = Menu(menu_bar)
124   file_menu.add_command(label="New")
125   file_menu.add_command(label="Exit")
126   menu_bar.add_cascade(label="File", menu=file_menu)
127
128   name_entered.focus()        # Place cursor into name Entry
129   #======================
130   # Start GUI
131   #======================
132   win.mainloop()
```

Running the code produces the following result:

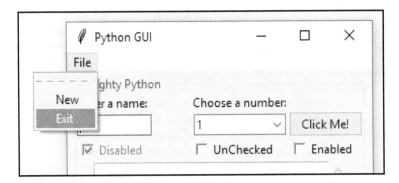

We can add a separator line between the menu items by adding this line of code in between the existing menu items:

GUI_menubar_separator.py

```
# Creating a Menu Bar
menu_bar = Menu(win)
win.config(menu=menu_bar)

# Add menu items
file_menu = Menu(menu_bar)
file_menu.add_command(label="New")
file_menu.add_separator()
file_menu.add_command(label="Exit")
menu_bar.add_cascade(label="File", menu=file_menu)
```

Now, we can see a separator line in between our two menu items:

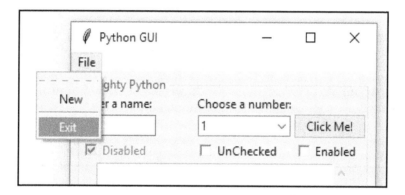

By passing in the `tearoff` property to the constructor of the menu, we can remove the first dashed line that, by default, appears above the first menu item in a menu:

```
# Add menu items
file_menu = Menu(menu_bar, tearoff=0)
file_menu.add_command(label="New")
file_menu.add_separator()
```

Now, the dashed line no longer appears, and our GUI looks so much better:

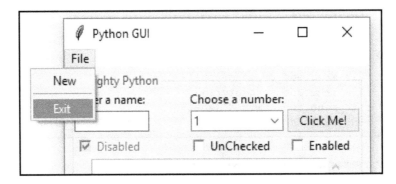

Next, we'll add a second menu, which will be horizontally placed to the right of the first menu. We'll give it one menu item, which we name **About** and, in order for this to work, we have to add this second menu to the menu bar.

File and **Help** | **About** are very common Windows GUI layouts we are all familiar with, and we can create those same menus using Python and tkinter:

GUI_menubar_help.py

```
# Creating a Menu Bar
menu_bar = Menu(win)
win.config(menu=menu_bar)

# Add menu items
file_menu = Menu(menu_bar, tearoff=0)
file_menu.add_command(label="New")
file_menu.add_separator()
file_menu.add_command(label="Exit")
menu_bar.add_cascade(label="File", menu=file_menu)

# Add another Menu to the Menu Bar and an item
help_menu = Menu(menu_bar, tearoff=0)
menu_bar.add_cascade(label="Help", menu=help_menu)
help_menu.add_command(label="About")

name_entered.focus()       # Place cursor into name Entry
#========================
# Start GUI
#========================
win.mainloop()
```

Now, we have a second menu with a menu item in the menu bar:

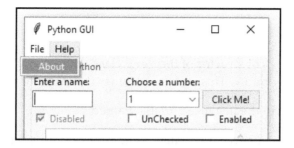

At this point, our GUI has a menu bar and two menus that contain some menu items. Clicking on them does not do much until we add some commands. That's what we will do next. Add the following code above the creation of the menu bar:

```
# Exit GUI cleanly
def _quit():
    win.quit()
    win.destroy()
    exit()
```

Next, we'll bind the **File** | **Exit** menu item to this function by adding the following command to the menu item:

GUI_menubar_exit_quit.py

```
# Exit GUI cleanly
def _quit():
    win.quit()
    win.destroy()
    exit()

# Creating a Menu Bar
menu_bar = Menu(win)
win.config(menu=menu_bar)

# Add menu items
file_menu = Menu(menu_bar, tearoff=0)
file_menu.add_command(label="New")
file_menu.add_separator()
file_menu.add_command(label="Exit", command=_quit)
menu_bar.add_cascade(label="File", menu=file_menu)
```

Now, when we click the `Exit` menu item, our application will indeed exit.

How it works...

First, we call the `tkinter` constructor of the `Menu` class. Then, we assign the newly created menu to our main GUI window. This, in fact, becomes the menu bar.

We save a reference to it in the instance variable named `menu_bar`.

Next, we create a menu and add a menu item to it. We then add a second menu item to the menu. The `add_cascade()` method aligns the menu items one below the other, in a vertical layout.

Then, we add a separator line between the two menu items. This is generally used to group related menu items and separate them from less related items (hence, the name).

Finally, we disable the `tearoff` dashed line to make our menu look much better.

 Without disabling this default feature, the user can tear off the menu from the main window. I find this capability of little value. Feel free to play around with it by double-clicking the dashed line (before disabling this feature). If you are using a Mac, this feature might not be enabled, so you do not have to worry about it at all.

Check the following GUI:

We then add a second menu to the menu bar. We can keep on adding menus through this technique.

Next, we create a function to quit our GUI application cleanly. This is the recommended Pythonic way to end the main event loop.

We bind the function we created to the menu item, using the tkinter's `command` property. Whenever we want our menu items to actually do something, we have to bind each of them to a function.

 We are using a recommended Python naming convention by preceding our `quit` function with one single underscore, to indicate that this is a private function not to be called by the clients of our code.

There's more...

We will add the **Help** | **About** functionality in `Chapter 3`, *Look and Feel Customization* ,which introduces message boxes and much more.

Creating tabbed widgets

In this recipe, we will create tabbed widgets to further organize our expanding GUI written in tkinter.

Getting ready

In order to improve our Python GUI using tabs, we will start at the beginning, using the minimum amount of code necessary. In this recipe, we will create a simple GUI and then add widgets from the previous recipes and place them into this new tabbed layout.

How to do it...

Create a new Python module and place the following code into this module:

GUI_tabbed.py

```
6  #=======================
7  # imports
8  #=======================
9  import tkinter as tk
10 from tkinter import ttk
11
12 win = tk.Tk()                              # Create instance
13 win.title("Python GUI")                    # Add a title
14 tabControl = ttk.Notebook(win)             # Create Tab Control
15 tab1 = ttk.Frame(tabControl)               # Create a tab
16 tabControl.add(tab1, text='Tab 1')         # Add the tab
17 tabControl.pack(expand=1, fill="both")     # Pack to make visible
18
19 #=======================
20 # Start GUI
21 #=======================
22 win.mainloop()
```

This creates the following GUI:

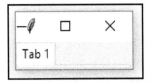

While not amazingly impressive as of yet, this widget adds another very powerful tool to our GUI design toolkit. It comes with its own limitations in the minimalist example above (for example, we can neither reposition the GUI nor does it show the entire GUI title).

While we used the grid layout manager for simpler GUIs in the previous recipes, we can use a simpler layout manager, and pack is one of them.

In the preceding code, we pack the tabControl and ttk.Notebook widgets into the main GUI form, expanding the notebook-tabbed control to fill in all the sides.

We can add a second tab to our control and click between them:

GUI_tabbed_two.py

```
tabControl = ttk.Notebook(win)          # Create Tab Control

tab1 = ttk.Frame(tabControl)            # Create a tab
tabControl.add(tab1, text='Tab 1')      # Add the tab
tab2 = ttk.Frame(tabControl)            # Add a second tab
tabControl.add(tab2, text='Tab 2')      # Add second tab

tabControl.pack(expand=1, fill="both")  # Pack to make visible

#=======================
# Start GUI
#=======================
win.mainloop()
```

Now, we have two tabs. Click on **Tab 2** to give it the focus:

We would really like to see our windows title; so, to do this, we have to add a widget to one of our tabs. The widget has to be wide enough to expand our GUI dynamically to display our window title:

GUI_tabbed_two_mighty.py

```
# LabelFrame using tab1 as the parent
mighty = ttk.LabelFrame(tab1, text=' Mighty Python ')
mighty.grid(column=0, row=0, padx=8, pady=4)

# Label using mighty as the parent
a_label = ttk.Label(mighty, text="Enter a name:")
a_label.grid(column=0, row=0, sticky='W')
```

Now we got our **Mighty Python** inside **Tab1**. This expands our GUI, but the added widgets are not large enough to make the GUI title visible:

After adding a second label plus some spacing around them, we stretch the layout enough to be able to see our GUI title again:

GUI_tabbed_two_mighty_labels.py

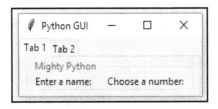

We can keep placing all the widgets we have created so far into our newly created tab controls:

GUI_tabbed_all_widgets.py

Now, all the widgets reside inside **Tab 1**. Let's move some to **Tab 2**. First, we create a second `LabelFrame` to be the container of our widgets relocating to **Tab 2**:

```
mighty2 = ttk.LabelFrame(tab2, text=' The Snake ')
mighty2.grid(column=0, row=0, padx=8, pady=4)
```

Next, we move the Check and Radiobuttons to **Tab 2**, by specifying the new parent container, which is a new variable that we name `mighty2`. Here is an example that we apply to all the controls that relocate to **Tab 2**:

```
chVarDis = tk.IntVar()
check1 = tk.Checkbutton(mighty2, text="Disabled", variable=chVarDis, state='disabled')
```

When we run the code, our GUI now looks different. **Tab 1** has fewer widgets than it had before, when it contained all of our previously created widgets:

GUI_tabbed_all_widgets_both_tabs.py

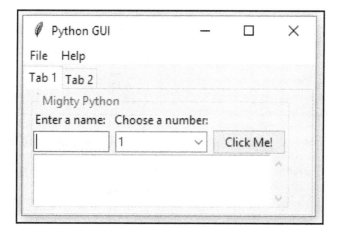

We can now click on **Tab 2** and see our relocated widgets:

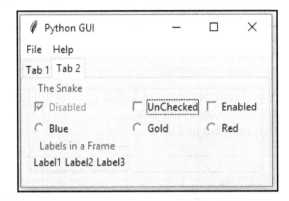

Clicking the relocated Radiobutton no longer has any effect, so we will change their actions to rename the text property, from the title of the LabelFrame widget, to the name the Radiobuttons display. When we click the **Gold** Radiobutton, we no longer set the background of the frame to the color gold but here replace the LabelFrame text title instead. Python **The Snake** now becomes **Gold**.

```
def radCall():
    radSel=radVar.get()
    if   radSel == 0: mighty2.configure(text='Blue')
    elif radSel == 1: mighty2.configure(text='Gold')
    elif radSel == 2: mighty2.configure(text='Red')
```

Now, selecting any of the RadioButton widgets will change the name of the LabelFrame:

GUI_tabbed_all_widgets_both_tabs_radio.py

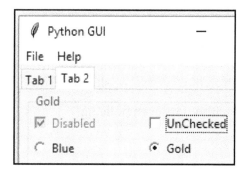

How it works...

After creating a second tab, we moved some of the widgets that originally resided in **Tab 1** to **Tab 2**. Adding tabs is another excellent way to organize our ever-increasing GUI. This is a very nice way to handle the complexity in our GUI design. We can arrange widgets in groups, where they naturally belong and free our users from clutter by using tabs.

In tkinter, creating tabs is done via the Notebook widget, which is the tool that allows us to add tabbed controls. The tkinter notebook widget, like so many other widgets, comes with additional properties that we can use and configure. An excellent place to start exploring additional capabilities of the tkinter widgets at our disposal is the official website: https://docs .python.org/3.1/library/tkinter.ttk.html#notebook.

Using the grid layout manager

The grid layout manager is one of the most useful layout tools at our disposal. We have already used it in many recipes because it is just so powerful.

Getting ready...

In this recipe, we will review some of the techniques of the grid layout manager. We have already used them and here we will explore them further.

How to do it...

In this chapter, we have created rows and columns, which truly is a database approach to GUI design (MS Excel does the same). We hardcoded the first rows, but then we forgot to give the next row a specification of where we wish it to reside.

Tkinter did fill this in for us without us even noticing.

Here is what we did in our code:

```
# Using a scrolled Text control
scrol_w  = 30
scrol_h  = 3
scr = scrolledtext.ScrolledText(mighty, width=scrol_w, height=scrol_h, wrap=tk.WORD)
# scr.grid(column=0, row=2, sticky='WE', columnspan=3)
scr.grid(column=0, sticky='WE', columnspan=3)                      # row not specified
```

Tkinter automatically adds the missing row where we did not specify any particular row. We might not realize this.

We laid out the Entry widgets on row 1, then we forgot to specify the row for our ScrolledText widget which we reference via the scr variable, and then we added the Radiobutton widgets to be laid out in row 3.

This works nicely because tkinter automatically incremented the row position for our ScrolledText widget to use the next highest row number, which was row 2.

Looking at our code and not realizing that we forgot to explicitly position our ScrolledText widget to row 2, we might think nothing resides there.

So, we might try the following. If we set the variable curRad to use row 2, we might get an unpleasant surprise:

GUI_grid_layout.py

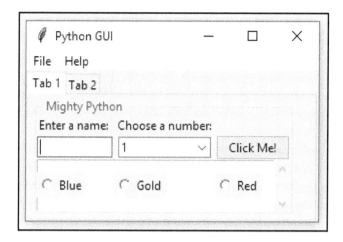

How it works...

Note how our row of `RadioButton`(s) suddenly ended up in the middle of our `ScrolledText` widget! This is definitely not what we intended our GUI to look like!

 If we forget to explicitly specify the row number, by default, tkinter will use the next available row.

We also used the `columnspan` property to make sure our widgets did not get limited to just one column. Here is how we made sure that our `ScrolledText` widget spans all the columns of our GUI:

```
# Using a scrolled Text control
scrol_w  = 30
scrol_h  = 3
scr = scrolledtext.ScrolledText(mighty, width=scrol_w, height=scrol_h, wrap=tk.WORD)
scr.grid(column=0, row=2, sticky='WE', columnspan=3)                    # using columnspan
```

3
Look and Feel Customization

In this chapter, we will customize our GUI using Python 3.6 and above. We will cover the following recipes:

- Creating message boxes – information, warning, and error
- How to create independent message boxes
- How to create the title of a tkinter window form
- Changing the icon of the main root window
- Using a spin box control
- Relief, sunken, and raised appearance of widgets
- Creating tooltips using Python
- Adding a progressbar to the GUI
- How to use the canvas widget

Introduction

In this chapter, we will customize some of the widgets in our GUI by changing some of their properties. We will also introduce a few new widgets that tkinter offers us.

The *Creating tooltips using Python* recipe will create a `ToolTip` OOP-style class, which will be a part of the single Python module that we have been using until now.

Here is the overview of the Python modules for this chapter:

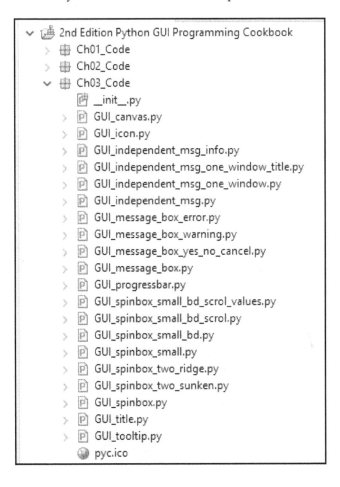

Creating message boxes – information, warning, and error

A message box is a pop-up window that gives feedback to the user. It can be informational, hinting at potential problems as well as catastrophic errors.

Using Python to create message boxes is very easy.

Getting ready

We will add functionality to the **Help** | **About** menu item we created in the previous chapter, in the *Creating tabbed widgets* recipe.

The code is from `GUI_tabbed_all_widgets_both_tabs.py`. The typical feedback to the user when clicking the **Help** | **About** menu in most applications is informational. We start with this information and then vary the design pattern to show warnings and errors.

How to do it...

Add the following line of code to the top of the module where the import statements live:

```
#========================
# imports
#========================
import tkinter as tk
from tkinter import ttk
from tkinter import scrolledtext
from tkinter import Menu
from tkinter import messagebox as msg
```

Next, create a callback function that will display a message box. We have to locate the code of the callback above the code where we attach the callback to the menu item, because this is still procedural and not OOP code.

Add the following code just above the lines where we create the help menu:

`GUI_message_box.py`

```
# Display a Message Box
def _msgBox():
    msg.showinfo('Python Message Info Box', 'A Python GUI created using tkinter:\nThe year is 2017.')

# Add another Menu to the Menu Bar and an item
help_menu = Menu(menu_bar, tearoff=0)
help_menu.add_command(label="About", command=_msgBox)    # display messagebox when clicked
menu_bar.add_cascade(label="Help", menu=help_menu)
```

Clicking **Help** | **About** now causes the following pop-up window to appear:

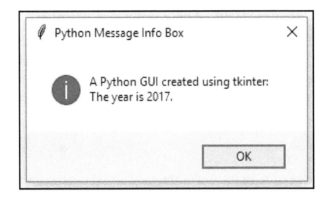

Let's transform this code into a warning message box pop-up window, instead. Comment out the previous line and add the following code:

```
# Display a Message Box
def _msgBox():
#       msg.showinfo('Python Message Info Box', 'A Python GUI created using tkinter:'
#                    '\nThe year is 2017.')
    msg.showwarning('Python Message Warning Box', 'A Python GUI created using tkinter:'
                    '\nWarning: There might be a bug in this code.')
```

Running the preceding code will now result in the following slightly modified message box:

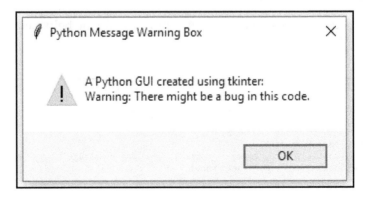

Displaying an error message box is simple and usually warns the user of a serious problem. As we did in the previous code snippet, comment out the previous line and add the following code, as we have done here:

```
# Display a Message Box
def _msgBox():
#    msg.showinfo('Python Message Info Box', 'A Python GUI created using tkinter:\nThe year is 2017.')
#    msg.showwarning('Python Message Warning Box', 'A Python GUI created using tkinter:'
#                    '\nWarning: There might be a bug in this code.')
    msg.showerror('Python Message Error Box', 'A Python GUI created using tkinter:'
                  '\nError: Houston ~ we DO have a serious PROBLEM!')
```

The error message looks like this:

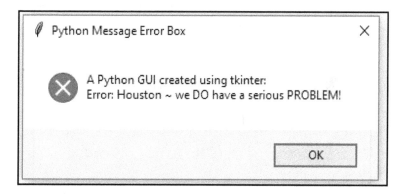

How it works...

We added another callback function and attached it as a delegate to handle the click event. Now, when we click the **Help** | **About** menu, an action takes place. We are creating and displaying the most common pop-up message box dialogs. They are modal, so the user can't use the GUI until they click the **OK** button.

In the first example, we display an information box, as can be seen by the icon to its left. Next, we create warning and error message boxes, which automatically change the icon associated with the popup. All we have to do is specify which message box we want to display.

There are different message boxes that display more than one **OK** button, and we can program our responses according to the user's selection.

The following is a simple example that illustrates this technique:

```
# Display a Message Box
def _msgBox():
#    msg.showinfo('Python Message Info Box', 'A Python GUI created using tkinter:\nThe year is 2017.')
#    msg.showwarning('Python Message Warning Box', 'A Python GUI created using tkinter:\nWarning: There might be a bug in this code.')
#    msg.showerror('Python Message Error Box', 'A Python GUI created using tkinter:\nError: Houston ~ we DO have a serious PROBLEM!')
    answer = msg.askyesnocancel("Python Message Multi Choice Box", "Are you sure you really wish to do this?")
    print(answer)
```

Running this GUI code results in a popup whose user response can be used to branch on the answer of this event-driven GUI loop, by saving it in the answer variable:

GUI_message_box_yes_no_cancel.py

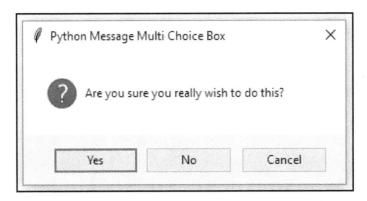

The console output using Eclipse shows that clicking the **Yes** button results in the Boolean value of True being assigned to the answer variable:

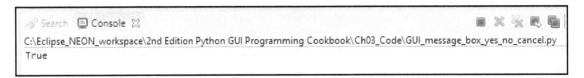

For example, we could use the following code:

```
If answer == True:
    <do something>
```

Clicking **No** returns False and **Cancel** returns None.

How to create independent message boxes

In this recipe, we will create our tkinter message boxes as standalone top-level GUI windows.

You will first notice that, by doing so, we end up with an extra window, so we will explore ways to hide this window.

In the previous recipe, we invoked tkinter message boxes via our **Help** | **About** menu from our main GUI form.

So, why would we wish to create an independent message box?

One reason is that we might customize our message boxes and reuse them in several of our GUIs. Instead of having to copy and paste the same code into every Python GUI we design, we can factor it out of our main GUI code. This can create a small reusable component which we can then import into different Python GUIs.

Getting ready

We have already created the title of a message box in the previous recipe, *Creating message boxes - information, warning, and error*. We will not reuse the code from the previous recipe but build a new GUI using very few lines of Python code.

How to do it...

We can create a simple message box, as follows:

```
from tkinter import messagebox as msg
msg.showinfo('Python GUI created using tkinter:\nThe year is 2017')
```

This will result in the following two windows:

GUI_independent_msg.py

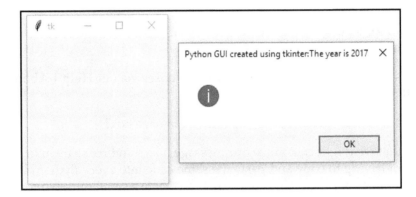

This does not look like what we had in mind. Now, we have two windows, one undesired and the second with its text displayed as its title.

Oops!

Let's solve this now. We can change the Python code by adding a single or double quote, followed by a comma:

```
from tkinter import messagebox as msg
msg.showinfo('', 'Python GUI created using tkinter:\nThe year is 2017')
```

Now, we do not have a title but our text ended up inside the popup, as we had intended:

GUI_independent_msg_info.py

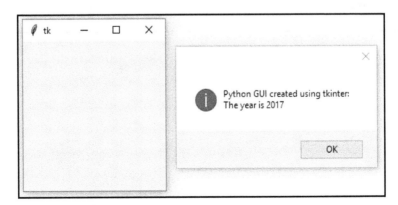

The first parameter is the title and the second is the text displayed in the pop-up message box. By adding an empty pair of single or double quotes, followed by a comma, we can move our text from the title into the pop-up message box.

We still need a title and we definitely want to get rid of this unnecessary second window. The second window is caused by a Windows event loop. We can get rid of it by suppressing it.

Add the following code:

```
from tkinter import messagebox as msg
from tkinter import Tk
root = Tk()
root.withdraw()
msg.showinfo('', 'Python GUI created using tkinter:\nThe year is 2017')
```

Now, we have only one window. The `withdraw()` function removes the debug window that we are not interested in having floating around:

`GUI_independent_msg_one_window.py`

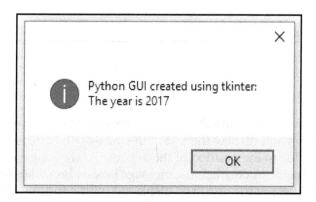

In order to add a title, all we have to do is place some string into our empty first argument.

For example, consider the following code snippet:

```
from tkinter import messagebox as msg
from tkinter import Tk
root = Tk()
root.withdraw()
msg.showinfo('This is a Title', 'Python GUI created using tkinter:\nThe year is 2017')
```

Now our dialog has a title, as shown in the following screenshot:

`GUI_independent_msg_one_window_title.py`

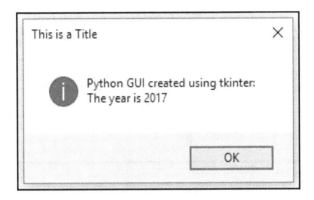

How it works...

We are passing more arguments into the tkinter constructor of the message box to add a title to the window form and display the text in the message box instead of displaying it as its title. This happens due to the position of the arguments we are passing. If we leave out an empty quote or a double quote, then the message box widget takes the first position of the arguments as the title, not the text to be displayed within the message box. By passing an empty quote followed by a comma, we change where the message box displays the text we are passing into the function.

We suppress the second pop-up window, which automatically gets created by the tkinter message box widget, by calling the withdraw() method on our main root window.

How to create the title of a tkinter window form

The principle of changing the title of a tkinter main root window is the same as what we discussed in the previous recipe: *How to create independent message boxes*. We just pass in a string as the first argument to the constructor of the widget.

Getting ready

Instead of a pop-up dialog window, we create the main root window and give it a title.

How to do it...

The following code creates the main window and adds a title to it. We have already done this in the previous recipes, for example, in *Creating tabbed widgets*, in Chapter 2, *Layout Management*. Here we just focus on this aspect of our GUI:

```
import tkinter as tk
win = tk.Tk()                  # Create instance
win.title("Python GUI")        # Add a title
```

How it works...

This gives a title to the main root window by using the built-in tkinter title property. After we create a Tk() instance, we can use all the built-in tkinter properties to customize our GUI.

Changing the icon of the main root window

One way to customize our GUI is to give it an icon different from the default icon that ships out of the box with tkinter. Here is how we do this.

Getting ready

We are improving our GUI from the recipe, *Creating tabbed widgets*, in Chapter 2, *Layout Management*. We will use an icon that ships with Python but you can use any icon you find useful. Make sure you have the full path to where the icon lives in your code, or you might get errors.

How to do it...

For this example, I have copied the icon from where I installed Python 3.6 to the same folder where the code lives.

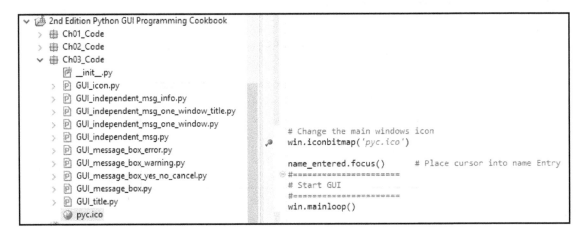

Place the following code somewhere above the main event loop:

```
# Change the main windows icon
win.iconbitmap('pyc.ico')
```

Note how the *feather* default icon in the top-left corner of the GUI changed:

GUI_icon.py

How it works...

This is another property that ships with tkinter, which ships with Python 3.6 and above. We use the iconbitmap property to change the icon of our main root window form, by passing in a relative path to an icon. This overrides the default icon of tkinter, replacing it with our icon of choice.

Using a spin box control

In this recipe, we will use a Spinbox widget, and we will also bind the *Enter* key on the keyboard to one of our widgets.

Getting ready

We will use our tabbed GUI and add a Spinbox widget above the ScrolledText control. This simply requires us to increment the ScrolledText row value by one and to insert our new Spinbox control in the row above the Entry widget.

How to do it...

First, we add the Spinbox control. Place the following code above the ScrolledText widget:

```
# Adding a Spinbox widget
spin = Spinbox(mighty, from_=0, to=10)
spin.grid(column=0, row=2)
```

This will modify our GUI as follows:

`GUI_spinbox.py`

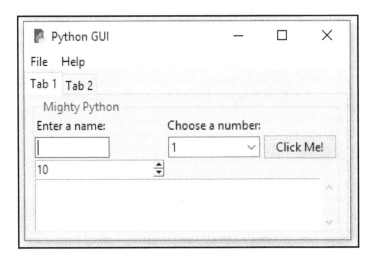

Next, we will reduce the size of the `Spinbox` widget:

```
spin = Spinbox(mighty, from_=0, to=10, width=5)
```

Running the preceding code results in the following GUI:

`GUI_spinbox_small.py`

Next, we add another property to customize our widget further; bd is a short-hand notation for the `borderwidth` property:

```
spin = Spinbox(mighty, from_=0, to=10, width=5 , bd=8)
```

Running the preceding code results in the following GUI:

`GUI_spinbox_small_bd.py`

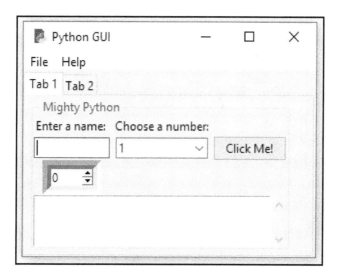

Here, we add functionality to the widget by creating a callback and linking it to the control.

This will print the selection of the `Spinbox` into `ScrolledText` as well as onto `stdout`. The variable named `scrol` is our reference to the `ScrolledText` widget:

```
# Spinbox callback
def _spin():
    value = spin.get()
    print(value)
    scrol.insert(tk.INSERT, value + 'n')

spin = Spinbox(mighty, from_=0, to=10, width=5, bd=8,
                command=_spin)
```

Running the preceding code results in the following GUI:

`GUI_spinbox_small_bd_scrol.py`

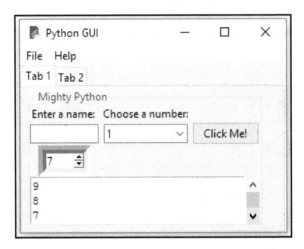

Instead of using a range, we can also specify a set of values:

```
# Adding a Spinbox widget using a set of values
spin = Spinbox(mighty, values=(1, 2, 4, 42, 100), width=5, bd=8,
               command=_spin)
spin.grid(column=0, row=2)
```

This will create the following GUI output:

`GUI_spinbox_small_bd_scrol_values.py`

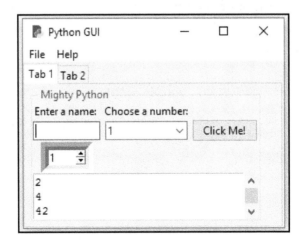

How it works...

Note how, in the first screenshot, our new Spinbox control defaulted to a width of 20, pushing out the column width of all controls in this column. This is not what we want.

We gave the widget a range from 0 to 10.

In the second screenshot, we reduced the width of the Spinbox control, which aligned it in the center of the column.

In the third screenshot, we added the borderwidth property of the Spinbox, which automatically made the entire Spinbox appear no longer flat, but three-dimensional.

In the fourth screenshot, we added a callback function to display the number chosen in the ScrolledText widget and print it to the standard out stream. We added \n to print on new lines. Notice how the default value does not get printed. It is only when we click the control that the callback function gets called. By clicking the down arrow with a default of 0, we can print the 0 value.

Lastly, we restrict the values available to a hardcoded set. This could also be read in from a data source (for example, a text or XML file).

Relief, sunken and raised appearance of widgets

We can control the appearance of our Spinbox widgets by using a property that makes them appear in different sunken or raised formats.

Getting ready

We will add one more Spinbox control to demonstrate the available appearances of widgets, using the relief property of the Spinbox control.

How to do it...

First, let's increase the `borderwidth` to distinguish our second `Spinbox` from the first `Spinbox`:

```
# Adding a second Spinbox widget
spin = Spinbox(mighty, values=(0, 50, 100), width=5, bd=20,
               command=_spin)
spin.grid(column=1, row=2)
```

This will create the following GUI output:

`GUI_spinbox_two_sunken.py`

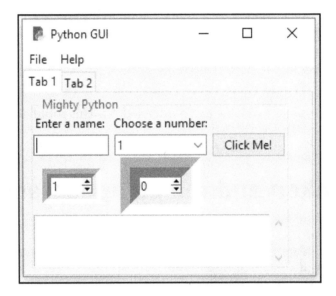

Both our preceding `Spinbox` widgets have the same relief style. The only difference is that our new widget to the right of the first `Spinbox` has a much larger border width.

In our code, we did not specify which relief property to use, so the relief defaulted to `tk.SUNKEN`.

 We imported `tkinter` as `tk`. This is why we can call the relief property as `tk.SUNKEN`.

Here are the available relief property options that can be set:

`tk.SUNKEN`	`tk.RAISED`	`tk.FLAT`	`tk.GROOVE`	`tk.RIDGE`

By assigning the different available options to the relief property, we can create different appearances for this widget.

Assigning the `tk.RIDGE` relief and reducing the border width to the same value as our first `Spinbox` widget results in the following GUI:

`GUI_spinbox_two_ridge.py`

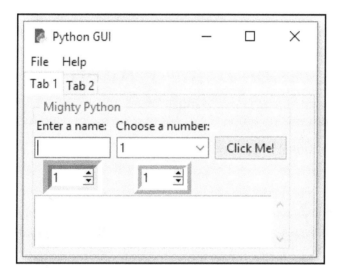

How it works...

First, we created a second `Spinbox` aligned in the second column (index == 1). It defaults to SUNKEN, so it looks similar to our first `Spinbox`. We distinguished the two widgets by increasing the border width of the second control (the one on the right).

Next, we explicitly set the relief property of the `Spinbox` widget. We made the border width the same as our first `Spinbox` because, by giving it a different relief, the differences became visible without having to change any other properties.

Here is an example of the different options:

```
# Adding a second Spinbox widget displaying its relief options with larger borderline
# uncomment each next code line to see the different effects
# spin = Spinbox(mighty, values=(0, 50, 100), width=5, bd=20, command=_spin)     # default value is: tk.SUNKEN
# spin = Spinbox(mighty, values=(0, 50, 100), width=5, bd=20, command=_spin, relief=tk.FLAT)
# spin = Spinbox(mighty, values=(0, 50, 100), width=5, bd=20, command=_spin, relief=tk.RAISED)
# spin = Spinbox(mighty, values=(0, 50, 100), width=5, bd=20, command=_spin, relief=tk.SUNKEN) # default
# spin = Spinbox(mighty, values=(0, 50, 100), width=5, bd=20, command=_spin, relief=tk.GROOVE)
# spin = Spinbox(mighty, values=(0, 50, 100), width=5, bd=20, command=_spin, relief=tk.RIDGE)
```

Creating tooltips using Python

This recipe will show us how to create tooltips. When the user hovers the mouse over a widget, additional information will be available in the form of a tooltip.

We will code this additional information into our GUI.

Getting ready

We will be adding more useful functionality to our GUI. Surprisingly, adding a tooltip to our controls should be simple, but it is not as simple as we'd wish it to be.

In order to achieve this desired functionality, we will place our tooltip code into its own OOP class.

How to do it...

Add the following class just below the import statements:

```python
#==============================================================
class ToolTip(object):
    def __init__(self, widget):
        self.widget = widget
        self.tip_window = None

    def show_tip(self, tip_text):
        "Display text in a tooltip window"
        if self.tip_window or not tip_text:
            return
        x, y, _cx, cy = self.widget.bbox("insert")        # get size of widget
        x = x + self.widget.winfo_rootx() + 25            # calculate to display tooltip
        y = y + cy + self.widget.winfo_rooty() + 25       # below and to the right
        self.tip_window = tw = tk.Toplevel(self.widget)   # create new tooltip window
        tw.wm_overrideredirect(True)                      # remove all Window Manager (wm) decorations
#        tw.wm_overrideredirect(False)                    # uncomment to see the effect
        tw.wm_geometry("+%d+%d" % (x, y))                 # create window size

        label = tk.Label(tw, text=tip_text, justify=tk.LEFT,
                  background="#ffffe0", relief=tk.SOLID, borderwidth=1,
                  font=("tahoma", "8", "normal"))
        label.pack(ipadx=1)

    def hide_tip(self):
        tw = self.tip_window
        self.tip_window = None
        if tw:
            tw.destroy()


#==============================================================
def create_ToolTip(widget, text):
    toolTip = ToolTip(widget)        # create instance of class
    def enter(event):
        toolTip.show_tip(text)
    def leave(event):
        toolTip.hide_tip()
    widget.bind('<Enter>', enter)    # bind mouse events
    widget.bind('<Leave>', leave)
```

In an **Object Oriented Programming (OOP)** approach, we create a new class in our Python module. Python allows us to place more than one class into the same Python module and it also enables us to *mix-and-match* classes and regular functions in the same module.

The preceding code does exactly this.

The ToolTip class is a Python class, and in order to use it, we have to instantiate it.

If you are not familiar with OOP programming, instantiating an object to create an instance of the class, may sound rather boring.

The principle is quite simple and very similar to creating a Python function via a def statement and then, later in the code, actually calling this function.

In a very similar manner, we first create a blueprint of a class and simply assign it to a variable by adding parentheses to the name of the class, as follows:

```
class AClass():
    pass
instance_of_a_class = AClass()
print(instance_of_a_class)
```

The preceding code prints out a memory address and also shows that our variable now has a reference to this class instance.

The cool thing about OOP is that we can create many instances of the same class.

In our tooltip code, we declare a Python class and explicitly make it inherit from object, which is the foundation of all Python classes. We can also leave it out, as we did in the AClass code example, because it is the default for all Python classes.

After all the necessary tooltip creation code that occurs within the ToolTip class, we switch over to non-OOP Python programming by creating a function just below it.

We define the create_ToolTip() function, and it expects one of our GUI widgets to be passed in as an argument, so we can display a tooltip when we hover our mouse over this control.

The create_ToolTip() function actually creates a new instance of our ToolTip class for every widget we call it for.

We can add a tooltip for our Spinbox widget, as follows:

```
# Add a Tooltip
create_ToolTip(spin, 'This is a Spin control')
```

We could do the same for all of our other GUI widgets in the very same manner. We just have to pass in a reference to the widget we wish to have a tooltip, displaying some extra information. For our `ScrolledText` widget, we made the `scrol` variable point to it, so this is what we pass into the constructor of our tooltip creation function:

```
# Using a scrolled Text control
scrol_w = 30
scrol_h = 3
scrol = scrolledtext.ScrolledText(mighty, width=scrol_w, height=scrol_h, wrap=tk.WORD)
scrol.grid(column=0, row=3, sticky='WE', columnspan=3)

# Add a Tooltip to the ScrolledText widget
create_ToolTip(scrol, 'This is a ScrolledText widget')
```

How it works...

This is the beginning of OOP programming in this book. This might appear a little bit advanced, but do not worry; we will explain everything and it does actually work.

Consider adding the following code just below the creation of the `Spinbox`:

```
# Add a Tooltip
create_ToolTip(spin, 'This is a Spin control.')
```

Now, when we hover the mouse over the Spinbox widget, we get a tooltip, providing additional information to the user:

GUI_tooltip.py

We call the function that creates the `ToolTip`, and then we pass in a reference to the widget and the text we wish to display when we hover the mouse over the widget.

The rest of the recipes in this book will use OOP when it makes sense. Here, we've shown the simplest OOP example possible. As a default, every Python class we create inherits from the `object` base class. Python, being the pragmatic programming language that it truly is, simplifies the class creation process.

We can write the following syntax:

```
class ToolTip(object):
    pass
```

We can also simplify it by leaving the default base class out:

```
class ToolTip():
    pass
```

Similarly, we can inherit and expand any `tkinter` class.

Adding a progressbar to the GUI

In this recipe, we will add a `Progressbar` to our GUI. It is very easy to add a `ttk.Progressbar`, and we will demonstrate how to start and stop a `Progressbar`. This recipe will also show you how to delay the stopping of a `Progressbar` and how to run it in a loop.

 `Progressbar` is typically used to show the current status of a long-running process.

Getting ready

We will add the progressbar to **Tab 2** of the GUI that we developed in the previous recipe: *Creating tooltips using Python*.

How to do it...

First, we add four buttons into `LabelFrame` on **Tab 2**, replacing the labels that were there before. We set the `Labelframe` text property to `ProgressBar`.

We then place a `ttk.Progressbar` widget below all other widgets on **Tab 2** and align this new widget with the other widgets.

Our GUI now looks as follows:

`GUI_progressbar.py`

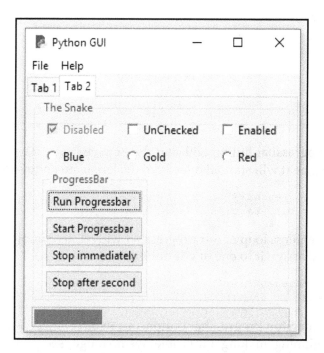

We connect each of our four new buttons to a new callback function, which we assign to their command property:

```
# Add Buttons for Progressbar commands
ttk.Button(buttons_frame, text=" Run Progressbar    ", command=run_progressbar).grid(column=0, row=0, sticky='W')
ttk.Button(buttons_frame, text=" Start Progressbar  ", command=start_progressbar).grid(column=0, row=1, sticky='W')
ttk.Button(buttons_frame, text=" Stop immediately  ", command=stop_progressbar).grid(column=0, row=2, sticky='W')
ttk.Button(buttons_frame, text=" Stop after second ", command=progressbar_stop_after).grid(column=0, row=3, sticky='W')
```

Clicking the **Run Progressbar** button will run the `Progressbar` from the left to the right, then the `Progressbar` will stop there, and the green bar will disappear.

Here is the code:

```
# Add a Progressbar to Tab 2
progress_bar = ttk.Progressbar(tab2, orient='horizontal', length=286, mode='determinate')
progress_bar.grid(column=0, row=3, pady=2)

# update progressbar in callback loop
def run_progressbar():
    progress_bar["maximum"] = 100
    for i in range(101):
        sleep(0.05)
        progress_bar["value"] = i      # increment progressbar
        progress_bar.update()          # have to call update() in loop
    progress_bar["value"] = 0          # reset/clear progressbar
```

Clicking the **Start Progressbar** button will start the `Progressbar`. The `Progressbar` will run to the end, and then it will start all over from the left, in an endless loop:

```
def start_progressbar():
    progress_bar.start()
```

In order to stop this endless loop of our progressbar widget, we simply create another callback function and assign it to one of our buttons:

```
def stop_progressbar():
    progress_bar.stop()
```

As soon as we click the **Stop Progressbar** button, our `Progressbar` will stop and it will reset itself to the beginning, making it invisible. We no longer see a green bar inside the `Progressbar`.

 If we click the **Run Progressbar** button and then click the **Stop Progressbar** button, the progress of the bar will temporarily halt, but then the loop will run to completion and so will the ProgressBar.

We can also delay the stopping of the running `ProgressBar`. While we might expect that a `sleep` statement would do the trick, it does not. Instead, we have to use the `after` function of `tkinter`, as follows:

```
def progressbar_stop_after(wait_ms=1000):
    win.after(wait_ms, progress_bar.stop)
```

Coding it this way will stop the running `ProgressBar` when we click this button after the time specified in the `wait_ms` variable, in milliseconds.

How it works...

We can specify a maximum value and use this value in a loop, together with a `sleep` statement.

We can start and stop the progress of the `ProgressBar`, using the `start` and `stop` commands built into the `ProgressBar` widget.

We can also delay the stopping of the progress in the bar by using tkinter's built-in `after` function.

We do this by calling the `after` function on the reference to our main GUI window, which we named `win`.

How to use the canvas widget

This recipe shows how to add dramatic color effects to our GUI by using the tkinter canvas widget.

Getting ready

We will improve our previous code from `GUI_tooltip.py`, and we'll improve the look of our GUI by adding some more colors to it.

How to do it...

First, we will create a third tab in our GUI in order to isolate our new code.

Here is the code to create the new third tab:

```
tabControl = ttk.Notebook(win)              # Create Tab Control

tab1 = ttk.Frame(tabControl)                # Create a tab
tabControl.add(tab1, text='Tab 1')          # Add the tab

tab2 = ttk.Frame(tabControl)
tabControl.add(tab2, text='Tab 2')          # Add a second tab

tab3 = ttk.Frame(tabControl)
tabControl.add(tab3, text='Tab 3')          # Add a third tab

tabControl.pack(expand=1, fill="both")      # Pack to make tabs visible
```

Next, we use another built-in widget of `tkinter`: `Canvas`. A lot of people like this widget because it has powerful capabilities:

```
# Tab Control 3 -------------------------------
tab3_frame = tk.Frame(tab3, bg='blue')
tab3_frame.pack()
for orange_color in range(2):
    canvas = tk.Canvas(tab3_frame, width=150, height=80,
                        highlightthickness=0, bg='orange')
    canvas.grid(row=orange_color, column=orange_color)
```

How it works...

After we have created the new tab, we place a regular `tk.Frame` into it and assign it a background color of blue. In the loop, we create two `tk.Canvas` widgets, making their color orange and assigning them to grid coordinates 0,0 and 1,1. This also makes the blue background color of the `tk.Frame` visible in the two other grid locations.

The following screenshot shows the result created by running the preceding code and clicking on the new **Tab 3**. It really is orange and blue when you run the code. In a non-colored printed book, this might not be visually obvious, but those colors are true; you can trust me on this.

You can check out the graphing and drawing capabilities by searching online. I will not go deeper into this widget in this book (but it is very cool):

`GUI_canvas.py`

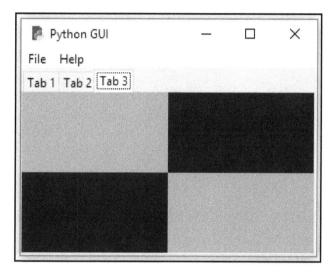

4
Data and Classes

In this chapter, we will use data and OOP classes using Python 3.6 and above. We will cover the following recipes:

- How to use `StringVar()`
- How to get data from a widget
- Using module-level global variables
- How coding in classes can improve the GUI
- Writing callback functions
- Creating reusable GUI components

Introduction

In this chapter, we will save our GUI data into `tkinter` variables. We will also start using OOP to extend the existing `tkinter` classes in order to extend the built-in functionality of tkinter. This will lead us into creating reusable OOP components.

Here is the overview of the Python modules for this chapter:

```
∨  🚢 2nd Edition Python GUI Programming Cookbook
    >  ⊞ Ch01_Code
    >  ⊞ Ch02_Code
    >  ⊞ Ch03_Code
    ∨  ⊞ Ch04_Code
          📄 _init_.py
       >  📄 GUI_const_42_777_global_print.py
       >  📄 GUI_const_42_777_global.py
       >  📄 GUI_const_42_777.py
       >  📄 GUI_const_42_print_func.py
       >  📄 GUI_const_42_print.py
       >  📄 GUI_const_42.py
       >  📄 GUI_data_from_widget.py
       >  📄 GUI_OOP_2_classes.py
       >  📄 GUI_OOP_class_imported_tooltip.py
       >  📄 GUI_OOP_class_imported.py
       >  📄 GUI_PyVar_defaults.py
       >  📄 GUI_PyVar_Get.py
       >  📄 GUI_StringVar.py
          🌐 pyc.ico
       >  📄 ToolTip.py
```

How to use StringVar()

There are built-in programming types in tkinter that differ slightly from the Python types we are used to programming with. StringVar() is one such tkinter type. This recipe will show you how to use the StringVar() type.

Getting ready

You will learn how to save data from the tkinter GUI into variables so we can use that data. We can set and get their values, which is very similar to the Java getter/setter methods.

Here are some of the available types of coding in tkinter:

strVar = StringVar()	**# Holds a string; the default value is an empty string ""**
intVar = IntVar()	# Holds an integer; the default value is 0
dbVar = DoubleVar()	# Holds a float; the default value is 0.0
blVar = BooleanVar()	# Holds a Boolean, it returns 0 for False and 1 for True

 Different languages call numbers with decimal points as floats or doubles. Tkinter calls them DoubleVar, what is known in Python as float datatype. Depending on the level of precision, float and double data can be different. Here, we are translating tkinter DoubleVar into what Python turns into a Python float type.

This becomes clearer when we add a DoubleVar with a Python float and look at the resulting type, which is a Python float and no longer a DoubleVar:

GUI_PyDoubleVar_to_Float_Get.py

```
import tkinter as tk

# Create instance of tkinter
win = tk.Tk()

# Create DoubleVar
doubleData = tk.DoubleVar()
print(doubleData.get())          # default value
doubleData.set(2.4)
print(type(doubleData))

add_doubles = 1.22222222222222222222222 + doubleData.get()
print(add_doubles)
print(type(add_doubles))
```

```
Console ⌗
<terminated> C:\Eclipse_NEON_workspace\2nd Edition Python GUI Programming Cookbook
0.0
<class 'tkinter.DoubleVar'>
3.6222222222222222
<class 'float'>
```

How to do it...

We will create a new Python module, and the following screenshot shows both the code and the resulting output:

GUI_StringVar.py

```
import tkinter as tk

# Create instance of tkinter
win = tk.Tk()

# Assign tkinter Variable to strData variable
strData = tk.StringVar()

# Set strData variable
strData.set('Hello StringVar')

# Get value of strData variable
varData = strData.get()

# Print out current value of strData
print(varData)
```

Search Console ⌗

<terminated> C:\Eclipse_NEON_workspace\2nd Edition Python GUI Programming Cookbook\Ch04_Code\GUI_StringVar.py
Hello StringVar

First, we import the `tkinter` module and alias it to the name `tk`.

Next, we use this alias to create an instance of the `Tk` class by appending parentheses to `Tk`, which calls the constructor of the class. This is the same mechanism as calling a function; only here, we create an instance of a class.

Usually, we use this instance assigned to the `win` variable to start the main event loop later in the code, but here, we are not displaying a GUI, rather, we are demonstrating how to use the tkinter `StringVar` type.

 We still have to create an instance of `Tk()`. If we comment out this line, we will get an error from `tkinter`, so this call is necessary.

Then, we create an instance of the tkinter `StringVar` type and assign it to our Python `strData` variable.

After that, we use our variable to call the `set()` method on `StringVar` and after setting to a value, we get the value, save it in a new variable named `varData`, and then print out its value.

In the Eclipse PyDev console, towards the bottom of the screenshot, we can see the output printed to the console, which is **Hello StringVar**.

Next, we will print the default values of tkinter `IntVar`, `DoubleVar`, and `BooleanVar` types:

`GUI_PyVar_defaults.py`

```
# Get value of strData variable
varData = strData.get()

# Print out current value of strData
print(varData)

# Print out the default tkinter variable values
print(tk.IntVar())
print(tk.DoubleVar())
print(tk.BooleanVar())
<
```

```
Search  Console ⊠                                          ▦ ✖ ✖ ☜

<terminated> C:\Eclipse_NEON_workspace\2nd Edition Python GUI Programming Cookbook\Ch04_Code\GUI_PyVar_defaults.py
Hello StringVar
PY_VAR1
PY_VAR2
PY_VAR3
```

How it works...

As can be seen in the preceding screenshot, the default values do not get printed, as we would have expected.

The online literature mentions default values but we won't see those values until we call the `get` method on them. Otherwise, we just get a variable name that automatically increments (for example, `PY_VAR3`, as can be seen in the preceding screenshot).

Assigning the `tkinter` type to a Python variable does not change the outcome. We still do not get the default value.

Here, we are focusing on the simplest code (which creates `PY_VAR0`):

The value is PY_VAR0, not the expected 0, until we call the get method. Now we can see the default value. We did not call set, so we see the default value automatically assigned to each tkinter type once we call the get method on each type:

GUI_PyVar_Get.py

Note how the default value of 0 gets printed to the console for the IntVar instance that we saved in the intData variable. We can also see the values in the Eclipse PyDev debugger window at the top of the screenshot.

How to get data from a widget

When the user enters data, we want to do something with it in our code. This recipe shows how to capture data in a variable. In the previous recipe, we created several `tkinter` class variables. They were standalone. Now, we are connecting them to our GUI, using the data we get from the GUI and storing it in Python variables.

Getting ready

We will continue using the Python GUI we were building in Chapter 3, *Look and Feel Customization*. We'll reuse and enhance the code from `GUI_progressbar.py` from that chapter.

How to do it...

We will assign a value from our GUI to a Python variable.

Add the following code towards the bottom of our module, just above the main event loop:

```
strData = spin.get()
print("Spinbox value: " + strData)

# Place cursor into name Entry
name_entered.focus()
#=======================
# Start GUI
#=======================
win.mainloop()
```

Running the code gives us the following result:

```
    strData = spin.get()
    print("Spinbox value: " + strData)

    <

 Search   Console       PyUnit
C:\Eclipse_NEON_workspace\2nd Edition Python GUI
Spinbox value: 1
```

We will retrieve the current value of the `Spinbox` control.

 We placed our code above the GUI main event loop, so the printing happens before the GUI becomes visible. We would have to place the code into a callback function if we wanted to print out the current value after displaying the GUI and changing the value of the `Spinbox` control.

We created our `Spinbox` widget using the following code, hardcoding the available values into it:

```
# Adding a Spinbox widget using a set of values
spin = Spinbox(mighty, values=(1, 2, 4, 42, 100), width=5, bd=8,
               command=_spin)
spin.grid(column=0, row=2)
```

We can also move the hardcoding of the data out of the creation of the `Spinbox` class instance and set it later:

```
# Adding a Spinbox widget assigning values after creation
spin = Spinbox(mighty, width=5, bd=8, command=_spin)
spin['values'] = (1, 2, 4, 42, 100)
spin.grid(column=0, row=2)
```

It does not matter how we create our widget and insert data into it because we can access this data by using the `get()` method on the instance of the widget.

How it works...

In order to get the values out of our GUI written using tkinter, we use the tkinter `get()` method on an instance of the widget we wish to get the value from.

In the preceding example, we used the `Spinbox` control, but the principle is the same for all widgets that have a `get()` method.

Once we have got the data, we are in a pure Python world, and tkinter did serve us well in building our GUI. Now that we know how to get the data out of our GUI, we can use this data.

Using module-level global variables

Encapsulation is a major strength in any programming language, enabling us to program using OOP. Python is both OOP as well as procedural. We can create `global` variables that are localized to the module they reside in. They are `global` only to this module, which is one form of encapsulation. Why do we want this? Because as we add more and more functionality to our GUI, we want to avoid naming conflicts that could result in bugs in our code.

 We do not want naming clashes creating bugs in our code! Namespaces are one way to avoid these bugs, and in Python, we can do this by using Python modules (which are unofficial namespaces).

Getting ready

We can declare module-level **globals** in any module just above and outside functions.

We then have to use the `global` Python keyword to refer to them. If we forget to use `global` in functions, we will accidentally create new local variables. This would be a bug and something we really do not want to do.

 Python is a dynamic, strongly typed language. We will notice bugs such as this (forgetting to scope variables with the `global` keyword) only at runtime.

How to do it...

Add the code shown on line 17 to the GUI we used in the previous recipe, *How to get data from a widget*, creating a module-level global variable. We use the C-style all uppercase convention, which is not truly Pythonic, but I think this does emphasize the principle we are addressing in this recipe:

```
 6  #=======================
 7  # imports
 8  #=======================
 9  import tkinter as tk
10  from tkinter import ttk
11  from tkinter import scrolledtext
12  from tkinter import Menu
13  from tkinter import messagebox as msg
14  from tkinter import Spinbox
15  from time import  sleep           # careful - this can freeze the GUI
16
17  GLOBAL_CONST = 42
18
```

Running the code results in a printout of the `global`. Note **42** being printed to the Eclipse console:

`GUI_const_42_print.py`

```
213  # Printing the Global works
214  print(GLOBAL_CONST)
215
216  name_entered.focus()
217  #=======================
218  # Start GUI
219  #=======================
220  win.mainloop()
     <
```

Search Console ☒ PyUnit

`<terminated> C:\Eclipse_NEON_workspace\2nd Edition`

`42`

How it works...

We define a `global` variable at the top of our module, and we print out its value later, towards the bottom of our module.

That works.

Add this function towards the bottom of our module:

GUI_const_42_print_func.py

```
213  def usingGlobal():
214        print(GLOBAL_CONST)
215
216  # call function
217  usingGlobal()
218
```

```
  Search    Console ⊠   PyUnit
C:\Eclipse_NEON_workspace\2nd Edition Python
42
```

In the preceding code snippet, we use the module-level global. It is easy to make a mistake by shadowing global, as demonstrated in the following:

GUI_const_42_777.py

```
213  def usingGlobal():
214        GLOBAL_CONST = 777
215        print(GLOBAL_CONST)
216
```

```
  Search    Console ⊠   PyUnit
C:\Eclipse_NEON_workspace\2nd Edition Python
777
```

Note how **42** becomes **777**, even though we are using the same variable name.

> There is no compiler in Python that warns us if we overwrite global variables in a local function. This can lead to difficulties in debugging at runtime.

Without using the `global` qualifier (line 214), we get an error.

```
213  def usingGlobal():
214  #      global GLOBAL_CONST
215        print(GLOBAL_CONST)
216        GLOBAL_CONST = 777
217        print(GLOBAL_CONST)
218
219
220  # call function
221  usingGlobal()
222
```

```
Search   Console ⋈   PyUnit

<terminated> C:\Eclipse_NEON_workspace\2nd Edition Python GUI Programming Cookbook\Ch04_Code\
Traceback (most recent call last):
  File "C:\Eclipse_NEON_workspace\2nd Edition Python GUI Programming Cookbook\Ch
    usingGlobal()
  File "C:\Eclipse_NEON_workspace\2nd Edition Python GUI Programming Cookbook\Ch
    print(GLOBAL_CONST)
UnboundLocalError: local variable 'GLOBAL_CONST' referenced before assignment
```

When we qualify our local variable with the `global` keyword, we can print out the value of the `global` variable as well as overwrite this value locally:

```
213  def usingGlobal():
214        global GLOBAL_CONST
215        print(GLOBAL_CONST)
216        GLOBAL_CONST = 777
217        print(GLOBAL_CONST)
218
219
220  # call function
221  usingGlobal()
222
```

```
Search   Console ⋈   PyUnit

C:\Eclipse_NEON_workspace\2nd Edition Python
42
777
```

The `global` variables can be very useful when programming small applications. They can help us make data available across methods and functions within the same Python module and sometimes the overhead of OOP is not justified.

As our programs grow in complexity, the benefit we gain from using globals can quickly diminish.

It is best to avoid globals and accidentally shadowing variables by using the same name in different scopes. We can use OOP instead of using global variables.

We played around with the `global` variables within procedural code and learned how it can lead to hard-to-debug bugs. In the next recipe, we will move on to OOP, which can eliminate such bugs.

How coding in classes can improve the GUI

So far, we have been coding in a procedural style. This is a quick scripting method from Python. Once our code gets larger and larger, we need to advance to coding in OOP.

Why?

Because, among many other benefits, OOP allows us to move code around by using methods. Once we use classes, we no longer have to physically place code above the code that calls it. This gives us great flexibility in organizing our code.

We can write related code next to other code and no longer have to worry that the code will not run because the code does not sit above the code that calls it.

We can take that to some rather fancy extremes by coding up modules that refer to methods that are not being created within that module. They rely on the runtime state having created those methods during the time the code runs.

If the methods we call have not been created by that time, we get a runtime error.

Getting ready

We will turn our entire procedural code into OOP very simply. We just turn it into a class, indent all the existing code, and prepend `self` to all variables.

It is very easy.

While at first it might feel a little bit annoying having to prepend everything with the `self` keyword making our code more verbose (hey, we are wasting so much paper…), in the end it is worth it.

How to do it…

In the beginning, all hell breaks loose, but we will soon fix this apparent mess.

Note that in Eclipse, the PyDev editor hints at coding problems by highlighting them in red on the right-hand side portion of the code editor.

Maybe we should not code in OOP after all, but this is what we do, and for very good reasons:

```
GUI_OOP_classes 23

60  class OOP():
61
62      # Create instance
63      win = tk.Tk()
64
65      # Add a title
66      win.title("Python GUI")
67
68      tabControl = ttk.Notebook(win)          # Create Tab Control
69
70      tab1 = ttk.Frame(tabControl)            # Create a tab
71      tabControl.add(tab1, text='Tab 1')      # Add the tab
72      tab2 = ttk.Frame(tabControl)            # Add a second tab
73      tabControl.add(tab2, text='Tab 2')      # Make second tab visible
74
75      tabControl.pack(expand=1, fill="both")  # Pack to make visible
76
77      # LabelFrame using tab1 as the parent
78      mighty = ttk.LabelFrame(tab1, text=' Mighty Python ')
79      mighty.grid(column=0, row=0, padx=8, pady=4)
80
81      # Modify adding a Label using mighty as the parent instead of win
82      a_label = ttk.Label(mighty, text="Enter a name:")
83      a_label.grid(column=0, row=0, sticky='W')
84
85      # Modified Button Click Function
86      def click_me():
87          action.configure(text='Hello ' + name.get() + ' ' +
88                                 number_chosen.get())
89
90      # Adding a Textbox Entry widget
91      name = tk.StringVar()
92      name_entered = ttk.Entry(mighty, width=12, textvariable=name)
```

Search   Console 23   PyUnit

\<terminated> C:\Eclipse_NEON_workspace\2nd Edition Python GUI Programming Cookbook\Ch04_Code\GUI_OOP_classes.py

We just have to prepend all the variables with the `self` keyword and also bind the functions to the class by using `self`, which officially and technically turns the functions into methods.

> There is a difference between functions and methods. Python makes this very clear. Methods are bound to a class while functions are not. We can even mix the two within the same Python module.

Let's prefix everything with `self` to get rid of the red so we can run our code again:

```
# Modified Button Click Function
def click_me(self):
    self.action.configure(text='Hello ' + self.name.get() + ' ' +
                    self.number_chosen.get())
```

Once we do this for all of the errors highlighted in red, we can run our Python code again. The `click_Me` function is now bound to the class and has officially become a method.

Unfortunately, starting in a procedural way and then translating it into OOP is not as simple as I stated earlier. The code has become a huge mess. This is a very good reason to start programming in Python using the OOP model of coding.

> Python is good at doing things the easy way. The easy code often becomes more complex (because it was easy to begin with). Once we get too complex, refactoring our procedural code into what truly could be OOP code becomes harder with every single line of code.

We are translating our procedural code into object-oriented code. Looking at all the troubles we got ourselves into, translating only 200+ lines of Python code into OOP could suggest that we might as well start coding in OOP from the beginning.

We actually did break some of our previously working functionality. Using **Tab 2** and clicking the radio buttons no longer works. We have to refactor more.

The procedural code was easy in the sense that it was simply top to bottom coding. Now that we have placed our code into a class, we have to move all the callback functions into methods. This works, but does take some work to translate our original code:

```
#######################################
# Our procedural code looked like this:
#######################################
# Button Click Function
```

```
def click_me():
    action.configure(text='Hello ' + name.get() + ' ' +
                      number_chosen.get())

# Adding a Textbox Entry widget
name = tk.StringVar()
name_entered = ttk.Entry(mighty, width=12, textvariable=name)
name_entered.grid(column=0, row=1, sticky='W')

# Adding a Button
action = ttk.Button(mighty, text="Click Me!", command=click_me)
action.grid(column=2, row=1)

ttk.Label(mighty, text="Choose a number:").grid(column=1, row=0)
number = tk.StringVar()
number_chosen = ttk.Combobox(mighty, width=12,
                              textvariable=number, state='readonly')
number_chosen['values'] = (1, 2, 4, 42, 100)
number_chosen.grid(column=1, row=1)
number_chosen.current(0)

*********************************************
The new OOP code looks like this:
*********************************************
class OOP():
    def __init__(self):                      # Initializer method
        # Create instance
        self.win = tk.Tk()

        # Add a title
        self.win.title("Python GUI")
        self.create_widgets()

    # Button callback
    def click_me(self):
        self.action.configure(text='Hello ' + self.name.get() + ' '
                              +self.number_chosen.get())
        # ... more callback methods

    def create_widgets(self):
        # Create Tab Control
        tabControl = ttk.Notebook(self.win)
        tab1 = ttk.Frame(tabControl)             # Create a tab
        tabControl.add(tab1, text='Tab 1')       # Add the tab
        tab2 = ttk.Frame(tabControl)             # Create second tab
        tabControl.add(tab2, text='Tab 2')       # Add second tab
        # Pack to make visible
        tabControl.pack(expand=1, fill="both")
```

```
# Adding a Textbox Entry widget - using self
self.name = tk.StringVar()
name_entered = ttk.Entry(mighty, width=12,
                             textvariable=self.name)
name_entered.grid(column=0, row=1, sticky='W')

# Adding a Button - using self
self.action = ttk.Button(mighty, text="Click Me!",
                             command=self.click_me)
self.action.grid(column=2, row=1)
# ...
#=======================
# Start GUI
#=======================
oop = OOP()             # create an instance of the class
# use instance variable to call mainloop via win
oop.win.mainloop()
```

We moved the callback methods to the top of the module, inside the new OOP class. We moved all the widget-creation code into one rather long method, which we call in the initializer of the class.

Technically, deep underneath the hood of the low-level code, Python does have a constructor, yet Python frees us from any worries about this. It is taken care of for us.

Instead, in addition to a real constructor, Python provides us with an initializer.

We are strongly encouraged to use this initializer. We can use it to pass in parameters to our class, initializing variables we wish to use inside our class instance.

 In Python, several classes can exist within the same Python module.

Unlike Java, which has a very rigid naming convention (without which it does not work), Python is much more flexible.

 We can create multiple classes within the same Python module. Unlike Java, we do not depend on a file name that has to match each class name. Python truly rocks!

Once our Python GUI gets large, we will break some classes out into their own modules but, unlike Java, we do not have to. In this book and project, we will keep some classes in the same module while, at the same time, we will break out some other classes into their own modules, importing them into what can be considered as a `main()` function (this is not C, but we can think C-like because Python is very flexible).

What we have achieved so far is adding the `ToolTip` class to our Python module and refactoring our procedural Python code into OOP Python code.

Here, in this recipe, we can see that more than one class can live in the same Python module.

Cool stuff, indeed!

```
 GUI_OOP_2_classes ⌧

20   #=================================================
21⊖ class ToolTip(object):
22⊖     def __init__(self, widget):
23           self.widget = widget
24           self.tip_window = None
25
26⊖     def show_tip(self, tip_text):
27           "Display text in a tooltip window"
```

Both the `ToolTip` class and the `OOP` class reside within the same Python module:

```
 GUI_OOP_2_classes ⌧

61   #=================================================
62⊖ class OOP():
63⊖     def __init__(self):           # Initializer method
64           # Create instance
65           self.win = tk.Tk()
66
67           create_ToolTip(self.win, 'Hello GUI')
68
69           # Add a title
70           self.win.title("Python GUI")
71           self.create_widgets()
```

How it works...

In this recipe, we advanced our procedural code into OOP code. Python enables us to write code in both a practical and a procedural style such as the C-programming language. At the same time, we have the option to code in an OOP style, such as Java, C#, and C++.

Writing callback functions

At first, callback functions can seem to be a little bit intimidating. You call the function, passing it some arguments, and then the function tells you that it is really very busy and it will call you back!

You wonder: Will this function ever call me back? And how long do I have to wait? In Python, even callback functions are easy and, yes, they usually do call you back. They just have to complete their assigned task first (hey, it was you who coded them in the first place...).

Let's understand a little bit more about what happens when we code callbacks into our GUI. Our GUI is event-driven. After it has been created and displayed onscreen, it typically sits there waiting for an event to happen. It is basically waiting for an event to be sent to it. We can send an event to our GUI by clicking one of its action buttons. This creates an event and, in a sense, we called our GUI by sending it a message.

Now, what is supposed to happen after we send a message to our GUI? What happens after clicking the button depends on whether we created an event handler and associated it with this button. If we did not create an event handler, clicking the button will have no effect. The event handler is a callback function (or method, if we use classes). The callback method is also sitting there passively, like our GUI, waiting to be invoked. Once our GUI gets its button clicked, it will invoke the callback.

The callback often does some processing and, when done, it returns the result to our GUI.

 In a sense, we can see that our callback function is calling our GUI back.

Getting ready

The Python interpreter runs through all the code in a module once, finding any syntax errors and pointing them out. You cannot run your Python code if you do not have the syntax right. This includes indentation (if not resulting in a syntax error, wrong indentation usually results in a bug).

On the next parsing round, the interpreter interprets our code and runs it.

At runtime, many GUI events can be generated and it is usually callback functions that add functionality to GUI widgets.

How to do it...

Here is the callback for the `Spinbox` widget:

```
37      # Spinbox callback
38      def _spin(self):
39          value = self.spin.get()
40          print(value)
41          self.scrol.insert(tk.INSERT, value + '\n')


124
125         # Adding a Spinbox widget
126         self.spin = Spinbox(mighty, values=(1, 2, 4, 42, 100), width=5, bd=9, command=self._spin)
127         self.spin.grid(column=0, row=2)
```

How it works...

We created a callback method in the OOP class which gets called when we select a value from the `Spinbox` widget because we bound the method to the widget via the `command` argument (`command=self._spin`). We use a leading underscore to hint at the fact that this method is meant to be respected like a private Java method.

Python intentionally avoids language restrictions, such as private, public, friend, and so on. In Python, we use naming conventions instead. Leading and trailing double underscores surrounding a keyword are expected to be restricted to the Python language and we are expected not to use them in our own Python code.

However, we can use a leading underscore prefix with a variable name or function to provide a hint that this name is meant to be respected as a private helper.

At the same time, we can postfix a single underscore if we wish to use what otherwise would be built-in Python names. For example, if we wished to abbreviate the length of a list, we could do the following:

```
len_ = len(aList)
```

Often, the underscore is hard to read and easy to oversee, so this might not be the best idea in practice.

Creating reusable GUI components

We will create reusable GUI components using Python. In this recipe, we will keep it simple by moving our `ToolTip` class into its own module. Then, we will import and use it for displaying tooltips over several widgets of our GUI.

Getting ready

We are building our code from Chapter 3, *Look and Feel Customization*: `GUI_tooltip.py`.

How to do it...

We will start by breaking out our `ToolTip` class into a separate Python module. We will slightly enhance it to pass in the control widget and the tooltip text that we wish to display when we hover the mouse over the control.

We create a new Python module and place the `ToolTip` class code into it and then import this module into our primary module.

We then reuse the imported `ToolTip` class by creating several tooltips, which can be seen when hovering the mouse over several of our GUI widgets.

Refactoring our common `ToolTip` class code out into its own module helps us reuse this code from other modules. Instead of copy/paste/modify, we use the DRY principle and our common code is located in only one place, so when we modify the code, all modules that import it will automatically get the latest version of our module.

DRY stands for **Don't Repeat Yourself**, and we will look at it again in a later chapter. We can do similar things by turning our **Tab 3** image into a reusable component. To keep this recipe's code simple, we removed **Tab 3**, but you can experiment with the code from the previous chapter. The code is reused from `GUI_tooltip.py`.

Consider running `GUI_tooltip.py`:

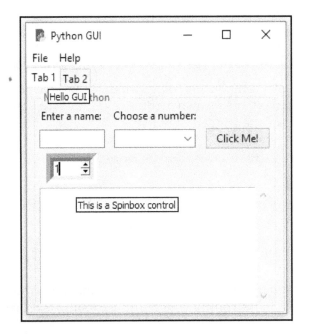

Consider the following code:

```
# Add a Tooltip to the Spinbox
tt.create_ToolTip(self.spin, 'This is a Spinbox control')

# Add Tooltips to more widgets
tt.create_ToolTip(self.name_entered, 'This is an Entry control')
tt.create_ToolTip(self.action, 'This is a Button control')
tt.create_ToolTip(self.scrol, 'This is a ScrolledText control')
```

This also works on the second tab:

The import statements look as follows:

```
   P GUI_OOP_class_imported_tooltip ⋈    P ToolTip
   13  from tkinter import messagebox as msg
   14  from tkinter import Spinbox
   15  from time import  sleep
   16  import Ch04_Code.ToolTip as tt
   17
   18  GLOBAL_CONST = 42
   19
   20  #=========================================================
   21⊖ class OOP():
   22⊖     def __init__(self):            # Initializer method
   23             # Create instance
   24             self.win = tk.Tk()
   25
   26             tt.create_ToolTip(self.win, 'Hello GUI')
   27
```

The new code structure looks like this now:

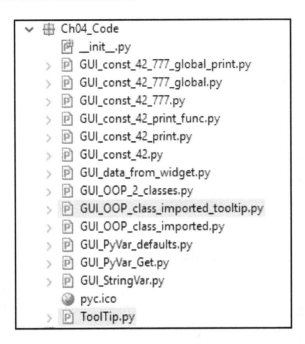

And the broken out (aka refactored) code in a separate module looks like this:

```
P GUI_OOP_class_imported_tooltip     P ToolTip 

  9  import tkinter as tk
 10
 11  #================================================
 12  class ToolTip(object):
 13      def __init__(self, widget):
 14          self.widget = widget
 15          self.tip_window = None
 16
 17      def show_tip(self, tip_text):
 18          "Display text in a tooltip window"
```

How it works...

In the preceding screenshots, we can see several tooltip messages being displayed. The one for the main window might appear a little bit annoying, so it is better not to display a tooltip for the main window, because we really wish to highlight the functionality of the individual widgets. The main window form has a title which explains its purpose; no need for a tooltip.

5
Matplotlib Charts

In this chapter, we will create beautiful charts using Python 3.6 with the `Matplotlib` module. We will cover the following recipes:

- Creating beautiful charts using `Matplotlib`
- Installing `Matplotlib` using `pip` with `whl` extension
- Creating our first chart
- Placing labels on charts
- How to give the chart a legend
- Scaling charts
- Adjusting the scale of charts dynamically

Introduction

In this chapter, we will create beautiful charts that visually represent data. Depending on the format of the data source, we can plot one or more columns of data in the same chart.

We will be using the Python `Matplotlib` module to create our charts.

In order to create these graphical charts, we need to download additional Python modules, and there are several ways to install them.

This chapter will explain how to download the `Matplotlib` Python module along with all other required Python modules and the ways to do this.

After we install the required modules, we will then create our own Pythonic charts.

Here is the overview of Python modules for this chapter:

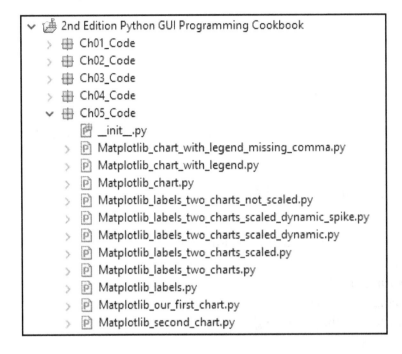

Creating beautiful charts using Matplotlib

This recipe introduces us to the `Matplotlib` Python module, which enables us to create visual charts using Python 3.6 and above.

The URL, `http://matplotlib.org/users/screenshots.html`, is a great place to start for exploring the world of `Matplotlib`, and it teaches us how to create many charts that are not presented in this chapter.

Getting ready

In order to use the `Matplotlib` Python module, we first have to install this module as well as several other related Python modules.

If you are running a version of Python older than 3.6, I would encourage you to upgrade your version, as we will be using the Python `pip` module throughout this chapter to install the required Python modules, and `pip` is installed with 3.6 and above.

 It is possible to install `pip` with the earlier versions of Python 3 but the process is not very intuitive, so it is definitely better to upgrade to 3.6 or above.

How to do it...

The following picture is an example of what incredible graphical charts can be created using Python with the `Matplotlib` module:

`Matplotlib_chart.py`

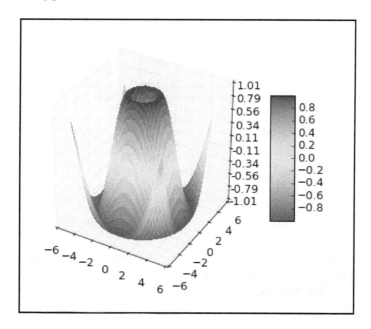

In the following code snippet, I have copied some code from the `http://matplotlib.org/` website, which creates this incredible chart. I have also added some comments to the code. There are many examples available on this site, and I encourage you to try them out until you find the kind of charts you would like to create.

Here is the code to create the chart in less than 25 lines of Python code, including white spaces:

```python
from mpl_toolkits.mplot3d import Axes3D
from matplotlib import cm
from matplotlib.ticker import LinearLocator, FormatStrFormatter
import matplotlib.pyplot as plt
import numpy as np

fig = plt.figure()                      # create a figure
ax = fig.gca(projection='3d')           # create a 3-dimensional axis
X = np.arange(-5, 5, 0.25)              # horizontal range
Y = np.arange(-5, 5, 0.25)              # vertical range
X, Y = np.meshgrid(X, Y)               # create a special grid
R = np.sqrt(X**2 + Y**2)               # calculate square root
Z = np.sin(R)                          # calculate sinus

## use #@UndefinedVariable below to ignore the error for cm.coolwarm
surf = ax.plot_surface(X, Y, Z, rstride=1, cstride=1,
                       cmap=cm.coolwarm, linewidth=0,
                       antialiased=False)
ax.set_zlim(-1.01, 1.01)               # z-axis is third dimension

ax.zaxis.set_major_locator(LinearLocator(10))
ax.zaxis.set_major_formatter(FormatStrFormatter('%.02f'))

fig.colorbar(surf, shrink=0.5, aspect=5)

plt.show()                             # display the figure
```

 Running the code using Python 3.6 or above with the Eclipse PyDev plugin might show some unresolved import and variable errors. You can simply disable these in Eclipse via `#@UnresolvedImport` and `#@UndefinedVariable`.

Just ignore those errors if you are developing using Eclipse, as the code will run successfully.

How it works...

In order to create beautiful graphs, as shown previously, we need to download Matplotlib as well as several other Python modules.

The following recipe will guide us through how to successfully download and install all the required modules that will enable us to create our own beautiful charts.

Installing Matplotlib using pip with whl extension

The usual way to download additional Python modules is by using pip. The pip module comes pre-installed with the latest version of Python (3.6 and above).

> If you are using an older version of Python, you may have to download both pip and setuptools yourself.

This recipe will show how to successfully install Matplotlib using pip. We will be using the .whl extension for this installation, so this recipe will also show you how to install the wheel module.

Getting ready

First, let's find out if you have the wheel module already installed. The wheel module is necessary to download and install Python packages that have the .whl extension.

We can find out what modules we have currently installed using pip.

From the Windows Command Prompt, run the `pip list` command:

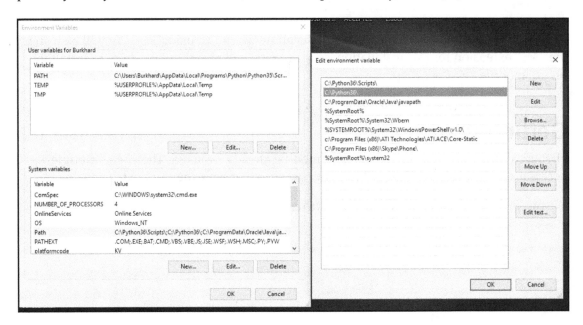

If you get an error running this command, you might want to check whether Python is on your environmental path. If it is currently not, add it to **System variables** | **Path** (bottom-left) by clicking the **Edit...** button. Then, click the **New** button (top-right) and type in the path to your Python installation. Also, add the Scripts directory, as the `pip.exe` lives there:

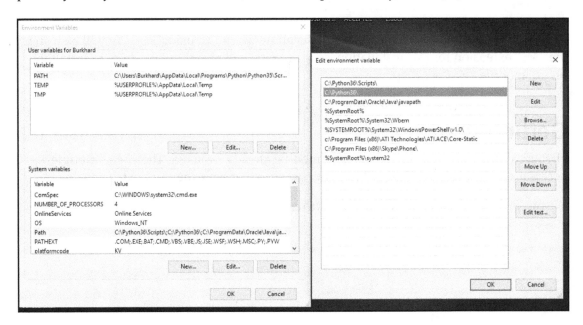

If you have more than one version of Python installed, it is a good idea to move Python 3.6 to the top of the list. When we type `pip install <module>`, the first version found in **System variables | Path** might be used and you might get some unexpected errors if an older version of Python is located above Python 3.6.

Let's run `pip install wheel` and then verify if it is successfully installed using `pip list`:

```
Administrator: Command Prompt

C:\WINDOWS\system32>pip install wheel
Collecting wheel
  Downloading wheel-0.29.0-py2.py3-none-any.whl (66kB)
    100% |                              | 71kB 54kB/s
Installing collected packages: wheel
Successfully installed wheel-0.29.0

C:\WINDOWS\system32>pip list
DEPRECATION: The default format will switch to columns i
conf under the [list] section) to disable this warning.
pip (9.0.1)
setuptools (28.8.0)
wheel (0.29.0)

C:\WINDOWS\system32>
```

If you are really very used to Python 2.7 and insist on running the code in Python 2.7, you can try this trick. After everything is working with Python 3.6, you can rename the 3.6 `python.exe` to `python3.exe` and then have fun using both 2.7 and 3.6 by typing `python.exe` or `python3.exe` in a command window to run the different Python executables. It is a hack. If you really wish to go on this road, your are on your own, but it can work.

How to do it…

With the wheel module installed, we can now download and install `Matplotlib` from `http://www.lfd.uci.edu/~gohlke/pythonlibs/`:

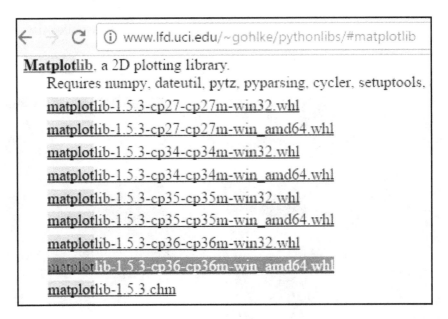

Make sure you download and install the `Matplotlib` version that matches the Python version you are using. For example, download and install **Matplotlib-1.5.3-cp36-cp36m-win-amd64.whl** if you have Python 3.6 installed on a 64-bit OS, such as Microsoft Windows 10.

 The **amd64** in the middle of the executable name means you are installing the 64-bit version. If you are using a 32-bit x86 system then installing **amd64** will not work. Similar problems can occur if you have installed a 32-bit version of Python and download 64-bit Python modules.

After downloading the wheel installer, we can now use `pip`. Depending upon what you have already installed on your system, running the `pip installMatplotlib-1.5.3-cp36-cp36m-win-amd64.whl` command might start fine, but then it might not run to completion. Here is a screenshot of what might happen during the installation:

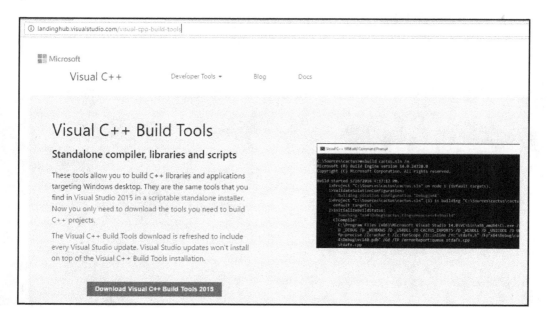

The installation ran into an error. The way to solve this is to download and install the **Microsoft Visual C++ Build Tools**, and we do this from the website that is mentioned in the preceding screenshot (`http://landinghub.visualstudio.com/visual-cpp-build-to ols`):

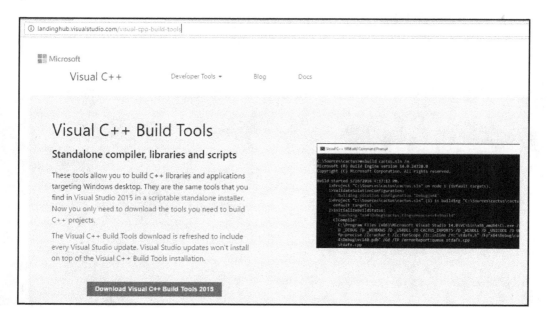

Starting the installation of the MS VC++ Build Tools looks as follows:

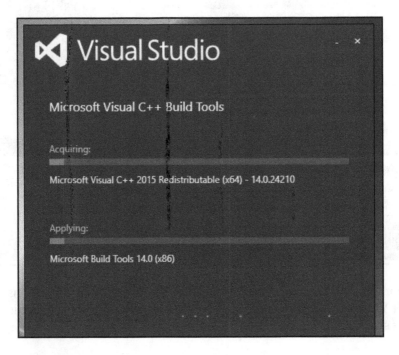

After we have successfully installed the Build Tools, we can now run our `Matplotlib` installation to completion. So, just type in the same `pip install` command we have used before:

```
Administrator: Command Prompt
Microsoft Windows [Version 10.0.14393]
(c) 2016 Microsoft Corporation. All rights reserved.

C:\WINDOWS\system32>cd C:\Users\Burkh\Desktop\2nd EDITION PACKT PYTHON GUI COOKBOOK\SW  DOWNLOADS

C:\Users\Burkh\Desktop\2nd EDITION PACKT PYTHON GUI COOKBOOK\SW  DOWNLOADS>pip install matplotlib-1.5.3-cp36-cp36m-win_amd64.whl
Processing c:\users\burkh\desktop\2nd edition packt python gui cookbook\sw  downloads\matplotlib-1.5.3-cp36-cp36m-win_amd64.whl
Requirement already satisfied: python-dateutil in c:\python36\lib\site-packages (from matplotlib==1.5.3)
Collecting cycler (from matplotlib==1.5.3)
  Using cached cycler-0.10.0-py2.py3-none-any.whl
Collecting pytz (from matplotlib==1.5.3)
  Using cached pytz-2016.7-py2.py3-none-any.whl
Collecting pyparsing!=2.0.0,!=2.0.4,!=2.1.2,>=1.5.6 (from matplotlib==1.5.3)
  Using cached pyparsing-2.1.10-py2.py3-none-any.whl
Collecting numpy>=1.6 (from matplotlib==1.5.3)
  Using cached numpy-1.11.2.tar.gz
Requirement already satisfied: six>=1.5 in c:\python36\lib\site-packages (from python-dateutil->matplotlib==1.5.3)
Installing collected packages: cycler, pytz, pyparsing, numpy, matplotlib
  Running setup.py install for numpy ... done
Successfully installed cycler-0.10.0 matplotlib-1.5.3 numpy-1.11.2 pyparsing-2.1.10 pytz-2016.7

C:\Users\Burkh\Desktop\2nd EDITION PACKT PYTHON GUI COOKBOOK\SW  DOWNLOADS>
```

We can verify that we have successfully installed `Matplotlib` by looking at our Python installation directory. After successful installation, the `Matplotlib` folder is added to `site-packages`. Depending upon where we installed Python, the full path to the site-packages folder on Windows can be:

```
C:\Python36\Lib\site-packages
```

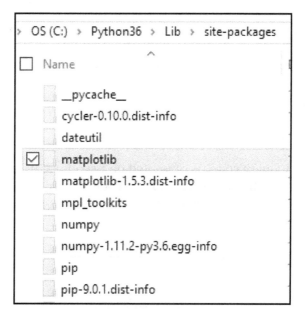

If you see the `matplotlib` folder added to the `site-packages` folder in your Python installation, then we have successfully installed `Matplotlib`.

How it works...

The common way to download Python modules is by using `pip`, shown previously. In order to install all the modules that `Matplotlib` requires, the download format of the main website where we can download them has changed, using a `whl` format.

> Installing Python modules using `pip` is usually very easy. Yet you might run into some unexpected troubles. Follow the preceding steps and your installation will succeed.

Creating our first chart

Now that we have all the required Python modules installed, we can create our own charts using Matplotlib.

We can create charts from only a few lines of Python code.

Getting ready

Successfully installing Matplotlib, as shown in the previous recipe, is a requirement for this recipe.

How to do it...

Using the minimum amount of code, as presented on the official Matplotlib website, we can create our first chart. Well, almost. The sample code shown on the website does not work until we import the show function from pylab and then call it:

Matplotlib_our_first_chart.py

```
import numpy as np
import matplotlib.pyplot as plt
from pylab import show

x = np.arange(0, 5, 0.1);
y = np.sin(x)
plt.plot(x, y)

show()          # call show()
```

We can simplify the code and even improve it by using another of the many examples provided on the official `Matplotlib` website. The `pylab` module comes with its own plotting function, so we do not need to import `matplotlib`, after all, if we wish to simplify the code:

`Matplotlib_second_chart.py`

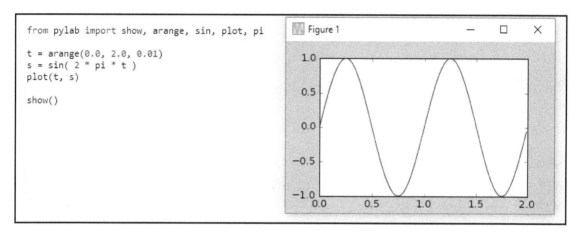

How it works...

The Python `Matplotlib` module, combined with add-ons such as `numpy`, creates a very rich programming environment that enables us to perform mathematical computations and plot them in visual charts very easily.

The `arange` method of `numpy` does not intend to arrange anything. It means to create a range, which is used instead of Python's built-in `range` operator. The `linspace` method can create a similar confusion. Who is *lin* and in what *space*?

As it turns out, the name means *linear spaced vector*.

The `pyglet` function `show` displays the graph we created. Calling `show()` has some side effects when you try to plot another graph after successfully creating the first one.

Placing labels on charts

So far, we have used the default `Matplotlib` GUI. Now, we will create some `tkinter` GUIs using `Matplotlib`.

This will require a few more lines of Python code and importing some more libraries, and it is well worth the effort, because we are gaining control of our paintings using canvases.

We will position labels onto both the horizontal and the vertical axes, that is, *x* and *y*. We will do this by creating a `Matplotlib` figure upon which we will draw.

You will also learn how to use subplots, which will enable you to draw more than one graph in the same window.

Getting ready

With the necessary Python modules installed and knowing where to find the official online documentation and tutorials, we can now carry on with our creation of `Matplotlib` charts.

How to do it...

While `plot` is the easiest way to create a `Matplotlib` chart, using `Figure` in combination with `Canvas` creates a more custom-made graph, which looks much better and also enables us to add buttons and other widgets to it:

Matplotlib_labels.py

```
from matplotlib.figure import Figure
from matplotlib.backends.backend_tkagg import FigureCanvasTkAgg
import tkinter as tk
#------------------------------------------------------------
fig = Figure(figsize=(12, 8), facecolor='white')
#------------------------------------------------------------
# axis = fig.add_subplot(111)      # 1 row,  1 column, only graph
axis = fig.add_subplot(211)        # 2 rows, 1 column, Top graph
#------------------------------------------------------------
xValues = [1,2,3,4]
yValues = [5,7,6,8]
axis.plot(xValues, yValues)
axis.set_xlabel('Horizontal Label')
axis.set_ylabel('Vertical Label')
# axis.grid()                      # default line style
axis.grid(linestyle='-')           # solid grid lines
```

```
#---------------------------------------------------------------
def _destroyWindow():
     root.quit()
     root.destroy()
#---------------------------------------------------------------
root = tk.Tk()
root.withdraw()
root.protocol('WM_DELETE_WINDOW', _destroyWindow)
#---------------------------------------------------------------
canvas = FigureCanvasTkAgg(fig, master=root)
canvas._tkcanvas.pack(side=tk.TOP, fill=tk.BOTH, expand=1)
#---------------------------------------------------------------
root.update()
root.deiconify()
root.mainloop()
```

Running the preceding code results in the following chart:

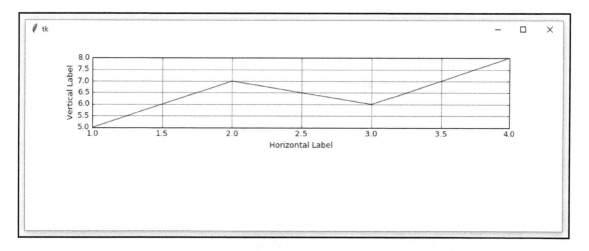

In the first line of code, after the import statements, we create an instance of a `Figure` object. Next, we add subplots to this figure by calling `add_subplot(211)`. The first number in `211` tells the figure how many plots to add, the second number determines the number of columns, and the third tells the figure the order in which to display the plots.

This might become clearer by giving an example based on the Matplotlib website:

```
from matplotlib.figure import Figure
from matplotlib.backends.backend_tkagg import FigureCanvasTkAgg
import tkinter as tk
#---------------------------------------------------------------
fig = Figure(figsize=(12, 8), facecolor='white')
```

```
xValues = [1,2,3,4]
yValues = [5,7,6,8]
#----------------------------------------------------------------
axis1 = fig.add_subplot(221)
axis2 = fig.add_subplot(222, sharex=axis1, sharey=axis1)
axis3 = fig.add_subplot(223, sharex=axis1, sharey=axis1)
axis4 = fig.add_subplot(224, sharex=axis1, sharey=axis1)
#----------------------------------------------------------------
axis1.plot(xValues, yValues)
axis1.set_xlabel('Horizontal Label 1')
axis1.set_ylabel('Vertical Label 1')
axis1.grid(linestyle='-') # solid grid lines
#----------------------------------------------------------------
axis2.plot(xValues, yValues)
axis2.set_xlabel('Horizontal Label 2')
axis2.set_ylabel('Vertical Label 2')
axis2.grid(linestyle='-') # solid grid lines
#----------------------------------------------------------------
axis3.plot(xValues, yValues)
axis3.set_xlabel('Horizontal Label3')
axis3.set_ylabel('Vertical Label 3')
axis3.grid(linestyle='-') # solid grid lines
#----------------------------------------------------------------
axis4.plot(xValues, yValues)
axis4.set_xlabel('Horizontal Label 4')
axis4.set_ylabel('Vertical Label 4')
axis4.grid(linestyle='-') # solid grid lines
#----------------------------------------------------------------
def _destroyWindow():
    root.quit()
    root.destroy()
#----------------------------------------------------------------
root = tk.Tk()
root.withdraw()
root.protocol('WM_DELETE_WINDOW', _destroyWindow)
#----------------------------------------------------------------
canvas = FigureCanvasTkAgg(fig, master=root)
canvas._tkcanvas.pack(side=tk.TOP, fill=tk.BOTH, expand=1)
#----------------------------------------------------------------
root.update()
root.deiconify()
root.mainloop()
```

Running the preceding code results in the following chart being created:

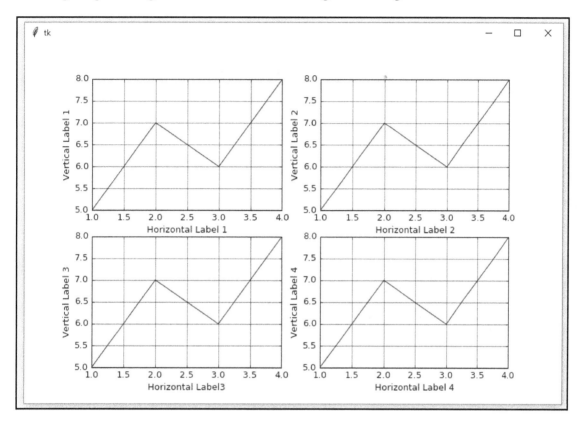

 The important thing to notice here is that we create one axis, which is then used as the shared *x* and *y* axes for the other graphs within the chart. In this way, we can achieve a database-like layout of the chart.

We also add a grid and change its default line style. Even though we only display one plot in the chart, by choosing 2 for the number of subplots, we are moving the plot up, which results in an extra white space at the bottom of the chart. This first plot now only occupies 50% of the screen, which affects how large the grid lines of this plot are when being displayed.

Experiment with the code by uncommenting the code for `axis` = and `axis.grid()` to see the different effects.

We can add more sub plots by assigning them to the second position using `add_subplot(212)`:

`Matplotlib_labels_two_charts.py`

```python
from matplotlib.figure import Figure
from matplotlib.backends.backend_tkagg import FigureCanvasTkAgg
import tkinter as tk
#----------------------------------------------------------------
fig = Figure(figsize=(12, 8), facecolor='white')
#----------------------------------------------------------------
axis = fig.add_subplot(211)     # 2 rows, 1 column, Top graph
#----------------------------------------------------------------
xValues = [1,2,3,4]
yValues = [5,7,6,8]
axis.plot(xValues, yValues)
axis.set_xlabel('Horizontal Label')
axis.set_ylabel('Vertical Label')
axis.grid(linestyle='-')         # solid grid lines
#----------------------------------------------------------------
axis1 = fig.add_subplot(212)    # 2 rows, 1 column, Bottom graph
#----------------------------------------------------------------
xValues1 = [1,2,3,4]
yValues1 = [7,5,8,6]
axis1.plot(xValues1, yValues1)
axis1.grid()                     # default line style
#----------------------------------------------------------------
def _destroyWindow():
    root.quit()
    root.destroy()
#----------------------------------------------------------------
root = tk.Tk()
root.withdraw()
root.protocol('WM_DELETE_WINDOW', _destroyWindow)
#----------------------------------------------------------------
canvas = FigureCanvasTkAgg(fig, master=root)
canvas._tkcanvas.pack(side=tk.TOP, fill=tk.BOTH, expand=1)
#----------------------------------------------------------------
root.update()
root.deiconify()
root.mainloop()
```

Running the slightly modified code now adds `axis1` to the chart. For the grid of the bottom plot, we left the line style as its default:

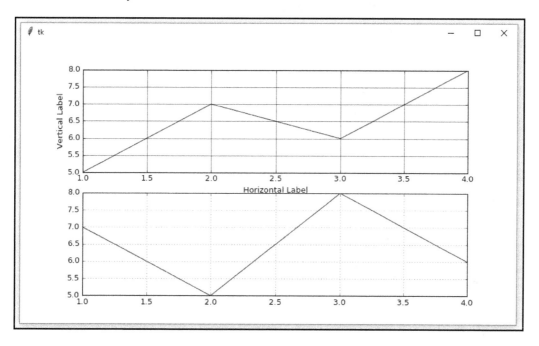

How it works...

We imported the necessary `Matplotlib` modules to create a figure and a canvas onto which to draw the chart. We gave it some values for the *x* and *y* axes and set a few of the many configuration options.

We created our own `tkinter` window in which to display the chart, and we customized the positioning of the plots.

As we saw in previous chapters, in order to create a `tkinter` GUI, we first have to import the `tkinter` module and then create an instance of the `Tk` class. We assign this class instance to a variable we name `root`, which is a name often used in examples that you find online.

Our `tkinter` GUI will not become visible until we start the main event loop and, to do so, we use `root.mainloop()`.

How to give the chart a legend

Once we start plotting more than one line of data points, things might become a little bit unclear. So by adding a legend to our graphs, we can tell which data is what, and what it actually means.

We do not have to choose different colors to represent the different data. `Matplotlib` automatically assigns a different color to each line of the data points.

All we have to do is create the chart and add a legend to it.

Getting ready

In this recipe, we will enhance the chart from the previous recipe, *Placing labels on charts*. We will only plot one chart.

How to do it...

First, we will plot more lines of data on the same chart, and then we will add a legend to the chart.

We'll do this by modifying the code from the previous recipe:

Matplotlib_chart_with_legend.py

```
from matplotlib.figure import Figure
from matplotlib.backends.backend_tkagg import FigureCanvasTkAgg
import tkinter as tk
#-------------------------------------------------------------
fig = Figure(figsize=(12, 5), facecolor='white')
#-------------------------------------------------------------
axis  = fig.add_subplot(111)              # 1 row, 1 column

xValues  = [1,2,3,4]

yValues0 = [6,7.5,8,7.5]
yValues1 = [5.5,6.5,8,6]
yValues2 = [6.5,7,8,7]

t0, = axis.plot(xValues, yValues0)
t1, = axis.plot(xValues, yValues1)
t2, = axis.plot(xValues, yValues2)
```

```
axis.set_ylabel('Vertical Label')
axis.set_xlabel('Horizontal Label')

axis.grid()

fig.legend((t0, t1, t2), ('First line', 'Second line', 'Third
            line'), 'upper right')

#-------------------------------------------------------------
def _destroyWindow():
    root.quit()
    root.destroy()
#-------------------------------------------------------------
root = tk.Tk()
root.withdraw()
root.protocol('WM_DELETE_WINDOW', _destroyWindow)
#-------------------------------------------------------------
canvas = FigureCanvasTkAgg(fig, master=root)
canvas._tkcanvas.pack(side=tk.TOP, fill=tk.BOTH, expand=1)
#-------------------------------------------------------------
root.update()
root.deiconify()
root.mainloop()
```

Running the modified code creates the following chart, which has a legend in the upper-right corner:

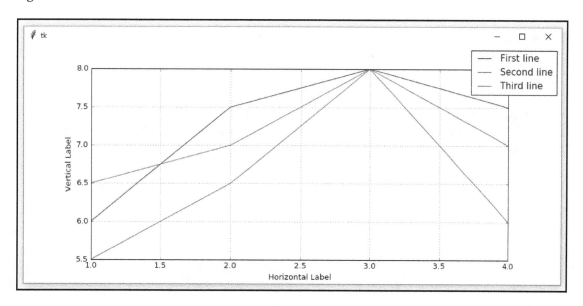

We are only plotting one graph in this recipe, and we do this by changing `fig.add_subplot(111)`. We also slightly modify the size of the figure via the `figsize` property.

Next, we create three Python lists that contain the values to be plotted. When we plot the data, we save the references to the plots in local variables.

We create the legend by passing in a tuple with the references to the three plots, another tuple that contains the strings that are then displayed in the legend, and in the third argument, we position the legend within the chart.

The default settings of `Matplotlib` assign a color scheme to the lines being plotted.

We can easily change this default setting of colors to the colors we prefer by setting a property when we plot each axis.

We do this by using the `color` property and assigning it an available color value:

Matplotlib_chart_with_legend.py

```
t0, = axis.plot(xValues, yValues0, color = 'purple')
t1, = axis.plot(xValues, yValues1, color = 'red')
t2, = axis.plot(xValues, yValues2, color = 'blue')
```

Note that the comma after the variable assignments of `t0`, `t1`, and `t2` is not a mistake. It is required in order to create the legend.

The comma after each variable turns a list into a tuple. If we leave this out, our legend will not be displayed.

The code will still run, just without the intended legend.

When we remove the comma after the `t0` assignment, we get an error and the first line no longer appears in the figure. The chart and legend still get created but without the first line appearing in the legend.

```
# the commas after t0, t1 and t2 are required
t0 = axis.plot(xValues, yValues0)          # no comma here
t1, = axis.plot(xValues, yValues1)
t2, = axis.plot(xValues, yValues2)
```

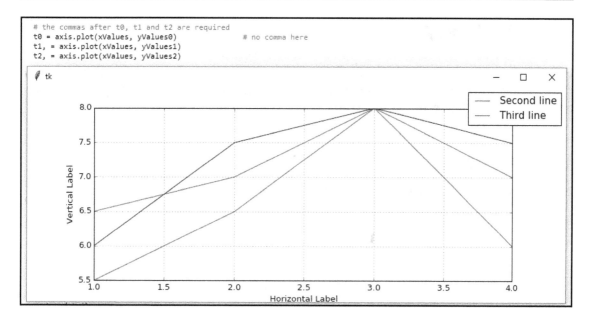

How it works...

We enhanced our chart by plotting three lines of data in the same chart and giving it a legend in order to distinguish the data that those three lines plot.

Scaling charts

In the previous recipes, while creating our first charts and enhancing them, we hardcoded the scaling of how those values are visually represented.

While this served us well for the values we were using, we often plot charts from very large databases.

Depending on the range of that data, our hardcoded values for the vertical y-dimension might not always be the best solution, and may make it hard to see the lines in our charts.

Getting ready

We will improve our code from the previous recipe, *How to give the chart a legend*. If you have not typed in all of the code from the previous recipes, just download the code for this chapter, and it will get you started (and then you can have a lot of fun creating GUIs, charts, and so on, using Python).

How to do it...

Modify the `yValues1` line of code from the previous recipe to use `50` as the third value:

`Matplotlib_labels_two_charts_not_scaled.py`

```
axis    = fig.add_subplot(111)        # 1 row, 1 column
xValues  = [1,2,3,4]
yValues0 = [6,7.5,8,7.5]
yValues1 = [5.5,6.5,50,6]             # one very high value (50)
yValues2 = [6.5,7,8,7]
```

The only difference to the code that created the chart in the previous recipe is one data value.

By changing one value that is not close to the average range of all the other values for all plotted lines, the visual representation of the data has dramatically changed, we lost a lot of details about the overall data, and we now mainly see one high spike:

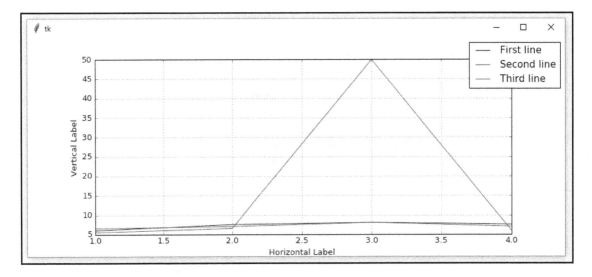

So far, our charts have adjusted themselves according to the data they visually represent.

While this is a practical feature of `Matplotlib`, this is not always what we want. We can restrict the scale of the chart being represented by limiting the vertical *y*-dimension:

`Matplotlib_labels_two_charts_scaled.py`

```
yValues0 = [6,7.5,8,7.5]
yValues1 = [5.5,6.5,50,6]              # one very high value (50)
yValues2 = [6.5,7,8,7]

axis.set_ylim(5, 8)                    # limit the vertical display
```

The `axis.set_ylim(5, 8)` line of code now limits the beginning value to 5 and the ending value of the vertical display to 8.

Now, when we create our chart, the high value peak no longer has the impact it had before:

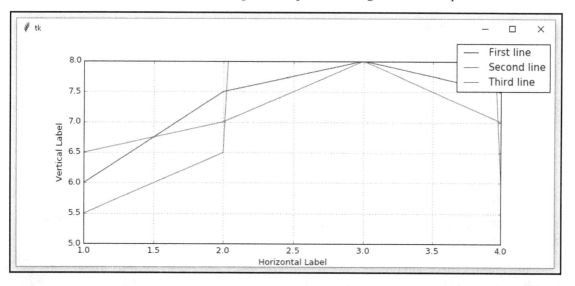

How it works...

We increased one value in the data, which resulted in a dramatic effect. By setting limits to the vertical and horizontal displays of the chart, we can see the data we are most interested in.

Spikes, like the ones just shown, can be of great interest too. It all depends on what we are looking for. The visual representation of the data is of great value.

 A picture is worth a thousand words.

Adjusting the scale of charts dynamically

In the previous recipe, we learned how we can limit the scaling of our charts. In this recipe, we will go one step further by dynamically adjusting the scaling by setting both a limit and analyzing our data before we represent it.

Getting ready

We will enhance the code from the previous recipe, *Scaling charts*, by reading in the data we are plotting dynamically, averaging it, and then adjusting our chart.

While we would typically read in the data from an external source, in this recipe we'll create the data we are plotting using Python lists, as can be seen in the code in the following section.

How to do it…

We are creating our own data in our Python module by assigning lists with data to the xValues and yValues variables.

In many graphs, the beginning of the *x* and *y* coordinate system starts at (0, 0). This is usually a good idea, so let's adjust our chart coordinate code accordingly.

Let's modify the code to set limits on both the *x* and *y* dimensions:

Matplotlib_labels_two_charts_scaled_dynamic.py

```
xValues  = [1,2,3,4]

yValues0 = [6,7.5,8,7.5]
yValues1 = [5.5,6.5,50,6]          # one very high value (50)
yValues2 = [6.5,7,8,7]

axis.set_ylim(0, 8)                # lower limit (0)
axis.set_xlim(0, 8)                # use same limits for x
```

Now that we have set the same limits for *x* and *y*, our chart might look more balanced. When we run the modified code, we get the following result:

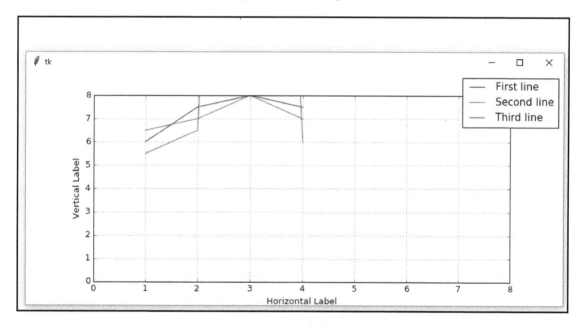

Maybe starting at (0, 0) was not such a great idea after all...

What we really want to do is adjust our chart dynamically according to the range of the data, while at the same time restricting the values that are too high or too low.

We can do this by parsing all the data to be represented in the chart while, at the same time, setting some explicit limits.

Modify the code as follows:

Matplotlib_labels_two_charts_scaled_dynamic.py

```
xValues  = [1,2,3,4]

yValues0 = [6,7.5,8,7.5]
yValues1 = [5.5,6.5,50,6]                # one very high value (50)
yValues2 = [6.5,7,8,7]
yAll = [yValues0, yValues1, yValues2]  # list of lists

# flatten list of lists retrieving minimum value
minY = min([y for yValues in yAll for y in yValues])

yUpperLimit = 20
# flatten list of lists retrieving max value within defined limit
maxY = max([y for yValues in yAll for y in yValues if y <
            yUpperLimit])

# dynamic limits
axis.set_ylim(minY, maxY)
axis.set_xlim(min(xValues), max(xValues))

t0, = axis.plot(xValues, yValues0)
t1, = axis.plot(xValues, yValues1)
t2, = axis.plot(xValues, yValues2)
```

Running the code results in the following chart. We adjusted both its *x* and *y* dimensions dynamically. Note how the *y*-dimension now starts at **5.5** instead of **5.0**, as it did before. The chart also no longer starts at (0, 0), giving us more valuable information about our data:

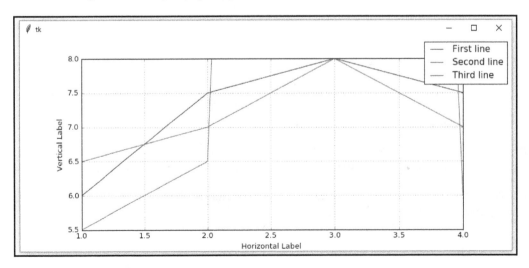

We are creating a list of lists for the *y*-dimension data and then using a list comprehension wrapped into a call to Python's `min()` and `max()` functions.

If list comprehensions seem to be a little bit advanced, what they basically are is a very compressed loop.

They are also designed to be faster than a regular programming loop.

In the preceding Python code, we created three lists that hold the *y*-dimensional data to be plotted. We then created another list that holds those three lists, which creates a list of lists, as follows:

```
yValues0 = [6,7.5,8,7.5]
yValues1 = [5.5,6.5,50,6]              # one very high value (50)
yValues2 = [6.5,7,8,7]
yAll = [yValues0, yValues1, yValues2]  # list of lists
```

We are interested in getting both the minimum value of all of the *y*-dimensional data and the maximum value contained within these three lists.

We can do this via a Python list comprehension:

```
# flatten list of lists retrieving minimum value
minY = min([y for yValues in yAll for y in yValues])
```

After running the list comprehension, `minY` is `5.5`.

The preceding line of code is the list comprehension that runs through all the values of all the data contained within the three lists and finds the minimum value using the Python `min` keyword.

In the very same pattern, we find the maximum value contained in the data we wish to plot. This time, we'll also set a limit within our list comprehension, which ignores all the values that are above the limit we specified, as follows:

```
yUpperLimit = 20
# flatten list of lists retrieving max value within defined limit
maxY = max([y for yValues in yAll for y in yValues if y <
            yUpperLimit])
```

After running the preceding code with our chosen restriction, maxY has the value of 8 (not 50).

We applied a restriction to the max value, according to a predefined condition choosing 20 as the maximum value to be displayed in the chart.

For the *x*-dimension, we simply called min() and max() in the Matplotlib method to scale the limits of the chart dynamically.

How it works...

In this recipe, we have created several Matplotlib charts and adjusted some of the many available properties. We also used core Python to control the scaling of the charts dynamically.

6

Threads and Networking

In this chapter, we will create threads, queues, and TCP/IP sockets using Python 3.6 and above. We will cover the following recipes:

- How to create multiple threads
- Starting a thread
- Stopping a thread
- How to use queues
- Passing queues among different modules
- Using dialog widgets to copy files to your network
- Using TCP/IP to communicate via networks
- Using urlopen to read data from websites

Introduction

In this chapter, we will extend the functionality of our Python GUI using threads, queues, and network connections.

 A tkinter GUI is single-threaded application. Every function that involves sleep or wait time has to be called in a separate thread; otherwise, the tkinter GUI freezes.

When we run our Python GUI in Windows Task Manager, we can see that a new `python.exe` process has been launched. When we give our Python GUI a `.pyw` extension, then the process created will be `python.pyw`, as can be seen in the Task Manager.

When a process is created, the process automatically creates a main thread to run our application. This is called a single-threaded application.

For our Python GUI, a single-threaded application will lead to our GUI becoming frozen as soon as we call a longer running task, such as clicking a button that has a sleep time of a few seconds. In order to keep our GUI responsive, we have to use multithreading, and this is what we will study in this chapter. We can also create multiple processes by creating multiple instances of our Python GUI, as can be seen in the Task Manager.

Processes are isolated from each other by design and do not share common data. In order to communicate between separate processes, we would have to use **Inter Process Communication** (**IPC**), which is an advanced technique. Threads, on the other hand, do share common data, code, and files, which makes communication between threads within the same process much easier than when using IPC.

 A great explanation of threads can be found at `https://www.cs.uic.edu /~jbell/CourseNotes/OperatingSystems/4_Threads.html`.

In this chapter, we will learn how to keep our Python GUI responsive and keep it from freezing.

Here is the overview of Python modules for this chapter:

```
  ∨  🏛 2nd Edition Python GUI Programming Cookbook
    >  ⊞ Ch01_Code
    >  ⊞ Ch02_Code
    >  ⊞ Ch03_Code
    >  ⊞ Ch04_Code
    >  ⊞ Ch05_Code
    ∨  ⊞ Ch06_Code
      >  ⊞ Backup
         🗋 _init_.py
      >  🅟 GUI_copy_files_limit.py
      >  🅟 GUI_copy_files.py
      >  🅟 GUI_multiple_threads_sleep_freeze.py
      >  🅟 GUI_multiple_threads_starting_a_thread.py
      >  🅟 GUI_multiple_threads_stopping_a_thread.py
      >  🅟 GUI_multiple_threads_thread_in_method.py
      >  🅟 GUI_multiple_threads.py
      >  🅟 GUI_passing_queues_member.py
      >  🅟 GUI_passing_queues.py
      >  🅟 GUI_queues_put_get_loop_endless_threaded.py
      >  🅟 GUI_queues_put_get_loop_endless.py
      >  🅟 GUI_queues_put_get_loop.py
      >  🅟 GUI_queues_put_get.py
      >  🅟 GUI_queues.py
      >  🅟 GUI_TCP_IP.py
      >  🅟 GUI_URL.py
         🌐 pyc.ico
      >  🅟 Queues.py
      >  🅟 TCP_Server.py
      >  🅟 ToolTip.py
      >  🅟 URL.py
```

How to create multiple threads

We will create multiple threads using Python. This is necessary in order to keep our GUI responsive.

A thread is like weaving a fabric made out of yarn and is nothing to be afraid of.

Getting ready

Multiple threads run within the same computer process memory space. There is no need for IPC, which would complicate our code. In this recipe, we will avoid IPC by using threads.

How to do it...

First we will increase the size of our ScrolledText widget, making it larger. Let's increase scrol_w to 40 and scrol_h to 10:

```
# Using a scrolled Text control
scrol_w = 40; scrol_h = 10                          # increase sizes
self.scrol = scrolledtext.ScrolledText(mighty, width=scrol_w,
                                       height=scrol_h,
                                       wrap=tk.WORD)
self.scrol.grid(column=0, row=3, sticky='WE', columnspan=3)
```

When we now run the resulting GUI, the Spinbox widget is center-aligned in relation to the Entry widget above it, which does not look good. We'll change this by left-aligning the widget.

Add sticky='W' to the grid control to left-align the Spinbox widget:

```
# Adding a Spinbox widget
self.spin = Spinbox(mighty, values=(1, 2, 4, 42, 100), width=5,
                    bd=9, command=self._spin)
self.spin.grid(column=0, row=2, sticky='W')          # align left
```

The GUI could still look better, so now we will increase the size of the Entry widget to get a more balanced GUI layout.

Increase the width to 24, as shown in the following code snippet:

```
# Adding a Textbox Entry widget
self.name = tk.StringVar()
self.name_entered = ttk.Entry(mighty, width=24,
                              textvariable=self.name)
self.name_entered.grid(column=0, row=1, sticky='W')
```

Let's also slightly increase the `width` of `Combobox` to `14`:

```
ttk.Label(mighty, text="Choose a number:").grid(column=1, row=0)
number = tk.StringVar()
self.number_chosen = ttk.Combobox(mighty, width=14,
                                  textvariable=number,
                                  state='readonly')
self.number_chosen['values'] = (1, 2, 4, 42, 100)
self.number_chosen.grid(column=1, row=1)
self.number_chosen.current(0)
```

Running the modified and improved code results in a larger GUI, which we will use for this and the following recipes:

`GUI_multiple_threads.py`

In order to create and use threads in Python, we have to import the `Thread` class from the `threading` module:

```
#=======================
# imports
#=======================
import tkinter as tk
```

```
from tkinter import ttk
from tkinter import scrolledtext
from tkinter import Menu
from tkinter import messagebox as msg
from tkinter import Spinbox
from time import sleep
import Ch06_Code.ToolTip as tt
from threading import Thread

GLOBAL_CONST = 42
```

Let's add a method to be created in a thread to our OOP class:

```
class OOP():
    def method_in_a_thread(self):
        print('Hi, how are you?')
```

We can now call our threaded method in the code, saving the instance in a variable:

```
#========================
# Start GUI
#========================
oop = OOP()

# Running methods in Threads
run_thread = Thread(target=oop.method_in_a_thread)

oop.win.mainloop()
```

Now, we have a method that is threaded, but when we run the code, nothing gets printed to the console!

We have to start the thread first before it can run, and the next recipe will show us how to do this.

However, setting a breakpoint after the GUI main event loop proves that we did indeed create a thread object, as can be seen in the Eclipse IDE debugger:

Name	Value
> ˣ⁺ʸ "run_thread"	Thread: < Thread(Thread-5, initial)>

How it works...

In this recipe, we prepared our GUI to use threads by first increasing the GUI size so we can better see the results printed to the ScrolledText widget.

We then imported the Thread class from the Python threading module.

Next we created a method that we call in a thread from within our GUI.

Starting a thread

This recipe will show us how to start a thread. It will also demonstrate why threads are necessary to keep our GUI responsive during long-running tasks.

Getting ready

Let's first see what happens when we call a function or a method of our GUI that has some sleep associated with it without using threads.

> We are using sleep here to simulate a real-world application that might have to wait for a web server or database to respond, a large file transfer, or complex computations to complete its task.
> sleep is a very realistic placeholder and shows the principle involved.

Adding a loop into our button callback method with some sleep time results in our GUI becoming unresponsive and, when we try to close the GUI, things get even worse:
GUI_multiple_threads_sleep_freeze.py

```
# Button callback
def click_me(self):
    self.action.configure(text='Hello ' + self.name.get() + ' '
                            + self.number_chosen.get())
    # Non-threaded code with sleep freezes the GUI
    for idx in range(10):
        sleep(5)
        self.scrol.insert(tk.INSERT, str(idx) + 'n')
```

Running the preceding code file results in the following screenshot:

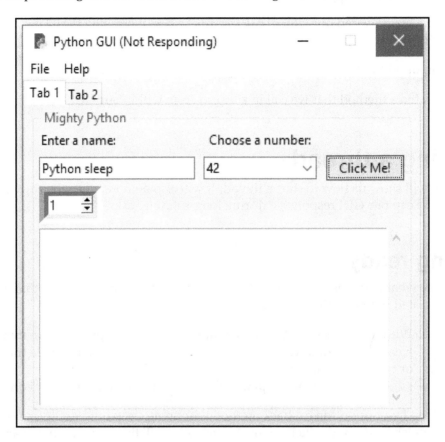

If we wait long enough, the method will eventually complete, but during this time, none of our GUI widgets respond to click events. We solve this problem by using threads.

In the previous recipe, we created a method to be run in a thread but, so far, the thread has not run!

Unlike regular Python functions and methods, we have to `start` a method that will be run in its own thread!

This is what we will do next.

How to do it...

First, let's move the creation of the thread into its own method and then call this method from the button `callback` method:

```
# Running methods in Threads
def create_thread(self):
    self.run_thread = Thread(target=self.method_in_a_thread)
    self.run_thread.start()                          # start the thread

# Button callback
def click_me(self):
    self.action.configure(text='Hello ' + self.name.get())
    self.create_thread()
```

Clicking the button now results in the `create_thread` method being called, which, in turn, calls the `method_in_a_thread` method.

First, we create a thread and target it at a method. Next, we start the thread that runs the targeted method in a new thread:

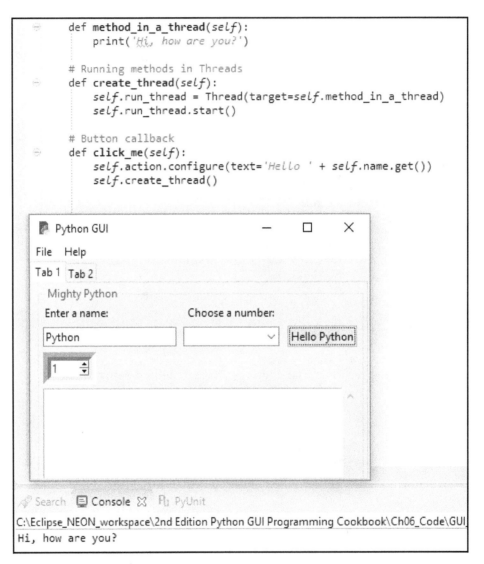

```python
    def method_in_a_thread(self):
        print('Hi, how are you?')

    # Running methods in Threads
    def create_thread(self):
        self.run_thread = Thread(target=self.method_in_a_thread)
        self.run_thread.start()

    # Button callback
    def click_me(self):
        self.action.configure(text='Hello ' + self.name.get())
        self.create_thread()
```

```
Search   Console ⊠   PyUnit
C:\Eclipse_NEON_workspace\2nd Edition Python GUI Programming Cookbook\Ch06_Code\GUI_
Hi, how are you?
```

 The GUI itself runs in its own thread, which is the main thread of the application.

We can print out the instance of the thread:

GUI_multiple_threads_thread_in_method.py

```
# Running methods in Threads
def create_thread(self):
    self.run_thread = Thread(target=self.method_in_a_thread)
    self.run_thread.start()                    # start the thread
    print(self.run_thread)
```

Clicking the button now creates the following printout:

```
🖥 Console ⋈

C:\Eclipse_NEON_workspace\2nd Edition Python GUI
Hi, how are you?
<Thread(Thread-1, started 7476)>
```

When we click the button several times, we can see that each thread gets assigned a unique name and ID:

```
🖥 Console ⋈

C:\Eclipse_NEON_workspace\2nd Edition Python GUI
Hi, how are you?
<Thread(Thread-1, started 7476)>
Hi, how are you?
<Thread(Thread-2, started 12484)>
Hi, how are you?
<Thread(Thread-3, started 12892)>
Hi, how are you?
<Thread(Thread-4, started 6124)>
```

Let's now move our code with sleep in a loop into the method_in_a_thread method to verify that threads really do solve our problem:

```
def method_in_a_thread(self):
    print('Hi, how are you?')
    for idx in range(10):
        sleep(5)
        self.scrol.insert(tk.INSERT, str(idx) + 'n')
```

When clicking the button, while the numbers are being printed into the `ScrolledText` widget with a five second delay, we can click around anywhere in our GUI, switch tabs, and so on. Our GUI has become responsive again because we are using threads!

`GUI_multiple_threads_starting_a_thread.py`

How it works...

In this recipe, we called the methods of our GUI class in their own threads and learned that we have to start the threads. Otherwise, the thread gets created but just sits there waiting for us to run its target method.

We noticed that each thread gets assigned a unique name and ID.

We simulated long-running tasks by inserting a `sleep` statement into our code, which showed us that threads can indeed solve our problem.

Stopping a thread

We have to start a thread to actually make it do something by calling the `start()` method, so intuitively, we would expect there to be a matching `stop()` method, but there is no such thing. In this recipe, we will learn how to run a thread as a background task, which is called a *daemon*. When closing the main thread, which is our GUI, all daemons will automatically be stopped as well.

Getting ready

When we call methods in a thread, we can also pass arguments and keyword arguments to the method. We start this recipe by doing exactly that.

How to do it...

By adding `args=[8]` to the thread constructor and modifying the targeted method to expect arguments, we can pass arguments to the threaded methods. The parameter to `args` has to be a sequence, so we will wrap our number in a Python list:

```
def method_in_a_thread(self, num_of_loops=10):
    print('Hi, how are you?')
    for idx in range(num_of_loops):
        sleep(5)
        self.scrol.insert(tk.INSERT, str(idx) + 'n')
```

In the following code, `run_thread` is a local variable, which we only access within the scope of the method inside which we created `run_thread`:

```
# Running methods in Threads
def create_thread(self):
    run_thread = Thread(target=self.method_in_a_thread, args=[8])
    run_thread.start()
```

By turning the local variable into a member, we can then check if the thread is still running by calling `isAlive` on it from another method:

```
# Running methods in Threads
def create_thread(self):
    self.run_thread = Thread(target=self.method_in_a_thread, args=
                                [8])
    self.run_thread.start()
    print(self.run_thread)
print('createThread():', self.run_thread.isAlive())
```

In the preceding code, we have elevated our local `run_thread` variable to a member of our class. This enables us to access the `self.run_thread` variable from any method in our class.

It is achieved like this:

```
def method_in_a_thread(self, num_of_loops=10):
    for idx in range(num_of_loops):
        sleep(1)
        self.scrol.insert(tk.INSERT, str(idx) + 'n')
    sleep(1)
    print('method_in_a_thread():', self.run_thread.isAlive())
```

When we click the button and then exit the GUI, we can see that the print statements in the `create_thread` method were printed, but we do not see the second print statement from `method_in_a_thread`.

Consider the following output:

```
Console ⊠
<terminated> C:\Eclipse_NEON_workspace\
Hi, how are you?
<Thread(Thread-1, started 4800)>
createThread(): True
method_in_a_thread(): True
```

Instead of the preceding output, we get the following **Runtime Error**:

```python
    def method_in_a_thread(self, num_of_loops=10):
        print('Hi, how are you?')
        for idx in range(num_of_loops):
            sleep(1)
            self.scrol.insert(tk.INSERT, str(idx) + '\n')
        print('method_in_a_thread():', self.run_thread.isAlive())

    # Running methods in Threads
    def create_thread(self):
        self.run_thread = Thread(target=self.method_in_a_thread, args=[8])
        self.run_thread.start()
        print(self.run_thread)
        print('createThread():', self.run_thread.isAlive())
```

```
Console ⊠
<terminated> C:\Eclipse_NEON_workspace\2nd Edition Python GUI Programming Cookbook\Ch06_Code\GUI
Hi, how are you?
<Thread(Thread-1, started 11304)>
createThread(): True
Exception in thread Thread-1:
Traceback (most recent call last):
  File "C:\Python36\lib\threading.py", line 916, in _bootstrap_inner
    self.run()
  File "C:\Python36\lib\threading.py", line 864, in run
    self._target(*self._args, **self._kwargs)
  File "C:\Eclipse NEON workspace\2nd Edition Python GUI Programming Cookbook\Ch06
    self.scrol.insert(tk.INSERT, str(idx) + '\n')
  File "C:\Python36\lib\tkinter\__init__.py", line 3266, in insert
    self.tk.call((self._w, 'insert', index, chars) + args)
RuntimeError: main thread is not in main loop
```

Threads are expected to finish their assigned task, so when we close the GUI while the thread has not completed, Python tells us that the thread we started is not in the main event loop.

We can solve this by turning the thread into a *daemon*, which will then execute as a background task.

What this gives us is that as soon as we close our GUI, which is our main thread starting other threads, the daemon threads will cleanly exit.

We can do this by calling the `setDaemon(True)` method on the thread before we start the thread:

```
# Running methods in Threads
def create_thread(self):
    self.run_thread = Thread(target=self.method_in_a_thread, args=
                             [8])
    self.run_thread.setDaemon(True)
    self.run_thread.start()
    print(self.run_thread)
```

When we now click the button and exit our GUI while the thread has not yet completed its assigned task, we no longer get any errors:

`GUI_multiple_threads_stopping_a_thread.py`

```
    # Running methods in Threads
⊖   def create_thread(self):
        self.run_thread = Thread(target=self.method_in_a_thread, args=[8])
        self.run_thread.setDaemon(True)
        self.run_thread.start()
        print(self.run_thread)
        print('createThread():', self.run_thread.isAlive())
```

```
⊟ Console ⊠
<terminated> C:\Eclipse_NEON_workspace\2nd Edition Python GUI Programming Cookbook\Ch06_Code\GUI_
Hi, how are you?
<Thread(Thread-1, started daemon 12264)>
createThread(): True
```

How it works...

While there is a start method to make threads run, surprisingly there isn't really an equivalent stop method.

In this recipe, we are running a method in a thread, which prints numbers to our `ScrolledText` widget.

When we exit our GUI, we are no longer interested in the thread that used to print to our widget, so by turning the thread into a daemon, we can exit our GUI cleanly.

How to use queues

A Python queue is a data structure that implements the first-in-first-out paradigm, basically working like a pipe. You shovel something into the pipe on one side and it falls out on the other side of the pipe.

The main difference between this queue shoveling and shoveling mud into physical pipes is that, in Python queues, things do not get mixed up. You put one unit in, and that unit comes back out on the other side. Next, you place another unit in (say, for example, an instance of a class), and this entire unit will come back out on the other end as one integral piece.

It comes back out at the other end in the exact order we inserted code into the queue.

 A queue is not a stack where we push and pop data. A stack is a **Last In First Out (LIFO)** data structure.

Queues are containers that hold data being fed into the queue from potentially different data sources. We can have different clients providing data to the queue whenever those clients have data available. Whichever client is ready to send data to our queue sends it and we can then display this data in a widget or send it forward to other modules.

Using multiple threads to complete assigned tasks in a queue is very useful when receiving the final results of processing and displaying them. The data is inserted at one end of the queue and then comes out of the other end in an ordered fashion, **First In First Out (FIFO)**.

Our GUI might have five different button widgets such that each kicks off a different task, which we want to display in our GUI in a widget (for example, a `ScrolledText` widget). These five different tasks take a different amount of time to complete.

Whenever a task has completed, we immediately need to know this and display this information in our GUI. By creating a shared Python queue and having the five tasks write their results to this queue, we can display the result of whichever task has been completed immediately, using the FIFO approach.

Getting ready

As our GUI is ever-increasing in its functionality and usefulness, it starts to talk to networks, processes, and websites, and will eventually have to wait for data to be made available for the GUI to represent.

Creating queues in Python solves the problem of waiting for data to be displayed inside our GUI.

How to do it...

In order to create queues in Python, we have to import the `Queue` class from the `queue` module. Add the following statement towards the top of our GUI module:

```
from threading import Thread
from queue import Queue
```

That gets us started.

Next, we create a queue instance:

```
def use_queues(self):
    gui_queue = Queue()                    # create queue instance
    print(gui_queue)                       # print instance
```

We call the method within our button click event:

```
# Button callback
def click_me(self):
    self.action.configure(text='Hello ' + self.name.get())
    self.create_thread()
    self.use_queues()
```

In the preceding code, we create a local `Queue` instance that is only accessible within this method. If we wish to access this queue from other places, we have to turn it into a member of our class by using the `self` keyword, which binds the local variable to the entire class, making it available from any other method within our class. In Python, we often create class instance variables in the `__init__(self)` method, but Python is very pragmatic and enables us to create those member variables anywhere in the code.

Now we have an instance of a queue. We can prove that this works by printing it out:

```
🖥 Console ⊠ 📖 Bookmarks
C:\Eclipse_NEON_workspace\2nd Edition Python GUI Programming Cookbook\Ch06_Code\GUI_queues.py
Hi, how are you?
<Thread(Thread-1, started daemon 6432)>
createThread(): True
<queue.Queue object at 0x0000023C005534A8>
method_in_a_thread(): True
```

In order to put the data into the queue, we use the put command. In order to get the data out of the queue, we use the get command:

```
# Create Queue instance
def use_queues(self):
    gui_queue = Queue()
    print(gui_queue)
    gui_queue.put('Message from a queue')
    print(gui_queue.get())
```

Running the modified code results in the message first being placed in the Queue, then being taken out of the Queue, and then being printed to the console:

```
        # Create Queue instance
⊖   def use_queues(self):
        gui_queue = Queue()
        print(gui_queue)
        gui_queue.put('Message from a queue')
        print(gui_queue.get())


🖥 Console ⊠ 📖 Bookmarks
<terminated> C:\Eclipse_NEON_workspace\2nd Edition Python GUI
<queue.Queue object at 0x000001B585C832B0>
Message from a queue
```

We can place many messages into the `Queue`:

```
# Create Queue instance
def use_queues(self):
    gui_queue = Queue()
    print(gui_queue)
    for idx in range(10):
        gui_queue.put('Message from a queue: ' + str(idx))
    print(gui_queue.get())
```

We have placed ten messages into `Queue`, but we are only getting the first one out. The other messages are still inside `Queue`, waiting to be taken out in a FIFO fashion:

```
Console 🛠   Bookmarks
<terminated> C:\Eclipse_NEON_workspace\2nd Edition Python GUI Programming Cookbook\Ch06_Code\GUI_queues.py
<queue.Queue object at 0x000001F5F7DE32E8>
Message from a queue: 0
```

In order to get all the messages that have been placed into `Queue` out, we can create an endless loop:

`GUI_queues_put_get_loop_endless.py`

```
# Create Queue instance
def use_queues(self):
    gui_queue = Queue()
    print(gui_queue)
    for idx in range(10):
        gui_queue.put('Message from a queue: ' + str(idx))
    while True:
        print(gui_queue.get())
```

Running the preceding code results in the following screenshot:

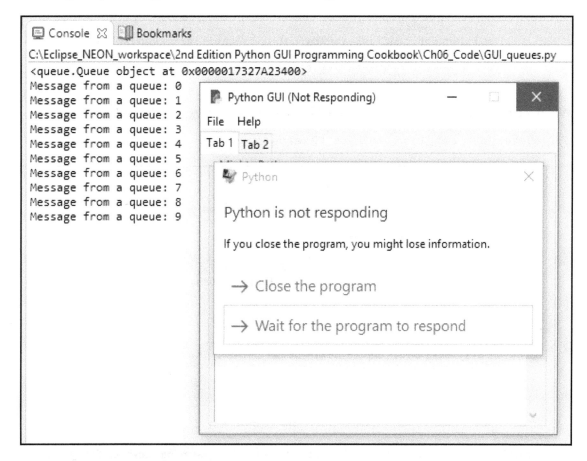

While this code works, unfortunately, it freezes our GUI. In order to fix this, we have to call the method in its own thread, as we did in the previous recipes.

Let's run our `Queue` method in a thread:

```
# Running methods in Threads
def create_thread(self):
    self.run_thread = Thread(target=self.method_in_a_thread, args=
                            [8])
    self.run_thread.setDaemon(True)
    self.run_thread.start()

    # start queue in its own thread
    write_thread = Thread(target=self.use_queues, daemon=True)
```

```
            write_thread.start()

    # Button callback
    def click_me(self):
        self.action.configure(text='Hello ' + self.name.get())
        self.create_thread()
        # now started as a thread in create_thread()
        # self.use_queues()
```

When we now click the action button, the GUI no longer freezes and the code works:

GUI_queues_put_get_loop_endless_threaded.py

```
    # Running methods in Threads
    def create_thread(self):
        self.run_thread = Thread(target=self.method_in_a_thread, args=[8])
        self.run_thread.setDaemon(True)
        self.run_thread.start()

        # start queue in its own thread
        write_thread = Thread(target=self.use_queues, daemon=True)
        write_thread.start()

    # Button callback
    def click_me(self):
        self.action.configure(text='Hello ' + self.name.get())
        self.create_thread()
        # self.use_queues()     # now started as a thread in create_thread()
```

```
Console ⌧   Bookmarks
<terminated> C:\Eclipse_NEON_workspace\2nd Edition Python GUI Programming Cookbook\Ch06_Code\GUI_
<queue.Queue object at 0x00000195FEB013C8>
Message from a queue: 0
Message from a queue: 1
Message from a queue: 2
Message from a queue: 3
Message from a queue: 4
Message from a queue: 5
Message from a queue: 6
Message from a queue: 7
Message from a queue: 8
Message from a queue: 9
```

How it works...

We created a Queue and placed messages into one side of the Queue in a FIFO fashion. We got the messages out of the Queue and then printed them to the console (stdout).

We realized that we have to call the method in its own thread because, otherwise, our GUI might freeze.

Passing queues among different modules

In this recipe, we will pass queues around different modules. As our GUI code increases in complexity, we want to separate the GUI components from the business logic, separating them out into different modules.

Modularization gives us code reuse and also makes the code more readable.

Once the data to be displayed in our GUI comes from different data sources, we will face latency issues, which is what queues solve. By passing instances of Queue among different Python modules, we are separating the different concerns of the modules' functionalities.

 The GUI code ideally would only be concerned with creating and displaying widgets.
The business logic modules' job is only to do the business logic.

We have to combine the two elements, ideally using as few relations among the different modules as possible, reducing code interdependence.

 The coding principle of avoiding unnecessary dependencies is usually called *loose coupling*.

In order to understand the significance of loose coupling, we can draw some boxes on a whiteboard or a piece of paper. One box represents our GUI class and code while the other boxes represent business logic, databases, and so on.

Next, we draw lines between the boxes, graphing out the interdependencies between those boxes which are our Python modules.

The fewer lines we have between our Python boxes, the more loosely coupled our design is.

Getting ready

In the previous recipe, *How to use queues,* we started to use queues. In this recipe, we will pass instances of a Queue from our main GUI thread to other Python modules, which will enable us to write to the ScrolledText widget from another module while keeping our GUI responsive.

How to do it...

First, we create a new Python module in our project. Let's call it Queues.py. We'll place a function into it (no OOP necessary yet).

We pass a self-reference of the class that creates the GUI form and widgets, which enables us to use all of the GUI methods from another Python module.

We do this in the button callback.

This is the magic of OOP. In the middle of a class, we pass ourselves into a function we are calling from within the class, using the self keyword.

The code now looks as follows:

```
import Ch06_Code.Queues as bq

class OOP():
    # Button callback
    def click_me(self):
        # Passing in the current class instance (self)
        print(self)
        bq.write_to_scrol(self)
```

The imported module contains the function we are calling:

```
def write_to_scrol(inst):
    print('hi from Queue', inst)
    inst.create_thread(6)
```

We have commented out the call to `create_thread` in the button callback because we are now calling it from our new module:

```
# Threaded method does not freeze our GUI
# self.create_thread()
```

 By passing in a self-reference from the class instance to the function that the class is calling in another module, we now have access to all our GUI elements from other Python modules.

Running the code yields the following result:

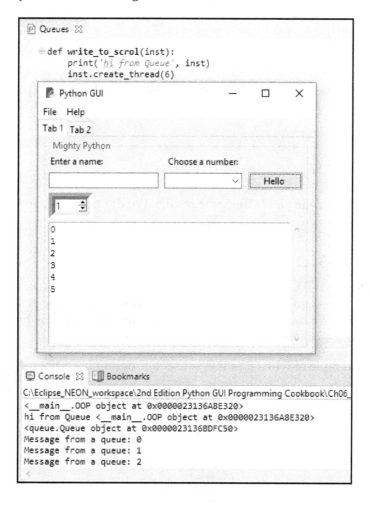

Next, we will create the `Queue` as a member of our class, placing a reference to it in the `__init__` method of the class:

```
class OOP():
    def __init__(self):
        # Create a Queue
        self.gui_queue = Queue()
```

Now, we can put messages into the queue from our new module by simply using the passed-in class reference to our GUI:

```
def write_to_scrol(inst):
    print('hi from Queue', inst)
    for idx in range(10):
        inst.gui_queue.put('Message from a queue: ' + str(idx))
    inst.create_thread(6)
```

The `create_thread` method in our GUI code now only reads from the `Queue`, which got filled in by the business logic residing in our new module, which has separated the logic from our GUI module:

```
def use_queues(self):
    # Now using a class member Queue
    while True:
        print(self.gui_queue.get())
```

Running our modified code yields the same results. We did not break anything (yet)!

How it works...

In order to separate the GUI widgets from the functionality that expresses the business logic, we created a class, made a queue a member of this class, and by passing an instance of the class into a function residing in a different Python module, we now have access to all the GUI widgets as well as the queue.

This recipe is an example of when it makes sense to program in OOP.

Using dialog widgets to copy files to your network

This recipe shows us how to copy files from your local hard drive to a network location.

We will do this by using one of Python's tkinter built-in dialogs which enables us to browse our hard drive. We can then select a file to be copied.

This recipe also shows us how to make Entry widgets read-only and to default Entry to a specified location, which speeds up the browsing of our hard drive.

Getting ready

We will extend **Tab 2** of the GUI we were building in the previous recipe, *Passing queues among different modules*.

How to do it...

Add the following code to our GUI in the `create_widgets()` method towards the bottom where we created Tab Control 2. The parent of the new widget frame is `tab2`, which we created at the very beginning of the `create_widgets()` method. As long as you place the following code physically below the creation of `tab2`, it will work:

```
############################################################
def create_widgets(self):
    # Create Tab Control
    tabControl = ttk.Notebook(self.win)
    # Add a second tab
    tab2 = ttk.Frame(tabControl)
    # Make second tab visible
    tabControl.add(tab2, text='Tab 2')

# Create Manage Files Frame
mngFilesFrame = ttk.LabelFrame(tab2, text=' Manage Files: ')
mngFilesFrame.grid(column=0, row=1, sticky='WE', padx=10, pady=5)

# Button Callback
def getFileName():
    print('hello from getFileName')

# Add Widgets to Manage Files Frame
lb = ttk.Button(mngFilesFrame, text="Browse to File...",
```

```
                         command=getFileName)
        lb.grid(column=0, row=0, sticky=tk.W)

        file = tk.StringVar()
        self.entryLen = scrol_w
        self.fileEntry = ttk.Entry(mngFilesFrame, width=self.entryLen,
                                   textvariable=file)
        self.fileEntry.grid(column=1, row=0, sticky=tk.W)

        logDir = tk.StringVar()
        self.netwEntry = ttk.Entry(mngFilesFrame,
                                   width=self.entryLen,
                                   textvariable=logDir)
        self.netwEntry.grid(column=1, row=1, sticky=tk.W)

        def copyFile():
            import shutil
            src = self.fileEntry.get()
            file = src.split('/')[-1]
            dst = self.netwEntry.get() + ''+ file
            try:
                shutil.copy(src, dst)
                msg.showinfo('Copy File to Network', 'Succes:
                             File copied.')
            except FileNotFoundError as err:
                msg.showerror('Copy File to Network',
                             '*** Failed to copy file! ***\n\n' +
                             str(err))
            except Exception as ex:
                msg.showerror('Copy File to Network',
                             '*** Failed to copy file! ***\n\n' + str(ex))

        cb = ttk.Button(mngFilesFrame, text="Copy File To : ",
                        command=copyFile)
        cb.grid(column=0, row=1, sticky=tk.E)

        # Add some space around each label
        for child in mngFilesFrame.winfo_children():
            child.grid_configure(padx=6, pady=6)
```

This will add two buttons and two entries to **Tab 2** of our GUI.

We are not yet implementing the functionality of our button callback function.

Running the code creates the following GUI:

Clicking the **Browse to File...** button currently prints to the console:

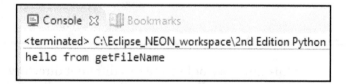

We can use tkinter's built-in file dialogs, so let's add the following `import` statements to the top of our Python GUI module:

```
from tkinter import filedialog as fd
from os import path
```

We can now use the dialogs in our code. Instead of hardcoding a path, we can use Python's `os` module to find the full path to where our GUI module resides:

```
def getFileName():
    print('hello from getFileName')
```

```
fDir  = path.dirname(__file__)
fName = fd.askopenfilename(parent=self.win, initialdir=fDir)
```

Clicking the browse button now opens up the `askopenfilename` dialog:

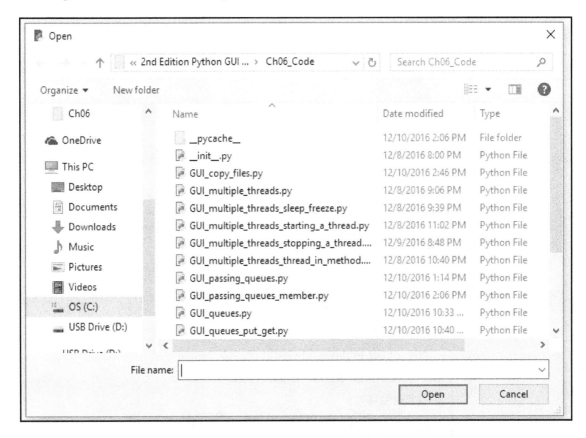

We can now open a file in this directory or browse to a different directory. After selecting a file and clicking the **Open** button in the dialog, we will save the full path to the file in the `fName` local variable.

It would be nice if, when we opened our Python `askopenfilename` dialog widget, we would automatically default to a directory so that we would not have to browse all the way to where we were looking for a particular file to be opened.

It is best to demonstrate how to do this by going back to our GUI **Tab 1**, which is what we will do next.

We can default the values into Entry widgets. Back on our **Tab 1**, this is very easy. All we have to do is add the following two lines of code to the creation of the Entry widget:

```
# Adding a Textbox Entry widget
self.name = tk.StringVar()
self.name_entered = ttk.Entry(mighty, width=24, textvariable=self.name)
self.name_entered.grid(column=0, row=1, sticky='W')
self.name_entered.delete(0, tk.END)
self.name_entered.insert(0, '< default name >')
```

When we now run the GUI, the `name_entered` entry has a default value:

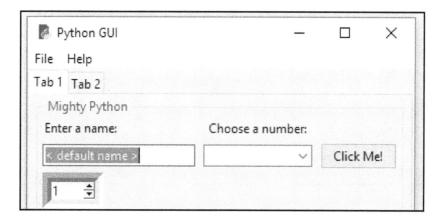

We can get the full path to the module we are using with the following Python syntax, and then we can create a new subfolder just below it. We can do this as a module-level global, or we can create the subfolder within a method:

```
# Module level GLOBALS
GLOBAL_CONST = 42
fDir   = path.dirname(__file__)
netDir = fDir + 'Backup'

def __init__(self):
    self.createWidgets()
    self.defaultFileEntries()

def defaultFileEntries(self):
    self.fileEntry.delete(0, tk.END)
    self.fileEntry.insert(0, fDir)
    if len(fDir) > self.entryLen:
        self.fileEntry.config(width=len(fDir) + 3)
        self.fileEntry.config(state='readonly')
```

```
self.netwEntry.delete(0, tk.END)
self.netwEntry.insert(0, netDir)
if len(netDir) > self.entryLen:
    self.netwEntry.config(width=len(netDir) + 3)
```

We set the defaults for both the Entry widgets, and after setting them, we make the local file Entry widget read-only.

 This order is important. We have to first populate the entry before we make it read-only.

We are also selecting **Tab 2** before calling the main event loop and no longer set the focus into the Entry of **Tab 1**. Calling `select` on our tkinter `notebook` is zero-based, so by passing in the value of `1`, we select **Tab 2**:

```
# Place cursor into name Entry
# name_entered.focus()
tabControl.select(1)
```

Running `GUI_copy_files.py` results in the following screenshot:

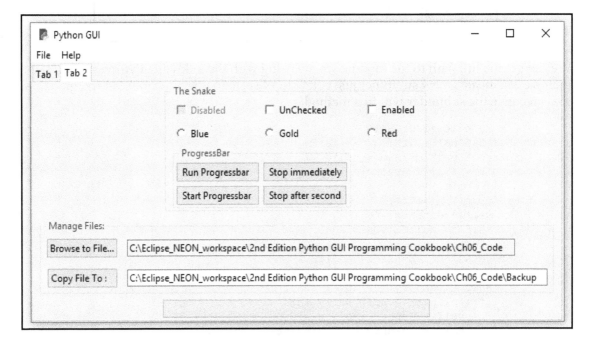

As we are not all on the same network, this recipe will use the local hard drive as an example for a network.

A UNC path is a **Universal Naming Convention** (**UNC**) and what this means is that by using double backslashes instead of the typical C:\, we can access a server on a network.

 You just have to use the UNC and replace C:\ with
\\<servername>\<folder>.

This example can be used to back up our code to a backup directory, which we can create if it does not exist by using os.makedirs:

```
# Module level GLOBALS
GLOBAL_CONST = 42

from os import makedirs
fDir   = path.dirname(__file__)
netDir = fDir + 'Backup'
if not path.exists(netDir):
    makedirs(netDir, exist_ok = True)
```

After selecting a file to copy to somewhere else, we import the Python shutil module. We need the full path to the source of the file to be copied and a network or local directory path, and then we append the file name to the path where we will copy it, using shutil.copy.

 Shutil is short-hand notation for shell utility.

We also give feedback to the user via a message box to indicate whether the copying succeeded or failed. In order to do this, import messagebox and alias it msg.

In the next code, we will mix two different approaches of where to place our import statements. In Python, we have some flexibility that other languages do not provide. We typically place all of the import statements towards the very top of each of our Python modules so that it is clear which modules we are importing. At the same time, a modern coding approach is to place the creation of variables close to the function or method where they are first being used.

In the next code, we import the message box at the top of our Python module, but then we also import the `shutil` Python module in a function. Why would we wish to do this? Does this even work? The answer is yes, it does work, and we are placing this `import` statement into a function because this is the only place in our code where we actually do need this module.

If we never call this method then we will never import the module this method requires. In a sense, you can view this technique as the lazy initialization design pattern. If we don't need it, we don't import it until we really do require it in our Python code. The idea here is that our entire code might require, let's say, 20 different modules. At runtime, which modules are really needed depends upon the user interaction. If we never call the `copyFile()` function, then there is no need to import `shutil`.

Once we click the button that invokes the `copyFile()` function in this function, we import the required module:

```python
from tkinter import messagebox as msg
def copyFile():
    import shutil                    #import module within function
    src = self.fileEntry.get()
    file = src.split('/')[-1]
    dst = self.netwEntry.get() + ''+ file
    try:
        shutil.copy(src, dst)
        msg.showinfo('Copy File to Network', 'Succes: File
                copied.')
    except FileNotFoundError as err:
        msg.showerror('Copy File to Network',
                    '*** Failed to copy file! ***\n\n' +
                    str(err))
    except Exception as ex:
        msg.showerror('Copy File to Network',
                    '*** Failed to copy file! ***\n\n' + str(ex))
```

When we now run our GUI, browse to a file, and click **Copy**, the file is copied to the location we specified in our Entry widget:

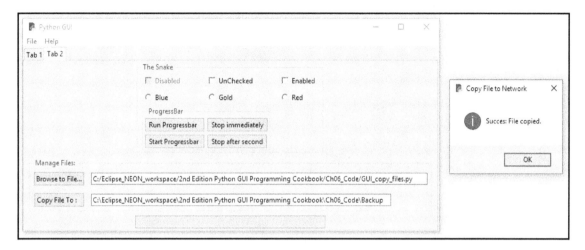

If the file does not exist or we forgot to browse to a file and are trying to copy the entire parent folder, the code will let us know this as well because we are using Python's built-in exception handling capabilities:

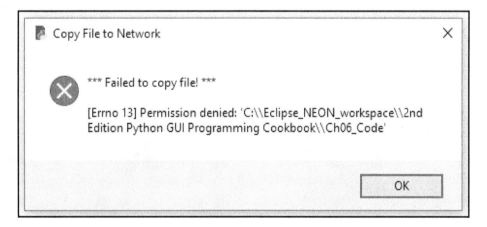

Our new Entry widgets did expand the width of the GUI. While it is sometimes nice to be able to see the entire path, at the same time, it pushes other widgets, making our GUI look not so good. We can solve this by restricting the width parameter of our Entry widgets:

```
 GUI_TCP_IP ⊠   P TCP_Server      P Queues

   46
   47             self.defaultFileEntries()
   48
   49⊖     def defaultFileEntries(self):
   50             self.fileEntry.delete(0, tk.END)
   51             self.fileEntry.insert(0, fDir)
   52             if len(fDir) > self.entryLen:
   53   #             self.fileEntry.config(width=len(fDir) + 3)
   54                 self.fileEntry.config(width=35)              # limit width to adjust GUI
   55                 self.fileEntry.config(state='readonly')
   56
   57             self.netwEntry.delete(0, tk.END)
   58             self.netwEntry.insert(0, netDir)
   59             if len(netDir) > self.entryLen:
   60   #             self.netwEntry.config(width=len(netDir) + 3)
   61                 self.netwEntry.config(width=35)              # limit width to adjust GUI
   62
```

This results in the following GUI size. We can right-arrow in the enabled Entry widget to get to the end of this widget:

```
GUI_copy_files_limit.py
```

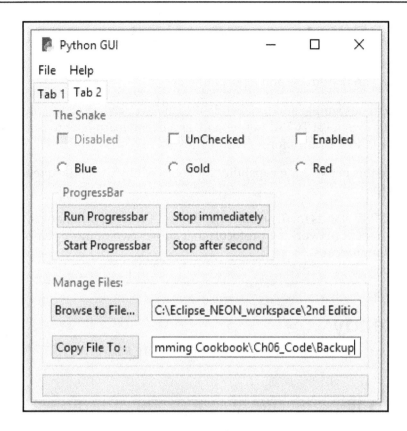

How it works...

We are copying files from our local hard drive to a network by using the Python shell utility. As most of us are not connected to the same local area network, we simulate the copying by backing up our code to a different local folder.

We are using one of tkinter's dialog controls, and by defaulting the directory paths, we can increase our efficiency in copying files.

Using TCP/IP to communicate via networks

This recipe shows you how to use `sockets` to communicate via TCP/IP. In order to achieve this, we need both an IP address and a port number.

In order to keep things simple and independent of the ever changing internet IP addresses, we will create our own local TCP/IP server and, as a client, learn how to connect to it and read data from a TCP/IP connection.

We will integrate this networking capability into our GUI by using the queues we created in the previous recipes.

 TCP/IP stands for Transmission Control Protocol/Internet Protocol, which is a set of networking protocols that allows two or more computers to communicate.

Getting ready

We will create a new Python module which will be the TCP server.

How to do it...

One way to implement a TCP server in Python is to inherit from the `socketserver` module. We subclass `BaseRequestHandler` and then override the inherited `handle` method. In very few lines of Python code, we can implement a TCP server:

```python
from socketserver import BaseRequestHandler, TCPServer

class RequestHandler(BaseRequestHandler):
    # override base class handle method
    def handle(self):
        print('Server connected to: ', self.client_address)
        while True:
            rsp = self.request.recv(512)
            if not rsp: break
            self.request.send(b'Server received: ' + rsp)

def start_server():
    server = TCPServer(('', 24000), RequestHandler)
    server.serve_forever()
```

We are passing in our `RequestHandler` class into a `TCPServer` initializer. The empty single quotes are a short cut for passing in localhost, which is our own PC. This is the IP address of `127.0.0.1`. The second item in the tuple is the port number. We can choose any port number that is not in use on our local PC.

We just have to make sure that we are using the same port on the client side of the TCP connection; otherwise, we would not be able to connect to the server. Of course, we have to start the server first before clients can connect to it.

We will modify our `Queues.py` module to become the TCP client:

```
# using TCP/IP
from socket import socket, AF_INET, SOCK_STREAM

def write_to_scrol(inst):
    print('hi from Queue', inst)
    sock = socket(AF_INET, SOCK_STREAM)
    sock.connect(('localhost', 24000))
    for idx in range(10):
        sock.send(b'Message from a queue: ' +
                    bytes(str(idx).encode()) )
        recv = sock.recv(8192).decode()
        inst.gui_queue.put(recv)
    inst.create_thread(6)
```

When we now click the **Click Me!** button, we are calling `bq.write_to_scrol(self)`, which then creates the socket and connection shown precedingly.
This is all the code we need to talk to the TCP server. In this example, we are simply sending some bytes to the server and the server sends them back, prepending some strings before returning the response.

 This shows the principle of how TCP communications via networks work.

Once we know how to connect to a remote server via TCP/IP, we will use whatever commands are designed by the protocol of the program we are interested in communicating with. The first step is to connect before we can send commands to specific applications residing on a server.

In the `writeToScrol` function, we will use the same loop as before, but now we will send the messages to the TCP server. The server modifies the received message and then sends it back to us. Next we place it into the GUI member queue, which, as in the previous recipes, runs in its own thread:

```
sock.send(b'Message from a queue: ' + bytes(str(idx).encode()) )
```

Note the `b` before the string and then, well, all the rest of the required casting.

We start the TCP server in its own thread in the initializer of the OOP class:

```
class OOP():
    def __init__(self):
    # Start TCP/IP server in its own thread
        svrT = Thread(target=startServer, daemon=True)
        svrT.start()
```

 In Python 3 we have to send strings over sockets in binary format. Adding the integer index now becomes a little bit convoluted as we have to cast it to a string, encode it, and then cast the encoded string into bytes!

Clicking the **Click Me!** button on **Tab 1** now creates the following output in our `ScrolledText` widget as well as on the console, and the response due to the use of threads is very fast:

`GUI_TCP_IP.py`

How it works...

We created a TCP server to simulate connecting to a server in our local area network or on the Internet. We turned our queues module into a TCP client. We are running both the queue and the server in their own background thread, which keeps our GUI very responsive.

Using urlopen to read data from websites

This recipe shows how we can easily read entire web pages by using Python's built-in modules. We will display the web page data first in its raw format and then decode it, and then we will display it in our GUI.

Getting ready

We will read the data from a webpage and then display it in the ScrolledText widget of our GUI.

How to do it...

First, we create a new Python module and name it URL.py. We then import the required functionality to read webpages using Python. We can do this in very few lines of code.

We wrap our code in a try...except block similar to Java and C#. This is a modern approach to coding, which Python supports. Whenever we have code that might not complete, we can experiment with this code and, if it works, all is fine. If the block of code in the try...except block does not work, the Python interpreter will throw one of several possible exceptions, which we can then catch. Once we have caught the exception, we can decide what to do next.

There is a hierarchy of exceptions in Python and we can also create our own classes that inherit from and extend the Python exception classes. In the following code, we are mainly concerned that the URL we are trying to open might not be available so, we wrap our code within a try...except code block. If the code succeeds in opening the requested URL, all is fine. If it fails, maybe because our Internet connection is down, we fall into the exception part of the code and print out that an exception has occurred:

```
from urllib.request import urlopen
link = 'http://python.org/'
```

```
try:
    http_rsp = urlopen(link)
    print(http_rsp)
    html = http_rsp.read()
    print(html)
    html_decoded = html.decode()
    print(html_decoded)
except Exception as ex:
    print('*** Failed to get Html! ***\n\n' + str(ex))
else:
    return html_decoded
```

 You can read more about Python exception handling at https://docs.py thon.org/3.6/library/exceptions.html.

By calling `urlopen` on the official Python website, we get the entire data as one long string. The first print statement prints this long string out to the console.

We then call `decode` on the result, and this time we get a little over 1,000 lines of web data, including some whitespace.

We also print out the type for calling `urlopen`, which is an `http.client.HTTPResponse` object. Actually, we print it out first:

```
Console ⌗   Bookmarks
<terminated> C:\Eclipse_NEON_workspace\2nd Edition Python GUI Programming Cookbook\Ch06_Code\URL.py
<http.client.HTTPResponse object at 0x000001F5148627F0>
b'<!doctype html>\n<!--[if lt IE 7]>    <html class="no-js ie6 lt-ie7 lt-ie8 lt-ie9">    <![endif]-->\n<!--[if IE 7]>
<!doctype html>
<!--[if lt IE 7]>    <html class="no-js ie6 lt-ie7 lt-ie8 lt-ie9">    <![endif]-->
<!--[if IE 7]>       <html class="no-js ie7 lt-ie8 lt-ie9">         <![endif]-->
<!--[if IE 8]>       <html class="no-js ie8 lt-ie9">                <![endif]-->
<!--[if gt IE 8]><!--><html class="no-js" lang="en" dir="ltr">  <!--<![endif]-->

<head>
    <meta charset="utf-8">
    <meta http-equiv="X-UA-Compatible" content="IE=edge">

    <link rel="prefetch" href="//ajax.googleapis.com/ajax/libs/jquery/1.8.2/jquery.min.js">
```

Here is the official Python webpage we just read. If you are a web developer, you probably have some good ideas about what to do with the parsed data:

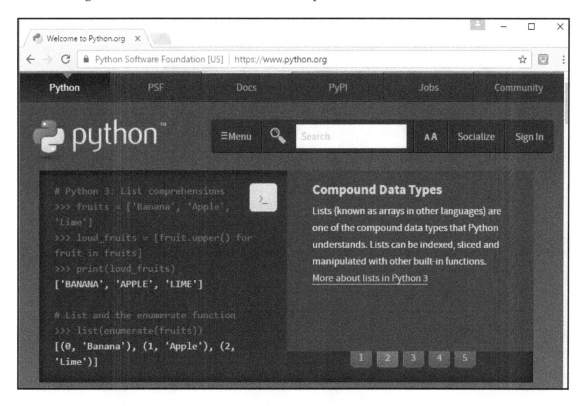

We then display this data in our GUI inside the `ScrolledText` widget. In order to do so, we have to connect our new module, which reads the data from the webpage to our GUI.

In order to do this, we need a reference to our GUI, and one way to do this is by tying our new module to the **Tab 1** button callback. We can return the decoded HTML data from the Python webpage to the `Button` widget, which we can then place into the `ScrolledText` control.

So, let's turn our code into a function and return the data to the calling code:

```
from urllib.request import urlopen
link = 'http://python.org/'

def get_html():
    try:
        http_rsp = urlopen(link)
        print(http_rsp)
        html = http_rsp.read()
        print(html)
        html_decoded = html.decode()
        print(html_decoded)
    except Exception as ex:
        print('*** Failed to get Html! ***\n\n' + str(ex))
    else:
        return html_decoded
```

We can now write the data from our button callback method to the `ScrolledText` control by first importing the new module and then inserting the data into the widget. We also give it some sleep after the call to `write_to_scrol`:

```
import Ch06_Code.URL as url

# Button callback
def click_me(self):
    self.action.configure(text='Hello ' + self.name.get())
    bq.write_to_scrol(self)
    sleep(2)
    html_data = url.get_html()
    print(html_data)
    self.scrol.insert(tk.INSERT, html_data)
```

The HTML data is now displayed in our GUI widget:

GUI_URL.py

How it works...

We create a new module to separate the code that gets the data from a webpage from our GUI code. This is always a good thing to do. We read in the webpage data and then return it to the calling code after decoding it. We then use the button callback function to place the returned data into the ScrolledText control.

This chapter introduced us to some advanced Python programming concepts, which we combined to produce a functional GUI program.

7
Storing Data in our MySQL Database via our GUI

In this chapter, we will enhance our Python GUI by connecting to a MySQL database. We will cover the following recipes:

- Installing and connecting to a MySQL server from Python
- Configuring the MySQL database connection
- Designing the Python GUI database
- Using the SQL INSERT command
- Using the SQL UPDATE command
- Using the SQL DELETE command
- Storing and retrieving data from our MySQL database
- Using the MySQL workbench

Introduction

Before we can connect to a MySQL server, we must have access to a MySQL server.

The first recipe in this chapter will show you how to install the free MySQL Server Community Edition.

After successfully connecting to a running instance of our MySQL server, we will design and create a database that will accept a book title, which could be our own journal or a quote we found somewhere on the Internet. We will require a page number for the book, which could be blank, and then, we will insert the quote we like from a book, journal, website, or a friend into our MySQL database using our GUI, built using Python 3.6 and above.

We will insert, modify, delete, and display our favorite quotes using our Python GUI to issue these SQL commands and to display the data.

 CRUD is a database term you might come across, which abbreviates the four basic SQL commands and stands for **Create**, **Read**, **Update**, and **Delete**.

Here is the overview of Python modules for this chapter:

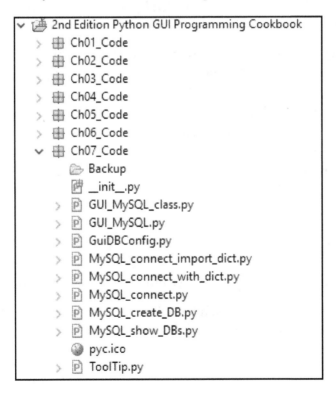

Installing and connecting to a MySQL server from Python

Before we can connect to a MySQL database, we have to connect to the MySQL Server. In order to do this, we need to know the IP address of the MySQL server as well as the port it is listening on.

We also have to be a registered user with a password in order to get authenticated by the MySQL server.

Getting ready

You will need to have access to a running MySQL Server instance and you also need to have administrator privileges in order to create databases and tables.

There is a free MySQL Community Edition available from the official MySQL website. You can download and install it on your local PC from `http://dev.mysql.com/downloads/windows/installer/5.7.html`:

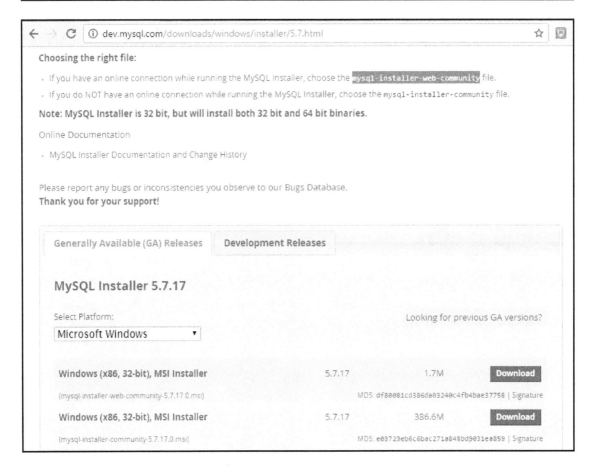

During the installation process, you will choose a password for the Root user, and you can also add more users. I recommend you add yourself as a **DB Admin** and choose a password as well:

Accounts and Roles

Root Account Password

Enter the password for the root account. Please remember to store this password in a secure place.

MySQL Root Password: ●●●●●●

Repeat Password: ●●●●●●

Password Strength: Weak

MySQL User Accounts

Create MySQL user accounts for your users and applications. Assign a role to the user that consists of a set of privileges.

	MySQL Username	Host	User Role		Add User
	Burkhard	%	DB Admin		Edit User
					Delete

 In this chapter, we are using the latest MySQL Community Server Release 5.7.17.

How to do it...

In order to connect to MySQL, we first need to install a special Python connector driver. This driver will enable us to talk to the MySQL server from Python. There is a freely available driver on the MySQL website and it comes with a very nice online tutorial:

`http://dev.mysql.com/doc/connector-python/en/index.html`

At the time of writing this book, this MySQL connector has not yet been updated to Python 3.6, so we will follow a slightly different approach.

From `http://www.lfd.uci.edu/~gohlke/pythonlibs/#mysqlclient`, we can download a package that lets us talk to our MySQL server via Python 3.6:

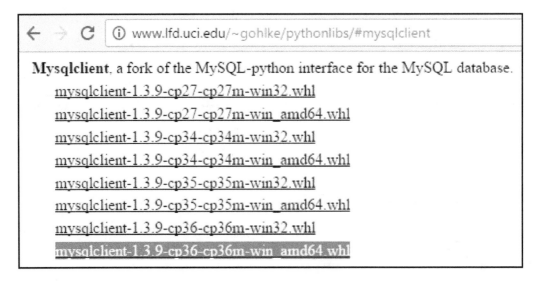

The highlighted wheel (`.whl`) installer package matches our Python 3.6 64-bit installation on a 64-bit Windows 10 OS.

One way to verify that we have installed the correct driver and that it lets Python talk to MySQL, is by looking into the Python `site-packages` directory. If your `site-packages` directory has a new `MySQLdb` folder as well as some other `_mysql` modules, the installation was successful:

Name	Date modified	Type	Size
MySQLdb	12/13/2016 8:13 PM	File folder	
numpy	12/4/2016 6:38 PM	File folder	
numpy-1.11.2-py3.6.egg-info	12/4/2016 6:38 PM	File folder	
pip	11/22/2016 8:45 PM	File folder	
pip-9.0.1.dist-info	11/22/2016 8:45 PM	File folder	
pkg_resources	11/22/2016 8:45 PM	File folder	
pyparsing-2.1.10.dist-info	12/4/2016 6:36 PM	File folder	
python_dateutil-2.6.0.dist-info	12/4/2016 4:48 PM	File folder	
pytz	12/4/2016 6:36 PM	File folder	
pytz-2016.7.dist-info	12/4/2016 6:36 PM	File folder	
setuptools	11/22/2016 8:45 PM	File folder	
setuptools-28.8.0.dist-info	11/22/2016 8:45 PM	File folder	
six-1.10.0.dist-info	12/4/2016 4:48 PM	File folder	
_mysql.cp36-win_amd64.pyd	12/13/2016 8:13 PM	Python Extension ...	3,784 KB
_mysql_exceptions.py	12/13/2016 8:13 PM	Python File	3 KB

OS (C:) > Python36 > Lib > site-packages   Search site-packages

First, let's verify that our MySQL server installation works by using the *MySQL Command Line Client*. At the `mysql>` prompt, type `SHOW DATABASES;` then press *Enter*:

```
MySQL 5.7 Command Line Client

Enter password: ******
Welcome to the MySQL monitor.  Commands end with ; or \g.
Your MySQL connection id is 8
Server version: 5.7.17-log MySQL Community Server (GPL)

Copyright (c) 2000, 2016, Oracle and/or its affiliates. All rights reserved.

Oracle is a registered trademark of Oracle Corporation and/or its
affiliates. Other names may be trademarks of their respective
owners.

Type 'help;' or '\h' for help. Type '\c' to clear the current input statement.

mysql> SHOW DATABASES;
+--------------------+
| Database           |
+--------------------+
| information_schema |
| mysql              |
| performance_schema |
| sakila             |
| sys                |
| world              |
+--------------------+
6 rows in set (0.00 sec)

mysql>
```

Next, we will verify that we can achieve the same results using Python 3.6:

 Replace the placeholder bracketed names `<adminUser>` and `<adminPwd>` with the real credentials you are using in your MySQL installation.

```
import MySQLdb as mysql
conn = mysql.connect(user=<adminUser>, password=<adminPwd>,
host='127.0.0.1')
print(conn)
conn.close()
```

If running the preceding code results in the following output printed to the console, then we are good:

```
MySQL_connect.py
```

> 🖥 Console ⌗ 📖 Bookmarks
> \<terminated\> C:\Eclipse_NEON_workspace\2nd Edition Python GUI Programming Cookbook\Ch07_Code\MySQL_connect.py
> \<_mysql.connection open to '127.0.0.1' at 605769b8\>

If you are not able to connect to the MySQL server via the *Command Line Client* or the Python *mysqlclient*, then something probably went wrong during the installation. If this is the case, try uninstalling, rebooting your PC, and then running the installation again.

How it works...

In order to connect our GUI to a MySQL server, we need to be able to connect to the server with administrative privileges if we want to create our own database. If the database already exists, then we just need the authorization rights to connect, insert, update, and delete data. We will create a new database on a MySQL server in the next recipe.

Configuring the MySQL database connection

In the previous recipe, we used the shortest way to connect to a MySQL server by hardcoding the credentials required for authentication into the `connection` method. While this is a fast approach for early development, we definitely do not want to expose our MySQL server credentials to anyone. Instead, we *grant* permission to access databases, tables, views, and related database commands to specific users.

A much safer way to get authenticated by a MySQL server is by storing the credentials in a configuration file, which is what we will do in this recipe. We will use our configuration file to connect to the MySQL server and then create our own database on the MySQL server.

 We will use this database in all of the following recipes.

Getting ready

Access to a running MySQL server with administrator privileges is required to run the code shown in this recipe.

 The previous recipe shows how to install the free Community Edition of MySQL Server. The administrator privileges will enable you to implement this recipe.

How to do it...

First, we create a dictionary in the same module of the `GUI_MySQL_class.py` code:

```
# create dictionary to hold connection info
dbConfig = {
    'user': <adminName>,        # use your admin name
    'password': <adminPwd>,     # not the real password
    'host': '127.0.0.1',        # IP address of localhost
    }
```

Next, in the connection method, we unpack the dictionary values. Take a look at the following code snippet:

```
mysql.connect('user': <adminName>,  'password': <adminPwd>, 'host':
'127.0.0.1')
```

Instead of using the preceding snippet, we use (`**dbConfig`), which achieves the same thing as the preceding one but is much shorter:

```
import MySQLdb as mysql
# unpack dictionary credentials
conn = mysql.connect(**dbConfig)
print(conn)
```

This results in the same successful connection to the MySQL server, but the difference is that the connection method no longer exposes any mission-critical information:

A database server is critical to your mission. You realize this once you have lost your valuable data...and can't find any recent backup!

`MySQL_connect_with_dict.py`

```
🖥 Console ⊠  📑 Bookmarks                                                    ⬛ ✖ ✖
<terminated> C:\Eclipse_NEON_workspace\2nd Edition Python GUI Programming Cookbook\Ch07_Code\MySQL_connect_with_dict.py
<_mysql.connection open to '127.0.0.1' at 62f229a8>
```

Now, placing the same username, password, database, and so on into a dictionary in the same Python module does not eliminate the risk of having the credentials seen by anyone perusing the code.

In order to increase database security, we first move the dictionary into its own Python module. Let's call the new Python module `GuiDBConfig.py`.

We then import this module and unpack the credentials as we did before:

```
import GuiDBConfig as guiConf
# unpack dictionary credentials
conn = mysql.connect(**guiConf.dbConfig)
print(conn)
```

 Once we place this module into a secure place, separated from the rest of the code, we have achieved a better level of security for our MySQL data.

Now that we know how to connect to MySQL and have administrator privileges, we can create our own database by issuing the following commands:

```
GUIDB = 'GuiDB'

# unpack dictionary credentials
conn = mysql.connect(**guiConf.dbConfig)

cursor = conn.cursor()

try:
    cursor.execute("CREATE DATABASE {}
                   DEFAULT CHARACTER SET 'utf8'".format(GUIDB))
```

```
except mysql.Error as err:
    print("Failed to create DB: {}".format(err))

conn.close()
```

In order to execute commands to MySQL, we create a cursor object from the connection object.

A cursor is usually a place in a specific row in a database table, which we move up or down the table, but here, we use it to create the database itself. We wrap the Python code into a `try...except` block and use the built-in error codes of MySQL to tell us if anything went wrong.

We can verify that this block works by executing the database-creating code twice. The first time, it will create a new database in MySQL, and the second time, it will print out an error message stating that this database already exists:

`MySQL_create_DB.py`

```
try:
    cursor.execute("CREATE DATABASE {} \
                    DEFAULT CHARACTER SET 'utf8'".format(GUIDB))
```

```
Console 🖾  📖 Bookmarks
<terminated> C:\Eclipse_NEON_workspace\2nd Edition Python GUI Programming Cookbook\Ch07_Code\MySQL_create_DB.py
Failed to create DB: (1007, "Can't create database 'guidb'; database exists")
```

We can verify which databases exist by executing the following MySQL command using the very same cursor object syntax. Instead of issuing the `CREATE DATABASE` command we create a cursor and use it to execute the `SHOW DATABASES` command, the result of which we fetch and print to the console output:

```
import MySQLdb as mysql
import GuiDBConfig as guiConf

# unpack dictionary credentials
conn = mysql.connect(**guiConf.dbConfig)

cursor = conn.cursor()

cursor.execute("SHOW DATABASES")
print(cursor.fetchall())

conn.close()
```

We retrieve the results by calling the `fetchall` method on the cursor object.

Running this code shows us which databases currently exist in our MySQL server instance. As we can see from the output, MySQL ships with several built-in databases such as `information_schema`, and so on. We have successfully created our own `guidb` database, which is shown in the output. All other databases illustrated come shipped with MySQL:

MySQL_show_DBs.py

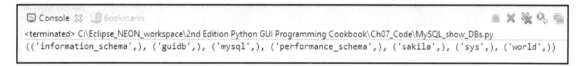
```
Console ⌧ 📑 Bookmarks                                                           🗑 ✖ ✂ ✎ 🖥
<terminated> C:\Eclipse_NEON_workspace\2nd Edition Python GUI Programming Cookbook\Ch07_Code\MySQL_show_DBs.py
(('information_schema',), ('guidb',), ('mysql',), ('performance_schema',), ('sakila',), ('sys',), ('world',))
```

Note how, even though we specified the database when we created it in mixed-case letters as GuiDB, the SHOW DATABASES command shows all existing databases in MySQL in lower-case and displays our database as `guidb`.

How it works...

In order to connect our Python GUI to a MySQL database, we first have to know how to connect to the MySQL server. This requires establishing a connection, and this connection will only be accepted by MySQL if we are able to provide the required credentials.

While it is easy to place strings into one line of Python code, when we deal with databases, we have to be really thoughtful because today's personal sandbox development environment could easily end up being accessible on the World Wide Web by tomorrow.

You do not want to compromise database security, and the first part of this recipe showed ways to be more secure by placing the connection credentials to the MySQL server into a separate file and, by placing this file into a location where it is not accessible from the outside world, our database system will become more secure.

In a real-world production environment, the MySQL server installation, connection credentials, and this `dbConfig` file would be handled by IT system administrators who would enable you to import the `dbConfig` file to connect to the MySQL server without you knowing what the actual credentials are. Unpacking `dbConfig` would not expose the credentials as it does in our code.

The second part created our own database in a MySQL server instance, and we will extend and use this database in the following recipes, combining it with our Python GUI.

Designing the Python GUI database

Before we start creating tables and inserting data into them, we have to design the database. Unlike changing local Python variable names, changing a database schema once it has been created and loaded with data is not that easy.

We would have to DROP the table, which means we would lose all the data that was in the table. So, before dropping a table, we would have to extract the data, then DROP the table, recreate it, and finally reimport the original data.

You get the picture...

Designing our GUI MySQL database means first thinking about what we want our Python application to do with it and then choosing names for our tables that match the intended purpose.

Getting ready

We are working with the MySQL database we created in the previous recipe, *Configuring the MySQL database connection*. A running instance of MySQL is necessary and the two previous recipes show how to install MySQL, all necessary additional drivers, as well as how to create the database we are using in this chapter.

How to do it...

First, we move the widgets from our Python GUI around between the two tabs we created in the previous recipes in order to organize our Python GUI better to connect to a MySQL database.

We rename several widgets and separate the code that accesses the MySQL data to what used to be named Tab 1, and we will move unrelated widgets to what we called Tab 2 in earlier recipes. We also adjust some internal Python variable names in order to understand our code better.

Code readability is a coding virtue and not a waste of time.

Our refactored Python GUI now looks like the following screenshot. We have renamed the first tab as **MySQL** and created two tkinter `LabelFrame` widgets. We labeled the one on the top Python database and it contains two labels and six tkinter entry widgets plus three buttons, which we aligned in four rows and three columns using the tkinter grid layout manager. We will enter book titles and pages into the entry widgets, and clicking the buttons will result in either inserting, retrieving, or modifying book quotations. The `LabelFrame` at the bottom has a label of **Book Quotation** and the `ScrolledText` widget that is part of this frame will display our books and quotations:

GUI_MySQL.py

We will create two SQL tables to hold our data. The first will hold the data for the book title and book page, and then, we will join with the second table, which will hold the book quotation. We will link the two tables together via primary to foreign key relations.

So, let's create the first database table now. Before we do that, let's verify first that our database does, indeed, have no tables. According to the online MySQL documentation, the command to view the tables that exist in a database is as follows:

14.7.5.37 SHOW TABLES Syntax

```
SHOW [FULL] TABLES [{FROM | IN} db_name]
    [LIKE 'pattern' | WHERE expr]
```

It is important to note that, in the preceding syntax, arguments in square brackets, such as FULL, are optional while arguments in curly braces, such as FROM, are required for the SHOW TABLES command. The pipe symbol between FROM and IN means that the MySQL syntax requires one or the other:

```
# unpack dictionary credentials
conn = mysql.connect(**guiConf.dbConfig)
# create cursor
cursor = conn.cursor()
# execute command
cursor.execute("SHOW TABLES FROM guidb")
print(cursor.fetchall())

# close connection to MySQL
conn.close()
```

When we execute the SQL command in Python, we get the expected result, which is an empty tuple showing us that our database currently has no tables:

GUI_MySQL_class.py

```
# show Tables from guidb DB
cursor.execute("SHOW TABLES FROM guidb")
print(cursor.fetchall())
```

🖳 Console ✕ 📖 Bookmarks

<terminated> C:\Eclipse_NEON_workspace\2nd Edition Python GUI Programming

()

We can also first select the database by executing the USE <DB> command and then we don't have to pass it into the SHOW TABLES command because we have already selected the database we want to talk to. The following code creates the same true result as the previous one:

```
cursor.execute("USE guidb")
cursor.execute("SHOW TABLES")
```

Now that we know how to verify that our database has no tables, let's create some. After we have created two tables, we will verify that they have truly made it into our database by using the same commands as before.

We create the first table, named Books, by executing the following code:

```
# connect by unpacking dictionary credentials
conn = mysql.connect(**guiConf.dbConfig)

# create cursor
cursor = conn.cursor()

# select DB
cursor.execute("USE guidb")

# create Table inside DB
cursor.execute("CREATE TABLE Books (
    Book_ID INT NOT NULL AUTO_INCREMENT,
    Book_Title VARCHAR(25) NOT NULL,
    Book_Page INT NOT NULL,
    PRIMARY KEY (Book_ID)
  ) ENGINE=InnoDB")

# close connection to MySQL
conn.close()
```

We can verify that the table has been created in our database by executing the following commands:

GUI_MySQL_class.py

```
# show Tables from guidb DB
cursor.execute("SHOW TABLES FROM guidb")
print(cursor.fetchall())
```

Console ⌗ Bookmarks
<terminated> C:\Eclipse_NEON_workspace\2nd Edition Python GUI Programming
((' books ',),)

Now the result is no longer an empty tuple but a tuple that contains a tuple, showing the books table we just created.

We can use the MySQL command-line client to see the columns in our table. In order to do this, we have to log in as the root user. We also have to append a semicolon to the end of the command.

 On Windows, you simply double-click the MySQL command-line client shortcut, which is automatically installed during the MySQL installation.

If you don't have a shortcut on your desktop, you can find the executable at the following path for a typical default installation:

C:\Program Files\MySQL\MySQL Server 5.7\bin\mysql.exe

Without a shortcut to run the MySQL client, you have to pass it some parameters:

- C:\Program Files\MySQL\MySQL Server 5.7\bin\mysql.exe
- -u root
- -p

Either double-clicking the shortcut or using the command line with the full path to the executable and passing in the required parameters, will bring up the MySQL command-line client, which prompts you to enter the password for the root user:

```
Command Prompt - "C:\Program Files\MySQL\MySQL Server 5.7\bin\mysql.exe" -u root -p

C:\>"C:\Program Files\MySQL\MySQL Server 5.7\bin\mysql.exe" -u root -p
Enter password: ******
Welcome to the MySQL monitor.  Commands end with ; or \g.
Your MySQL connection id is 35
Server version: 5.7.17-log MySQL Community Server (GPL)

Copyright (c) 2000, 2016, Oracle and/or its affiliates. All rights reserved.

Oracle is a registered trademark of Oracle Corporation and/or its
affiliates. Other names may be trademarks of their respective
owners.

Type 'help;' or '\h' for help. Type '\c' to clear the current input statement.

mysql>
```

If you remember the password you assigned to the root user during the installation, you can then run the `SHOW COLUMNS FROM books;` command, as shown in the following screenshot. This will display the columns of our `books` table from our guidb:

```
mysql> USE guidb
Database changed
mysql> SHOW COLUMNS FROM books;
+------------+-------------+------+-----+---------+----------------+
| Field      | Type        | Null | Key | Default | Extra          |
+------------+-------------+------+-----+---------+----------------+
| Book_ID    | int(11)     | NO   | PRI | NULL    | auto_increment |
| Book_Title | varchar(25) | NO   |     | NULL    |                |
| Book_Page  | int(11)     | NO   |     | NULL    |                |
+------------+-------------+------+-----+---------+----------------+
3 rows in set (0.11 sec)

mysql>
```

> When executing commands in the MySQL client, the syntax is not Pythonic.

Next, we will create the second table, which will store the book and journal quotations. We will create it by executing the following code:

```
# select DB
cursor.execute("USE guidb")

# create second Table inside DB
cursor.execute("CREATE TABLE Quotations (
        Quote_ID INT,
        Quotation VARCHAR(250),
        Books_Book_ID INT,
        FOREIGN KEY (Books_Book_ID)
            REFERENCES Books(Book_ID)
            ON DELETE CASCADE
    ) ENGINE=InnoDB")
```

Executing the SHOW TABLES command now shows that our database has two tables:

GUI_MySQL_class.py

```
# show Tables from guidb DB
cursor.execute("SHOW TABLES FROM guidb")
print(cursor.fetchall())
```

🖥 Console ✕ 📖 Bookmarks

<terminated> C:\Eclipse_NEON_workspace\2nd Edition Python GUI Programming
(('books',), ('quotations',))

We can see the columns by executing the SQL command using Python:

GUI_MySQL_class.py

```
# execute command
cursor.execute("SHOW COLUMNS FROM quotations")
print(cursor.fetchall())
```

🖥 Console ✕ 📖 Bookmarks

<terminated> C:\Eclipse_NEON_workspace\2nd Edition Python GUI Programming Cookbook\Ch07_Code\GUI_MySQL_class.py
(('Quote_ID', 'int(11)', 'NO', 'PRI', None, 'auto_increment'), ('Quotation', 'varchar(250)', 'YES',

Using the MySQL client might present the data in a better format. We could also use Python's pretty print (pprint) feature:

GUI_MySQL_class.py

```
from pprint import pprint
# execute command
cursor.execute("SHOW COLUMNS FROM quotations")
pprint(cursor.fetchall())
```

```
Console ⊠   Bookmarks
<terminated> C:\Eclipse_NEON_workspace\2nd Edition Python GUI Programming Cookbook
(('Quote_ID', 'int(11)', 'NO', 'PRI', None, 'auto_increment'),
 ('Quotation', 'varchar(250)', 'YES', '', None, ''),
 ('Books_Book_ID', 'int(11)', 'YES', 'MUL', None, ''))
```

The MySQL client still shows our columns in a clearer format, which can be seen when you run this client.

How it works...

We designed our Python GUI database and refactored our GUI in preparation to use our new database. We then created a MySQL database and created two tables within it.

We verified that the tables made it into our database by using both Python and the MySQL client that ships with the MySQL server.

In the next recipe, we will insert data into our tables.

Using the SQL INSERT command

This recipe presents the entire Python code that shows you how to create and drop MySQL databases and tables as well as how to display the existing databases, tables, columns, and data of our MySQL instance.

After creating the database and tables, we will insert data into the two tables we are creating in this recipe.

We are using a primary to foreign key relationship to connect the data of the two tables.

We will go into the details of how this works in the following two recipes, where we modify and delete the data in our MySQL database.

Getting ready

This recipe builds on the MySQL database we created in the previous recipe, *Designing the Python GUI database*, and also shows you how to drop and recreate the GuiDB.

Dropping the database, of course, deletes all the data the database had in its tables, so we'll show you how to re-insert that data as well.

How to do it...

The entire code of our GUI_MySQL_class.py module is present in the code folder of this chapter, which is available for download from https://github.com/PacktPublishing/Python-GUI-Programming-Cookbook-Second-Edition. It creates the database, adds tables to it, and then inserts data into the two tables we created.

Here, we will outline the code without showing all the implementation details in order to preserve space because it would take too many pages to show the entire code:

```
import MySQLdb as mysql
import Ch07_Code.GuiDBConfig as guiConf

class MySQL():
    # class variable
    GUIDB  = 'GuiDB'
    #---------------------------------------------------
    def connect(self):
        # connect by unpacking dictionary credentials
        conn = mysql.connector.connect(**guiConf.dbConfig)
        # create cursor
        cursor = conn.cursor()
        return conn, cursor
    #---------------------------------------------------
```

```python
    def close(self, cursor, conn):
        # close cursor
    #----------------------------------------------------
    def showDBs(self):
        # connect to MySQL
    #----------------------------------------------------
    def createGuiDB(self):
        # connect to MySQL
    #----------------------------------------------------
    def dropGuiDB(self):
        # connect to MySQL
    #----------------------------------------------------
    def useGuiDB(self, cursor):
        '''Expects open connection.'''
        # select DB
    #----------------------------------------------------
    def createTables(self):
        # connect to MySQL
        # create Table inside DB
    #----------------------------------------------------
    def dropTables(self):
        # connect to MySQL
    #----------------------------------------------------
    def showTables(self):
        # connect to MySQL
    #----------------------------------------------------
    def insertBooks(self, title, page, bookQuote):
        # connect to MySQL
        # insert data
    #----------------------------------------------------
    def insertBooksExample(self):
        # connect to MySQL
        # insert hard-coded data
    #----------------------------------------------------
    def showBooks(self):
        # connect to MySQL
    #----------------------------------------------------
    def showColumns(self):
        # connect to MySQL
    #----------------------------------------------------
    def showData(self):
        # connect to MySQL
#----------------------------------------------------
if __name__ == '__main__':
    # Create class instance
    mySQL = MySQL()
```

Running the preceding code creates the following tables and data in the database we created:

```
mysql> USE guidb
Database changed
mysql> SELECT * FROM books;
+---------+-------------------+-----------+
| Book_ID | Book_Title        | Book_Page |
+---------+-------------------+-----------+
|       1 | Design Patterns   |         7 |
|       2 | xUnit Test Patterns |      31 |
+---------+-------------------+-----------+
2 rows in set (0.10 sec)

mysql> SELECT * FROM quotations;
+----------+------------------------------------------------+---------------+
| Quote_ID | Quotation                                      | Books_Book_ID |
+----------+------------------------------------------------+---------------+
|        1 | Programming to an Interface, not an Implementation |          1 |
|        2 | Philosophy of Test Automation                  |             2 |
+----------+------------------------------------------------+---------------+
2 rows in set (0.00 sec)

mysql>
```

How it works...

We created a MySQL database, connected to it, and then created two tables that hold the data for a favorite book or journal quotation.

We distributed the data between two tables because the quotations tend to be rather large while the book titles and book page numbers are very short. By doing this, we can increase the efficiency of our database.

> In SQL database language, separating data into separate tables is called normalization.

Using the SQL UPDATE command

This recipe will use the code from the previous recipe, *Using the SQL INSERT command*, explain it in more detail, and then extend the code to update our data.

In order to update the data that we previously inserted into our MySQL database tables, we use the SQL UPDATE command.

Getting ready

This recipe builds on the previous recipe, *Using the SQL INSERT command*, so read and study the previous recipe in order to follow the coding in this recipe, where we modify the existing data.

How to do it...

First, we will display the data to be modified by running the following Python to MySQL command:

```python
import MySQLdb as mysql
import Ch07_Code.GuiDBConfig as guiConf

class MySQL():
    # class variable
    GUIDB  = 'GuiDB'
    #-----------------------------------------------------
    def showData(self):
        # connect to MySQL
        conn, cursor = self.connect()

        self.useGuiDB(cursor)

        # execute command
        cursor.execute("SELECT * FROM books")
        print(cursor.fetchall())

        cursor.execute("SELECT * FROM quotations")
        print(cursor.fetchall())

        # close cursor and connection
        self.close(cursor, conn)
#=============================================================
if __name__ == '__main__':
    # Create class instance
    mySQL = MySQL()
    mySQL.showData()
```

Running the code yields the following result:

`GUI_MySQL_class.py`

```
Console ✕  Bookmarks                                                    ▣ ✖ ✖ ✎
<terminated> C:\Eclipse_NEON_workspace\2nd Edition Python GUI Programming Cookbook\Ch07_Code\GUI_MySQL_class.py
((1, 'Design Patterns', 7), (2, 'xUnit Test Patterns', 31))
((1, 'Programming to an Interface, not an Implementation', 1), (2, 'Philosophy of Test Automation', 2))
```

We might not agree with the Gang of Four, so let's change their famous programming quote.

 The Gang of Four are the four authors who created the world-famous book called *Design Patterns*, which strongly influenced our entire software industry to recognize, think, and code using software design patterns.

We will do this by updating our database of favorite quotes. First, we retrieve the primary key value by searching for the book title and then we pass that value into our search for the quote:

```python
#-------------------------------------------------------
def updateGOF(self):
    # connect to MySQL
    conn, cursor = self.connect()

    self.useGuiDB(cursor)

    # execute command
    cursor.execute("SELECT Book_ID FROM books WHERE Book_Title =
                    'Design Patterns'")
    primKey = cursor.fetchall()[0][0]
    print("Primary key=" + str(primKey))

    cursor.execute("SELECT * FROM quotations WHERE Books_Book_ID =
                    (%s)", (primKey,))
    print(cursor.fetchall())

    # close cursor and connection
    self.close(cursor, conn)
#===========================================================
if __name__ == '__main__':
    mySQL = MySQL()              # Create class instance
    mySQL.updateGOF()
```

This gives us the following result:

`GUI_MySQL_class.py`

```
# execute command
cursor.execute("SELECT Book_ID FROM books WHERE Book_Title = 'Design Patterns'")
primKey = cursor.fetchall()[0][0]
print("Primary key=" + str(primKey))

cursor.execute("SELECT * FROM quotations WHERE Books_Book_ID = (%s)", (primKey,))
print(cursor.fetchall())
```

📄 Console ⊠ 📖 Bookmarks

```
<terminated> C:\Eclipse_NEON_workspace\2nd Edition Python GUI Programming Cookbook\Ch07_Code\GUI_MySQL_class.py
Primary key=1
((1, 'Programming to an Interface, not an Implementation', 1),)
```

Now that we know the primary key of the quote, we can update the quote by executing the following commands:

```
#--------------------------------------------------------
def showDataWithReturn(self):
    # connect to MySQL
    conn, cursor = self.connect()

    self.useGuiDB(cursor)

    # execute command
    cursor.execute("SELECT Book_ID FROM books WHERE Book_Title =
                'Design Patterns'")
    primKey = cursor.fetchall()[0][0]
    print(primKey)

    cursor.execute("SELECT * FROM quotations WHERE Books_Book_ID =
                (%s)", (primKey,))
    print(cursor.fetchall())

    cursor.execute("UPDATE quotations SET Quotation =
                (%s) WHERE Books_Book_ID = (%s)",
                ("Pythonic Duck Typing: If it walks like a duck and
                talks like a duck it probably is a duck...",
                primKey))

    # commit transaction
    conn.commit ()
```

```
            cursor.execute("SELECT * FROM quotations WHERE Books_Book_ID =
                            (%s)", (primKey,))
            print(cursor.fetchall())

            # close cursor and connection
            self.close(cursor, conn)

#================================================================
if __name__ == '__main__':
    # Create class instance
    mySQL = MySQL()
    #-----------------------
    mySQL.updateGOF()
    book, quote = mySQL.showDataWithReturn()
    print(book, quote)
```

By running the preceding code, we make this programming classic more Pythonic.

As can be seen in the following screenshot, before we ran the preceding code, our title with Book_ID 1 was related via a primary to foreign key relationship to the quotation in the Books_Book_ID column of the quotation table. This is the original quotation from the *Design Patterns* book.

We then updated the quotation related to this ID via the SQL UPDATE command.

None of the IDs have changed but the quotation that is now associated with Book_ID 1 has changed as can be seen in the second MySQL client window:

```
mysql> USE guidb
Database changed
mysql> SELECT * FROM books;
+---------+------------------+-----------+
| Book_ID | Book_Title       | Book_Page |
+---------+------------------+-----------+
|       1 | Design Patterns  |         7 |
|       2 | xUnit Test Patterns |      31 |
+---------+------------------+-----------+
2 rows in set (0.10 sec)

mysql> SELECT * FROM quotations;
+----------+--------------------------------------------------------+---------------+
| Quote_ID | Quotation                                              | Books_Book_ID |
+----------+--------------------------------------------------------+---------------+
|        1 | Programming to an Interface, not an Implementation     |             1 |
|        2 | Philosophy of Test Automation                          |             2 |
+----------+--------------------------------------------------------+---------------+
```

```
mysql> SELECT * FROM books;
+---------+------------------+-----------+
| Book_ID | Book_Title       | Book_Page |
+---------+------------------+-----------+
|       1 | Design Patterns  |         7 |
|       2 | xUnit Test Patterns |      31 |
+---------+------------------+-----------+
2 rows in set (0.00 sec)

mysql> SELECT * FROM quotations;
+----------+--------------------------------------------------------+
| Quote_ID | Quotation                                              |
D |
+----------+--------------------------------------------------------+
|        1 | Pythonic Duck Typing: If it walks like a duck and talks like a duck it probably is a duck... |
1 |
|        2 | Philosophy of Test Automation                          |
2 |
+----------+--------------------------------------------------------+
```

How it works...

In this recipe, we retrieved the existing data from our database and database tables that we created in earlier recipes. We inserted data into the tables and updated our data using the SQL UPDATE command.

Using the SQL DELETE command

In this recipe, we will use the SQL DELETE command to delete the data we created in the previous recipe, *Using the SQL UPDATE command*.

While deleting data might at first sight sound trivial, once we get a rather large database design in production, things might not be that easy any more.

Because we have designed our GUI database by relating two tables via a primary to foreign key relation, when we delete certain data, we do not end up with orphan records because this database design takes care of cascading deletes.

Getting ready

This recipe uses the MySQL database, tables, as well as the data inserted into those tables from the previous recipe, *Using the SQL UPDATE command*. In order to demonstrate how to create orphan records, we will have to change the design of one of our database tables.

How to do it...

We kept our database design simple by using only two database tables.

While this works when we delete data, there is always a chance of ending up with orphan records. What this means is that we delete data in one table but somehow do not delete the related data in another SQL table.

If we create our quotations table without a foreign key relationship to the books table, we can end up with orphan records:

```
# create second Table inside DB --
# No FOREIGN KEY relation to Books Table
cursor.execute("CREATE TABLE Quotations (
        Quote_ID INT AUTO_INCREMENT,
        Quotation VARCHAR(250),
        Books_Book_ID INT,
        PRIMARY KEY (Quote_ID)
    ) ENGINE=InnoDB")
```

After inserting data into the `books` and `quotations` tables, if we execute
a DELETE statement, we are only deleting the book with `Book_ID` 1 while the related
quotation with the `Books_Book_ID` 1 is left behind.

This in an *orphaned record*. There no longer exists a book record that has a `Book_ID` of 1:

```
mysql> SELECT * FROM books;
+---------+--------------------+-----------+
| Book_ID | Book_Title         | Book_Page |
+---------+--------------------+-----------+
|       2 | xUnit Test Patterns |        31 |
+---------+--------------------+-----------+
1 row in set (0.00 sec)

mysql> SELECT * FROM quotations;
+----------+------------------------------------------------+---------------+
| Quote_ID | Quotation                                      | Books_Book_ID |
+----------+------------------------------------------------+---------------+
|        1 | Programming to an Interface, not an Implementation |          1 |
|        2 | Philosophy of Test Automation                  |             2 |
+----------+------------------------------------------------+---------------+
2 rows in set (0.00 sec)

mysql>
```

This situation can create a mess, which we avoid by using cascading deletes.

We do this in the creation of the tables by adding certain database constraints. When we
created the table that holds the quotations in a previous recipe, we created our `quotations`
table with a foreign key constraint that explicitly references the primary key of the books
table, linking the two:

```
# create second Table inside DB
cursor.execute("CREATE TABLE Quotations (
        Quote_ID INT AUTO_INCREMENT,
        Quotation VARCHAR(250),
        Books_Book_ID INT,
        PRIMARY KEY (Quote_ID),
        FOREIGN KEY (Books_Book_ID)
            REFERENCES Books(Book_ID)
            ON DELETE CASCADE
    ) ENGINE=InnoDB")
```

The FOREIGN KEY relation includes the ON DELETE CASCADE attribute, which basically
tells our MySQL server to delete related records in this table when the records that this
foreign key relates to are deleted.

Without specifying the ON DELETE CASCADE attribute in the creation of our table we can neither delete nor update our data because an UPDATE is a DELETE followed by an INSERT.

Because of this design, no orphan records will be left behind, which is what we want.

In MySQL, we have to specify ENGINE=InnoDB on both the related tables in order to use primary to foreign key relations.

Let's display the data in our database:

```
#==============================================================
if __name__ == '__main__':
    # Create class instance
    mySQL = MySQL()
    mySQL.showData()
```

This shows us the following data in our database tables:

```
GUI_MySQL_class.py
```

```
Console 🔲 📖 Bookmarks                                                    ▦ ✖
<terminated> C:\Eclipse_NEON_workspace\2nd Edition Python GUI Programming Cookbook\Ch07_Code\GUI_MySQL_class.py
((1, 'Design Patterns', 7), (2, 'xUnit Test Patterns', 31))
((1, 'Programming to an Interface, not an Implementation', 1), (2, 'Philosophy of Test Automation', 2))
```

This shows us that we have two records that are related via primary to foreign key relationships.

When we now delete a record in the books table, we expect the related record in the quotations table to also be deleted by a cascading delete. Let's try this by executing the following SQL commands in Python:

```
import MySQLdb as mysql
import Ch07_Code.GuiDBConfig as guiConf

class MySQL():
    #-------------------------------------------------------
    def deleteRecord(self):
        # connect to MySQL
        conn, cursor = self.connect()
```

```
            self.useGuiDB(cursor)

            # execute command
            cursor.execute("SELECT Book_ID FROM books WHERE Book_Title =
                            'Design Patterns'")
            primKey = cursor.fetchall()[0][0]
            # print(primKey)

            cursor.execute("DELETE FROM books WHERE Book_ID = (%s)",
                            (primKey,))

            # commit transaction
            conn.commit ()

            # close cursor and connection
            self.close(cursor, conn)
    #============================================================
    if __name__ == '__main__':
        # Create class instance
        mySQL = MySQL()
        #------------------------
        mySQL.deleteRecord()
        mySQL.showData()
```

After executing the preceding commands to delete records, we get the following new results:

GUI_MySQL_class.py

```
        #------------------------
        mySQL.deleteRecord()
        mySQL.showData()

    <
```

🖥 Console ✕ 📖 Bookmarks

<terminated> C:\Eclipse_NEON_workspace\2nd Edition Python GUI Programming Cookbook\Ch07_Code\GUI_MySQL_class.py
((2, 'xUnit Test Patterns', 31),)
((2, 'Philosophy of Test Automation', 2),)

The famous Design Patterns are gone from our database of favorite quotations...

How it works...

We triggered cascading deletes in this recipe by designing our database in a solid fashion via primary to foreign key relationships with cascading deletes.

This keeps our data sane and integral.

In the next recipe, we will use the code of our `MySQL.py` module from our Python GUI.

Storing and retrieving data from our MySQL database

We will use our Python GUI to insert data into our MySQL database tables. We have already refactored the GUI we built in the previous recipes in our preparation for connecting and using a database.

We will use two textbox entry widgets into which we can type the book or journal title and the page number. We will also use a `ScrolledText` widget to type our favorite book quotations into, which we will then store in our MySQL database.

Getting ready

This recipe will build on the MySQL database and tables we created in the previous recipes.

How to do it...

We will insert, retrieve, and modify our favorite quotations using our Python GUI. We have refactored the MySQL tab of our GUI in preparation for this:

`GUI_MySQL.py`

In order to make the buttons do something, we will connect them to callback functions as we did in the previous recipes. We will display the data in the `ScrolledText` widget below the buttons.

In order to do this, we will import the `MySQL.py` module, as we did before. The entire code that talks to our MySQL server instance and database resides in this module, which is a form of encapsulating the code in the spirit of object-oriented programming.

We connect the **Insert Quote** button to the following callback function:

```
        # Adding a Button
        self.action = ttk.Button(self.mySQL, text="Insert Quote",
                                command=self.insertQuote)
        self.action.grid(column=2, row=1)

    # Button callback
    def insertQuote(self):
        title = self.bookTitle.get()
        page = self.pageNumber.get()
```

```
quote = self.quote.get(1.0, tk.END)
print(title)
print(quote)
self.mySQL.insertBooks(title, page, quote)
```

When we now run our code, we can insert data from our Python GUI into our MySQL database:

GUI_MySQL.py

After entering a book title and book page plus a quotation from the book or movie, we insert the data into our database by clicking the **Insert Quote** button.

Our current design allows for titles, pages, and a quotation. We can also insert our favorite quotations from movies. While a movie does not have pages, we can use the page column to insert the approximate time when the quotation occurred within the movie.

Next, we can verify that all of this data made it into our database tables by issuing the same commands we used previously:

GUI_MySQL.py

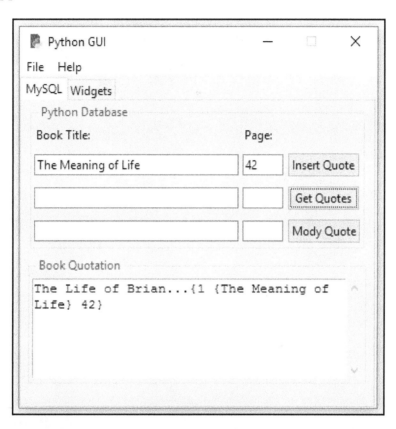

After inserting the data, we can verify that it made it into our two MySQL tables by clicking the **Get Quotes** button, which then displays the data we inserted into our two MySQL database tables, as shown in the preceding screenshot.

Clicking the **Get Quotes** button invokes the callback method we associated with the button click event. This gives us the data that we display in our ScrolledText widget:

```
# Adding a Button
    self.action1 = ttk.Button(self.mySQL, text="Get Quotes",
                             command=self.getQuote)
    self.action1.grid(column=2, row=2)

# Button callback
```

```
def getQuote(self):
    allBooks = self.mySQL.showBooks()
    print(allBooks)
    self.quote.insert(tk.INSERT, allBooks)
```

We use the `self.mySQL` class instance variable to invoke the `showBooks()` method, which is a part of the `MySQL` class we imported:

```
from Ch07_Code.GUI_MySQL_class import MySQL
class OOP():
    def __init__(self):
        # create MySQL instance
        self.mySQL = MySQL()

class MySQL():
    #------------------------------------------------------
    def showBooks(self):
        # connect to MySQL
        conn, cursor = self.connect()

        self.useGuiDB(cursor)

        # print results
        cursor.execute("SELECT * FROM Books")
        allBooks = cursor.fetchall()
        print(allBooks)

        # close cursor and connection
        self.close(cursor, conn)

        return allBooks
```

How it works...

In this recipe, we imported the Python module we wrote that contains all of the coding logic to connect to our MySQL database and knows how to insert, update, and delete data.

We have now connected our Python GUI to this SQL logic.

Using the MySQL workbench

MySQL has a very nice GUI that we can download for free. It is named the **MySQL Workbench**.

In this recipe, we will successfully install this workbench and then use it to run SQL queries against the GuiDB we created in the previous recipes, *Configuring the MySQL database connection*, *Designing the Python GUI database* and so on.

Getting ready

In order to use this recipe, you will need the MySQL database we developed in the previous recipes. You will also need a running MySQL server.

How to do it...

We can download the MySQL Workbench from the official MySQL website:

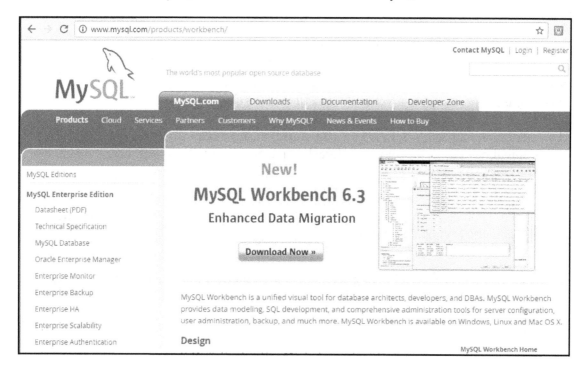

 The *MySQL Workbench* is a GUI in itself, very similar to the one we developed in the previous recipes. It does come with some additional features that are specific to working with MySQL.

When you installed MySQL, if you had the required components already installed on your PC, you might have MySQL Workbench already installed. If you do not have the Workbench installed, here are the steps to install the MySQL Workbench:

1. On the `http://www.mysql.com/products/workbench/` webpage, you can click the **Download** button, and this will bring you to the `http://dev.mysql.com/downloads/workbench/` webpage:

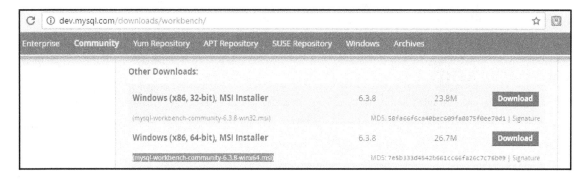

Download the MSI Installer that matches your operating system, for example, *mysql-workbench-community-6.3.8-winx64.msi*, for a typical Windows 10 running a 64-bit OS.

The installation may ask you to log in with your Oracle account, so if you don't yet have one, you will need to create your own Oracle developer account. Do not worry, it is free of charge.

 A few years ago, MySQL was acquired by Oracle. That is the reason why you need an Oracle account to download and install MySQL Server and the MySQL Workbench.

2. You will see the following screen, among others, until you have successfully installed the MySQL Workbench:

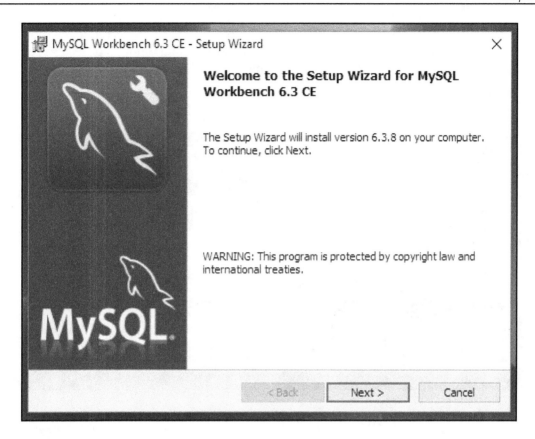

 The 6.3 CE in the installer window below is an abbreviation for **6.3 Community Edition**.

When you start up the MySQL Workbench, it will prompt you to connect. Use the root user and the password you created for it. MySQL Workbench is smart enough to recognize your running MySQL Server and the port it is listening on:

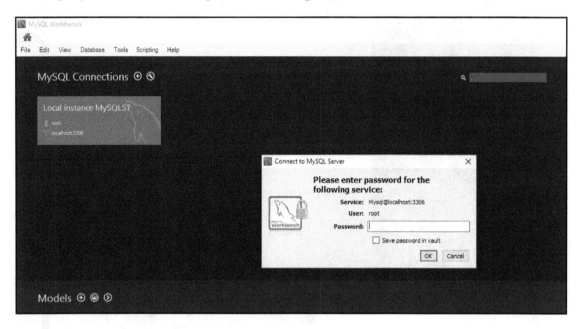

Once you are successfully logged into your MySQL Server instance, we can select our guidb:

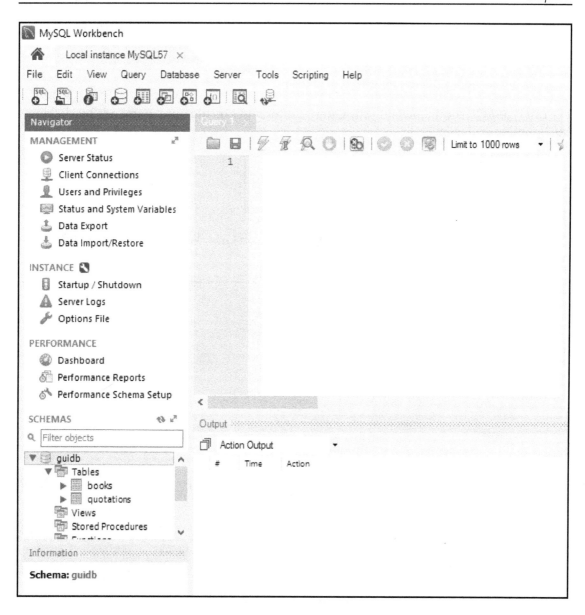

Towards the bottom left of the Workbench, we can find our **guidb** underneath the
SCHEMAS label.

In some literature and products, databases are often called **SCHEMAS**.

We can type SQL commands into the Query Editor and execute our commands by clicking the lightning bolt icon:

The following results are the Query editor in the Result Grid. We can click on the different tabs to see the different results:

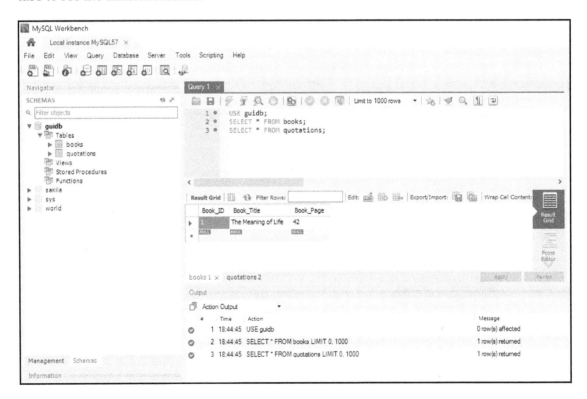

How it works...

We can now connect to our MySQL database via the *MySQL workbench* GUI. We can execute the same SQL commands we issued before and get the same results as we did when we executed them in our Python GUI.

There's more...

With the knowledge we gained throughout the recipes within this and the preceding chapters, we are now well-positioned to create our own GUIs written in Python, which can connect and talk to MySQL databases.

8
Internationalization and Testing

In this chapter, we will internationalize and test our Python GUI, covering the following recipes:

- Displaying widget text in different languages
- Changing the entire GUI language all at once
- Localizing the GUI
- Preparing the GUI for internationalization
- How to design a GUI in an agile fashion
- Do we need to test the GUI code?
- Setting debug watches
- Configuring different debug output levels
- Creating self-testing code using Python's __main__ section
- Creating robust GUIs using unit tests
- How to write unit tests using the Eclipse PyDev IDE

Introduction

In this chapter, we will internationalize our GUI by displaying text on labels, buttons, tabs, and other widgets, in different languages. We will start simply and then explore how we can prepare our GUI for internationalization at the design level.

We will also localize the GUI, which is slightly different from internationalization.

 As these words are long, they have been abbreviated to use the first character of the word, followed by the total number of characters in between the first and last character, followed by the last character of the word. So, internationalization becomes I18N and localization becomes L10N.

We will also test our GUI code, write unit tests, and explore the value unit tests can provide in our development efforts, which will lead us to the best practice of *refactoring* our code.

Here is the overview of Python modules for this chapter:

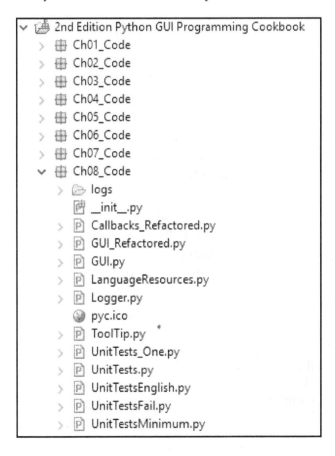

Displaying widget text in different languages

The easiest way to internationalize text strings in Python is by moving them into a separate Python module and then selecting the language to be displayed in our GUI by passing in a parameter to this module.

While this approach is not highly recommended, according to online search results, depending on the specific requirements of the application you are developing, this approach might still be the most pragmatic and fastest to implement.

Getting ready

We will reuse the Python GUI we created earlier. We have commented out one line of Python code that creates the MySQL tab because we do not talk to a MySQL database in this chapter.

How to do it...

In this recipe, we will start the I18N of our GUI by changing the Windows title from English to another language.

As the name GUI is the same in other languages, we will first expand the name which enables us to see the visual effects of our changes.

The following was our previous line of code:

```
self.win.title("Python GUI")
```

Let's change this to the following:

```
self.win.title("Python Graphical User Interface")
```

The preceding code change results in the following title for our GUI program:

`GUI_Refactored.py`

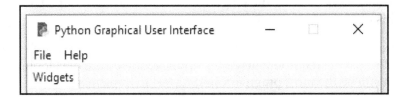

In this chapter, we will use English and German to exemplify the principle of internationalizing our Python GUI.

Hardcoding strings into code is never too good an idea, so the first thing we can do to improve our code is to separate all the strings that are visible in our GUI into a Python module of their own. This is the beginning of internationalizing the visible aspects of our GUI.

While we are into `I18N`, we will do this very positive refactoring and language translation, all in one step.

Let's create a new Python module and name it `LanguageResources.py`. Let's next move the English string of our GUI title into this module and then import this module into our GUI code.

We are separating the GUI from the languages it displays, which is an OOP design principle.

Our new Python module, containing internationalized strings, now looks as follows:

```
class I18N():
    '''Internationalization'''
    def __init__(self, language):
        if    language == 'en': self.resourceLanguageEnglish()
        elif  language == 'de': self.resourceLanguageGerman()
        else: raise NotImplementedError('Unsupported language.')

    def resourceLanguageEnglish(self):
```

```
        self.title = "Python Graphical User Interface"

def resourceLanguageGerman(self):
        self.title = 'Python Grafische Benutzeroberflaeche'
```

We import this new Python module into our main Python GUI code, and then use it:

```
from Ch08_Code.LanguageResources import I18N
class OOP():
    def __init__(self):
        self.win = tk.Tk()              # Create instance
        self.i18n = I18N('de')          # Select language
        self.win.title(self.i18n.title) # Add a title
```

Depending on which language we pass into the I18N class, our GUI will be displayed in that language.

Running the above code, we now get the following internationalized result:

GUI.py

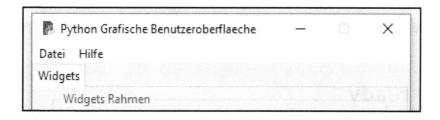

How it works...

We break out the hardcoded strings that are part of our GUI into their own separate modules. We do this by creating a class, and within the class's __init__() method, we select which language our GUI will display, depending on the passed-in language argument.

This works.

We can further modularize our code by separating the internationalized strings into separate files, potentially in XML or another format. We could also read them from a MySQL database.

This is a Separation of Concerns coding approach, which is at the heart of OOP programming.

Changing the entire GUI language, all at once

In this recipe, we will change all of the GUI display names, all at once, by refactoring all the previously hardcoded English strings into a separate Python module and then internationalizing those strings.

This recipe shows that it is a good design principle to avoid hardcoding any strings that our GUI displays but to separate the GUI code from the text that the GUI displays.

Designing our GUI in a modular way makes internationalizing it much easier.

Getting ready

We will continue to use the GUI from the previous recipe. In that recipe, we had already internationalized the title of the GUI.

How to do it...

In order to internationalize the text displayed in all of our GUI widgets, we have to move all hardcoded strings into a separate Python module, and this is what we'll do next.

Previously, strings of words that our GUI displayed were scattered all over our Python code.

Here is what our GUI looked like without I18N:

GUI_Refactored.py

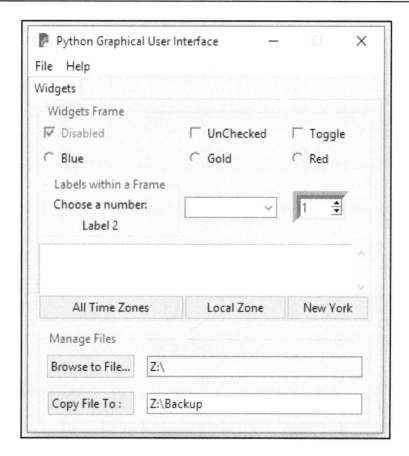

Every single string of every widget, including the title of our GUI, the tab control names, and so on, were all hardcoded and intermixed with the code that creates the GUI.

 It is a good idea to think about how we can best internationalize our GUI at the design phase of our GUI software development process.

The following is an excerpt of what our code looks like:

```
WIDGET_LABEL = ' Widgets Frame '
class OOP():
    def __init__(self):
        self.win = tk.Tk()                  # Create instance
        self.win.title("Python GUI")        # Add a title
```

```
# Radiobutton callback function
def radCall(self):
    radSel=self.radVar.get()
    if   radSel == 0: self.monty2.configure(text='Blue')
    elif radSel == 1: self.monty2.configure(text='Gold')
    elif radSel == 2: self.monty2.configure(text='Red')
```

 In this recipe, we are internationalizing all strings displayed in our GUI widgets. We are not internationalizing the text *entered* into our GUI, because this depends on the local settings on your PC.

The following is the code for the english internationalized strings:

```
classI18N():
'''Internationalization'''
    def __init__(self, language):
        if   language == 'en': self.resourceLanguageEnglish()
        elif language == 'de': self.resourceLanguageGerman()
        else: raiseNotImplementedError('Unsupported language.')

    def resourceLanguageEnglish(self):
        self.title = "Python Graphical User Interface"

        self.file  = "File"
        self.new   = "New"
        self.exit  = "Exit"
        self.help  = "Help"
        self.about = "About"

        self.WIDGET_LABEL = ' Widgets Frame '

        self.disabled  = "Disabled"
        self.unChecked = "UnChecked"
        self.toggle    = "Toggle"

        # Radiobutton list
        self.colors   = ["Blue", "Gold", "Red"]
        self.colorsIn = ["in Blue", "in Gold", "in Red"]

        self.labelsFrame  = ' Labels within a Frame '
        self.chooseNumber = "Choose a number:"
        self.label2       = "Label 2"

        self.mgrFiles = ' Manage Files '

        self.browseTo = "Browse to File..."
        self.copyTo   = "Copy File To :    "
```

In our Python GUI module, all previously hardcoded strings are now replaced by an instance of our new `I18N` class, which resides in the `LanguageResources.py` module.

Here is an example from our refactored `GUI.py` module:

```
from Ch08_Code.LanguageResources import I18N
class OOP():
    def __init__(self):
        self.win = tk.Tk()              # Create instance
        self.i18n = I18N('de')          # Select language
        self.win.title(self.i18n.title) # Add a title

    # Radiobutton callback function
    def radCall(self):
        radSel = self.radVar.get()
        if   radSel == 0: self.widgetFrame.configure(text=
                        self.i18n.WIDGET_LABEL + self.i18n.colorsIn[0])
        elif radSel == 1: self.widgetFrame.configure(text=
                        self.i18n.WIDGET_LABEL + self.i18n.colorsIn[1])
        elif radSel == 2: self.widgetFrame.configure(text=
                        self.i18n.WIDGET_LABEL + self.i18n.colorsIn[2])
```

Note how all of the previously hardcoded English strings have been replaced by calls to the instance of our new `I18N` class. An example is `self.win.title(self.i18n.title)`.

What this gives us is the ability to internationalize our GUI. We simply have to use the same variable names and combine them by passing in a parameter to select the language we wish to display.

We could change languages on the fly as part of the GUI as well, or we could read the local PC settings and decide which language our GUI text should display according to those settings.

 An example of how to read the local settings is covered in the next recipe, *Localizing the GUI*.

We can now implement the translation to German by simply filling in the variable names with the corresponding words:

```
class I18N():
    '''Internationalization'''
    def __init__(self, language):
        if   language == 'en': self.resourceLanguageEnglish()
        elif language == 'de': self.resourceLanguageGerman()
```

```
        else: raise NotImplementedError('Unsupported language.')

def resourceLanguageGerman(self):
        self.file   = "Datei"
        self.new    = "Neu"
        self.exit   = "Schliessen"
        self.help   = "Hilfe"
        self.about  = "Ueber"

        self.WIDGET_LABEL = ' Widgets Rahmen '

        self.disabled  = "Deaktiviert"
        self.unChecked = "Nicht Markiert"
        self.toggle    = "Markieren"

        # Radiobutton list
        self.colors   = ["Blau", "Gold", "Rot"]
        self.colorsIn = ["in Blau", "in Gold", "in Rot"]

        self.labelsFrame  = ' Etiketten im Rahmen '
        self.chooseNumber = "Waehle eine Nummer:"
        self.label2       = "Etikette 2"

        self.mgrFiles = ' Dateien Organisieren '

        self.browseTo = "Waehle eine Datei... "
        self.copyTo   = "Kopiere Datei zu :    "
```

In our GUI code, we can now change the entire GUI display language in one line of Python code:

```
classOOP():
    def __init__(self):
        self.win = tk.Tk()       # Create instance
        self.i18n = I18N('de')   # Pass in language
```

Running the preceding code creates the following internationalized GUI:

GUI.py

How it works...

In order to internationalize our GUI, we refactored hardcoded strings into a separate module and then used the same class members to internationalize our GUI by passing in a string as the initializer of our I18N class, effectively controlling the language our GUI displays.

Localizing the GUI

After the first step of internationalizing our GUI, the next step is to localize it. Why would we wish to do this?

Well, here in the United States of America, we are all cowboys and we live in different time zones.

So while we are internationalized to the USA, our horses do wake up in different time zones (and do expect to be fed according to their own inner horse time zone schedule).

This is where localization comes in.

Getting ready

We are extending the GUI we developed in the previous recipe by localizing it.

How to do it...

We start by first installing the Python `pytz` time zone module, using `pip`. We type the following command in a command processor prompt:

    pip install pytz

 In this book, we are using Python 3.6, which comes with the `pip` module built-in. If you are using an older version of Python, then you may have to install the `pip` module first.

When successful, we get the following result:

```
Administrator: Command Prompt                              —    □    ×

C:\WINDOWS\system32>pip install pytz
Collecting pytz
  Downloading pytz-2016.10-py2.py3-none-any.whl (483kB)
    100% |███████████████████████████████| 491kB 1.2MB/s
Installing collected packages: pytz
Successfully installed pytz-2016.10

C:\WINDOWS\system32>
```

The preceding screenshot shows that the command downloaded the `.whl` format. If you have not done so, you might have to install the Python `wheel` module first.

This installed the Python `pytz` module into the `site-packages` folder, so now we can import this module from our Python GUI code.

We can list all the existing time zones by running the following code, which will display the time zones in our `ScrolledText` widget. First, we add a new `Button` widget to our GUI:

```python
import pytz
class OOP():
    # TZ Button callback
    def allTimeZones(self):
        for tz in pytz.all_timezones:
            self.scr.insert(tk.INSERT, tz + '\n')

    def createWidgets(self):
        # Adding a TZ Button
        self.allTZs = ttk.Button(self.widgetFrame,
                                 text=self.i18n.timeZones,
                                 command=self.allTimeZones)
        self.allTZs.grid(column=0, row=9, sticky='WE')
```

Clicking our new `Button` widget results in the following output:

GUI.py

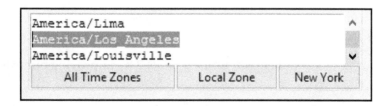

After we install the `tzlocal` Python module, we can print our current locale by running the following code:

```python
    # TZ Local Button callback
    def localZone(self):
        from tzlocal import get_localzone
        self.scr.insert(tk.INSERT, get_localzone())

    def createWidgets(self):
```

```
# Adding local TZ Button
self.localTZ = ttk.Button(self.widgetFrame,
                              text=self.i18n.localZone,
                              command=self.localZone)
self.localTZ.grid(column=1, row=9, sticky='WE')
```

We have internationalized the strings of our two new `Buttons` in `Resources.py`.

English version:

```
self.timeZones = "All Time Zones"
self.localZone = "Local Zone"
```

German version:

```
self.timeZones = "Alle Zeitzonen"
self.localZone = "Lokale Zone"
```

Clicking our new button now tells us which time zone we are in (hey, we didn't know that, did we...).

`GUI.py`

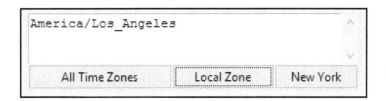

We can now translate our local time to a different time zone. Let's use USA Eastern Standard Time as an example.

We display our current local time in our unused Label 2 by improving our existing code.

When we run the code, our internationalized Label 2 (displayed as `Etikette 2` in German) will display the current local time:

GUI.py

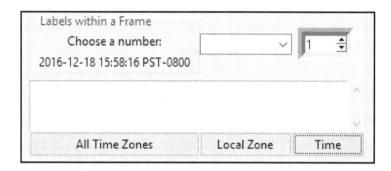

We can now change our local time to US EST by first converting it to **Coordinated Universal Time** (**UTC**) and then applying the `timezone` function from the imported `pytz` module:

```
import pytz
class OOP():
    # Format local US time with TimeZone info
    def getDateTime(self):
        fmtStrZone = "%Y-%m-%d %H:%M:%S %Z%z"
        # Get Coordinated Universal Time
        utc = datetime.now(timezone('UTC'))
        print(utc.strftime(fmtStrZone))

        # Convert UTC datetime object to Los Angeles TimeZone
        la = utc.astimezone(timezone('America/Los_Angeles'))
        print(la.strftime(fmtStrZone))

        # Convert UTC datetime object to New York TimeZone
        ny = utc.astimezone(timezone('America/New_York'))
        print(ny.strftime(fmtStrZone))

        # update GUI label with NY Time and Zone
        self.lbl2.set(ny.strftime(fmtStrZone))
```

Clicking the button, now renamed as New York, results in the following output:

GUI.py

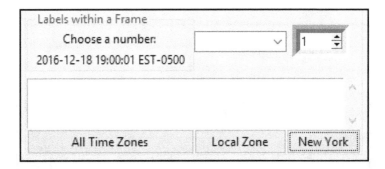

Our Label 2 got updated with the current time in New York and we are printing the UTC times of the cities, Los Angeles and New York, with their respective time zone conversions, relative to the UTC time on the Eclipse console, using a US date formatting string:

GUI.py

 UTC never observes Daylight Saving Time. During **Eastern Daylight Time (EDT)** UTC is four hours ahead and during **Standard Time (EST)** it is five hours ahead of the local time.

How it works...

In order to localize date and time information, we first need to convert our local time to UTC time. We then apply the `timezone` information and use the `astimezone` function from the `pytz` Python time zone module to convert to any time zone in the entire world!

In this recipe, we converted the local time of the USA west coast to UTC and then displayed the USA east coast time in Label 2 of our GUI.

Preparing the GUI for internationalization

In this recipe we will prepare our GUI for internationalization by realizing that not all is as easy as could be expected when translating English into foreign languages.

We still have one problem to solve, which is, how to properly display non-English Unicode characters from foreign languages.

One might expect that displaying the German ä, ö, and ü Unicode umlaut characters would be handled by Python 3.6 automatically, but this is not the case.

Getting ready

We will continue to use the Python GUI we developed in the recent chapters. First, we will change the default language to German in the GUI.py initialization code.

We do this by uncommenting the line, self.i18n = I18N('de').

How to do it...

When we change the word Ueber to the correct German Über using the umlaut character the Eclipse PyDev plugin is not too happy:

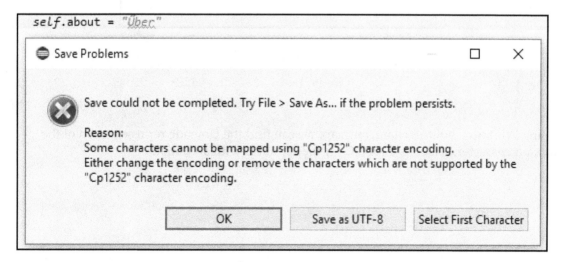

We get an error message, which is a little bit confusing because, when we run the same line of code from within the Eclipse PyDev Console, we get the expected result:

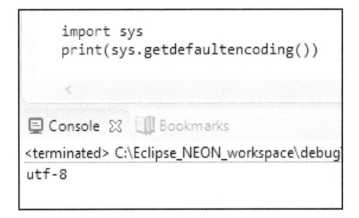

When we ask for the Python default encoding we get the expected result, which is utf-8:

```
import sys
print(sys.getdefaultencoding())
```

 We can, of course, always resort to the direct representation of Unicode.

Using Windows' built-in character map, we can find the Unicode representation of the umlaut character, which is **U+00DC** for the capital **U** with an umlaut:

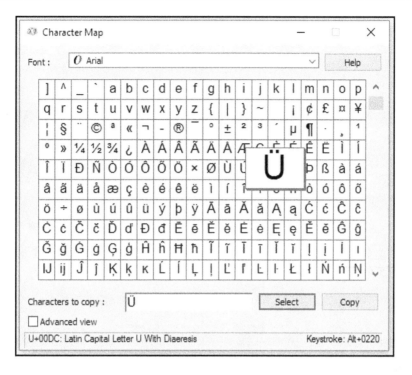

While this workaround is truly ugly, it does the trick. Instead of typing in the literal character Ü, we can pass in the Unicode of **U+00DC** to get this character correctly displayed in our GUI:

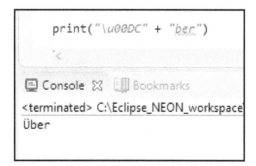

We can also just accept the change in the default encoding from *Cp1252* to **UTF-8** using PyDev with Eclipse but we may not always get the prompt to do so.

Instead, we might see the following error message displayed:

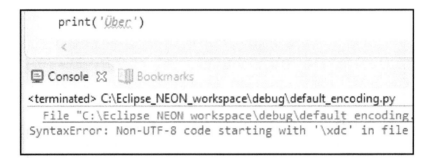

The way to solve this problem is to change the PyDev project's **Text file encoding** property to **UTF-8**:

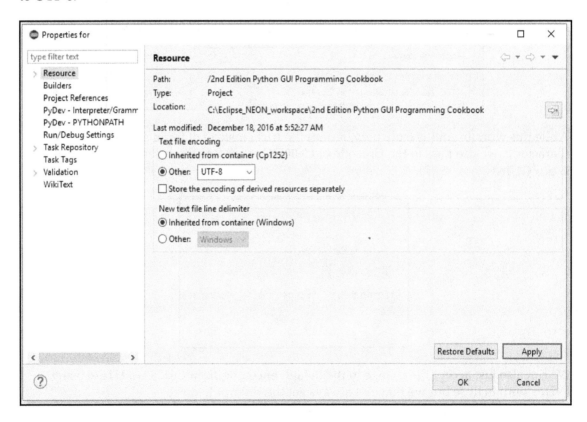

After changing the PyDev default encoding, we now can display those German umlaut characters. We also updated the title to use the correct German ä character:

GUI_Refactored.py

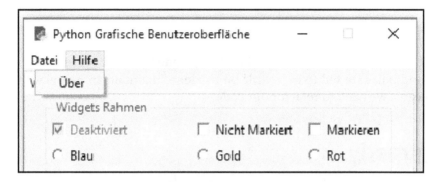

How it works...

Internationalization and working with foreign language Unicode characters is often not as straightforward as we would wish. Sometimes we have to find workarounds, and expressing Unicode characters via Python by using the direct representation by prepending \u can do the trick.

At other times, we just have to find the settings of our development environment to adjust.

How to design a GUI in an agile fashion

The modern agile software development approach to design and coding came out of the lessons learned by software professionals. This method applies to a GUI as much as to any other code. One of the main keys of agile software development is the continuously applied process of refactoring.

One practical example of how refactoring our code can help us in our software development work is by first implementing some simple functionality using functions.

As our code grows in complexity, we might want to refactor our functions into methods of a class. This approach would enable us to remove global variables and also to be more flexible about where we place the methods inside the class.

While the functionality of our code has not changed, the structure has.

In this process, we code, test, refactor, and then test again. We do this in short cycles and often start with the minimum code required to get some functionality to work.

 Test-driven software development is one particular style of the agile development methodology.

While our GUI is working nicely, our main GUI.py code has been ever-increasing in complexity, and it has started to get a little bit harder to maintain an overview of our code. This means, we need to refactor our code.

Getting ready

We will refactor the GUI we created in previous chapters. We will use the English version of the GUI.

How to do it...

We have already broken out all the names our GUI displays when we internationalized it in the previous recipe. That was an excellent start to refactoring our code.

 Refactoring is the process of improving the structure, readability, and maintainability of the existing code. We are not adding new functionality.

In the previous chapters and recipes, we have been extending our GUI in a top-to-bottom waterfall development approach, adding import to the top and code towards the bottom of the existing code.

While this was useful when looking at the code, it now looks a little bit messy and we can improve this to help our future development.

Let's first clean up our import statement section, which currently looks as follows:

```
#=======================
# imports
#=======================
import tkinter as tk
from tkinter import ttk
from tkinter import scrolledtext
```

```
from tkinter import Menu
from tkinter import Spinbox
import Ch08_Code.ToolTip as tt
from threading import Thread
from time import sleep
from queue import Queue
from tkinter import filedialog as fd
from os import path
from tkinter import messagebox as mBox
from Ch08_Code.LanguageResources import I18N
from datetime import datetime
from pytz import all_timezones, timezone

# Module level GLOBALS
GLOBAL_CONST = 42
```

By simply grouping related imports, we can reduce the number of lines of code, which improves the readability of our imports, making them appear less overwhelming:

```
#========================
# imports
#========================
import tkinter as tk
from tkinter import ttk, scrolledtext, Menu, Spinbox, filedialog as fd,
                     messagebox as mBox
from queue import Queue
from os import path
import Ch08_Code.ToolTip as tt
from Ch08_Code.LanguageResources import I18N
from Ch08_Code.Logger import Logger, LogLevel

# Module level GLOBALS
GLOBAL_CONST = 42
```

We can further refactor our code by breaking out the callback methods into their own modules. This improves readability by separating the different import statements into the modules they are required in.

Let's rename our GUI.py as GUI_Refactored.py and create a new module, which we name Callbacks_Refactored.py.

This gives us this new architecture:

```
#========================
# imports
#========================
import tkinter as tk
from tkinter import ttk, scrolledtext, Menu, Spinbox,
```

```
                        filedialog as fd, messagebox as mBox
from queue import Queue
from os import path
import Ch08_Code.ToolTip as tt
from Ch08_Code.LanguageResources import I18N
from Ch08_Code.Logger import Logger, LogLevel
from Ch08_Code.Callbacks_Refactored import Callbacks

# Module level GLOBALS
GLOBAL_CONST = 42

class OOP():
    def __init__(self):
        # Callback methods now in different module
        self.callBacks = Callbacks(self)
```

Note how we are passing an instance of our own GUI class (`self`) when calling the
`Callbacks` initializer.

Our new `Callbacks` class is as follows:

```
#======================
# imports
#======================
import tkinter as tk
from time import sleep
from threading import Thread
from pytz import all_timezones, timezone
from datetime import datetime

class Callbacks():
    def __init__(self, oop):
        self.oop = oop

    def defaultFileEntries(self):
        self.oop.fileEntry.delete(0, tk.END)
        self.oop.fileEntry.insert(0, 'Z:')              # bogus path
        self.oop.fileEntry.config(state='readonly')
        self.oop.netwEntry.delete(0, tk.END)
        self.oop.netwEntry.insert(0, 'Z:Backup')        # bogus path

    # Combobox callback
    def _combo(self, val=0):
        value = self.oop.combo.get()
        self.oop.scr.insert(tk.INSERT, value + '\n')
```

In the initializer of our new class, the passed-in GUI instance is saved under the name `self.oop` and used throughout this new Python class module.

Running the refactored GUI code still works. We have only increased its readability and reduced the complexity of our code in preparation for further development work.

How it works...

We have first improved the readability of our code by grouping the related import statements. We next broke out the callback methods into their own class and module, in order to further reduce the complexity of our code.

We had already taken the same OOP approach by having the `ToolTip` class reside in its own module and by internationalizing all GUI strings in the previous recipes. In this recipe, we went one step further in refactoring by passing our own instance into the callback method's class that our GUI relies upon. This enables us to use all of our GUI widgets.

Now that we better understand the value of a modular approach to software development, we will most likely start with this approach in our future software designs.

Do we need to test the GUI code?

Testing our software is an important activity during the coding phase as well as when releasing service packs or bug fixes.

There are different levels of testing. The first level is developer testing, which often starts with the compiler or interpreter not letting us run our buggy code, forcing us to test small parts of our code on the level of individual methods.

This is the first level of defense.

A second level of coding defensively is when our source code control system tells us about some conflicts to be resolved and does not let us check in our modified code.

This is very useful and absolutely necessary when we work professionally in a team of developers. The source code control system is our friend and points out changes that have been committed to a particular branch or top-of-tree, either by ourselves or by our other developers, and tells us that our local version of the code is both outdated and has some conflicts that need to be resolved before we can submit our code into the repository.

This part assumes you use a source control system to manage and store your code. Examples include git, mercurial, svn, and several others. Git is a very popular source control and it is free for a single user.

A third level is the level of APIs where we encapsulate potential future changes to our code by only allowing interactions with our code via published interfaces.

Another level of testing is integration testing, when half of the bridge we finally built meets the other half that the other development teams created and the two don't meet at the same height (say, one half ended up two meters or yards higher than the other half...).

Then, there is the end user testing. While we built what they specified, it is not really what they wanted.

All of the above examples are valid reasons why we need to test our code both in the design and implementation stages.

Getting ready

We will test the GUI we created in recent recipes and chapters. We will also show some simple examples of what can go wrong and why we need to keep testing our code and the code we call via APIs.

How to do it...

While many experienced developers grew up sprinkling `printf()` statements all over their code while debugging, many developers in the 21st century are accustomed to modern IDE development environments that efficiently speed up development time.

In this book, we are using the PyDev Python plugin for the Eclipse IDE.

If you are just starting to use an IDE, such as Eclipse with PyDev, it might be a little bit overwhelming at first. The Python IDLE tool that ships with Python 3.6 has a simpler debugger and you might wish to explore that first.

Whenever something goes wrong in our code, we have to debug it. The first step of doing this is to set break points and then step through our code, line by line, or method by method.

Stepping in and out of our code is a daily activity until the code runs smoothly.

In Python GUI programming, one of the first things that can go wrong is missing out on importing the required modules or importing the existing modules.

Here is a simple example:

GUI.py with the import statement # import tkinter as tk commented out:

```
#================================================
class OOP():
    def __init__(self, language='en'):
        # Create instance
        self.win = tk.Tk()

    <

Console   Bookmarks
<terminated> C:\Eclipse_NEON_workspace\2nd Edition Python
Traceback (most recent call last):
  File "C:\Eclipse NEON workspace\2nd Edition Py
    oop = OOP()
  File "C:\Eclipse NEON workspace\2nd Edition Py
    self.win = tk.Tk()
NameError: name 'tk' is not defined
```

We are trying to create an instance of the tkinter class, but things don't work as expected.

Well, we simply forgot to import the module and alias it as tk, and we can fix this by adding a line of Python code above our class creation, where the import statements live:

```
#========================
# imports
#========================
import tkinter as tk
```

This is an example in which our development environment does the testing for us. We just have to do the debugging and code fixing.

Another example more closely related to developer testing is when we code conditionals and, during our regular development, do not exercise all branches of logic.

Using an example from Chapter 7, *Storing Data in our MySQL Database via our GUI*, let's say we click on the **Get Quotes** button and this works, but we never clicked on the **Mody Quote** button. The first button click creates the desired result but the second throws an exception (because we had not yet implemented this code and probably forgot all about it):

`GUI_MySQL.py` in `Chapter 7`, *Storing Data in our MySQL Database via our GUI.*

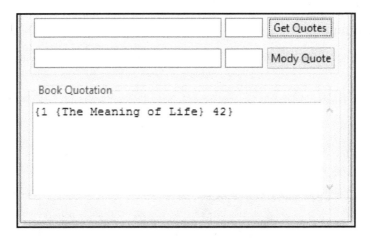

Clicking the **Mody Quote** button creates the following result:

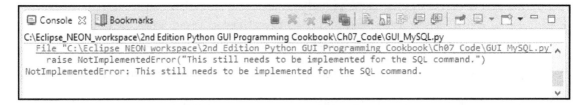

Another potential area of bugs is when a function or method suddenly no longer returns the expected result. Let's say we are calling the following function, which returns the expected result:

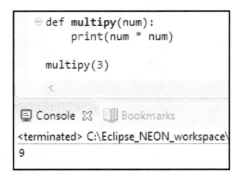

Then, someone makes a mistake, and we no longer get the previous results:

```
⊝ def multipy(num):
      print(num ** num)

   multipy(3)

   <

🖥 Console ⊠   📖 Bookmarks
<terminated> C:\Eclipse_NEON_workspace\
27
```

Instead of multiplying, we are raising by the power of the passed-in number, and the result is no longer what it used to be.

 In software testing, this sort of bug is called regression.

How it works...

In this recipe we emphasized the importance of software testing during several phases of the software development life cycle by showing several examples of where the code can go wrong and introduce software defects (aka bugs).

Setting debug watches

In modern **Integrated Development Environments (IDEs)**, such as the PyDev plugin in Eclipse or another IDE such as NetBeans, we can set debug watches to monitor the state of our GUI during the execution of our code.

This is very similar to the Microsoft IDEs of Visual Studio and the more recent versions of Visual Studio.NET.

Setting debug watches is a very convenient way to help our development efforts.

Getting ready

In this recipe, we will reuse the Python GUI we developed in the earlier recipes. We will step through the code we had previously developed, and we will set debug watches.

How to do it…

While this recipe applies to the PyDev plugin in the Java-based Eclipse IDE, its principles also apply to many modern IDEs.

The first position where we might wish to place a breakpoint is at the place where we make our GUI visible by calling the tkinter main event loop.

The green balloon symbol on the left is a breakpoint in PyDev/Eclipse. When we execute our code in debug mode, the execution of the code will be halted once the execution reaches the breakpoint. At this point, we can see the values of all the variables that are currently in scope. We can also type expressions into one of the debugger windows, which will execute them, showing us the results. If the result is what we want, we might decide to change our code using what we have just learned.

We normally step through the code by either clicking an icon in the toolbar of our IDE or by using a keyboard shortcut (such as pressing *F5* to step into code, *F6* to step over, and *F7* to step out of the current method):

GUI.py

```
#===========================
# Start GUI
#===========================
oop = OOP()
oop.win.mainloop()
```

Placing the breakpoint where we did and then stepping into this code turns out to be a problem because we end up in some low-level `tkinter` code we really do not wish to debug right now. We get out of the low-level `tkinter` code by clicking the Step-Out toolbar icon (which is the third yellow arrow on the right below the project menu) or by pressing *F7* (assuming we are using PyDev in Eclipse).

We started the debugging session by clicking the bug toolbar icon towards the right of the screenshot. If we execute without debugging, we click the green circle with the white triangle inside it, which is the icon to the right of the bug icon:

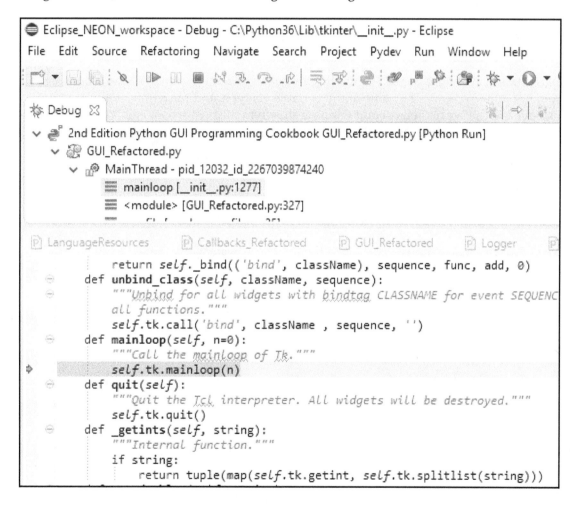

A better idea is to place our breakpoint closer to our own code in order to watch the values of some of our own Python variables. In the event-driven world of modern GUIs, we have to place our breakpoints at code that gets invoked during events, for example, button clicks.

Currently, one of our main functionalities resides in a button click event. When we click the button labelled **New York**, we create an event, which, then, results in something happening in our GUI.

Let's place a breakpoint at the **New York** button callback method, which we named `getDateTime()`.

When we now run a debug session, we will stop at the breakpoint and then we can enable watches of variables that are in scope.

Using PyDev in Eclipse, we can right-click a variable and then select the watch command from the pop-up menu. The name of the variable, its type, and the current value will be displayed in the expressions debug window shown in the next screenshot. We can also type directly into the expressions window.

The variables we are watching are not limited to simple data types. We can watch class instances, lists, dictionaries, and so on.

When watching these more complex objects, we can expand them in the Expressions window and drill down into all of the values of the class instances, dictionaries, and so on.

We do this by clicking on the triangle to the left of our watched variable that appears left-most under the **Name** column, next to each variable:

`Callbacks_Refactored.py`

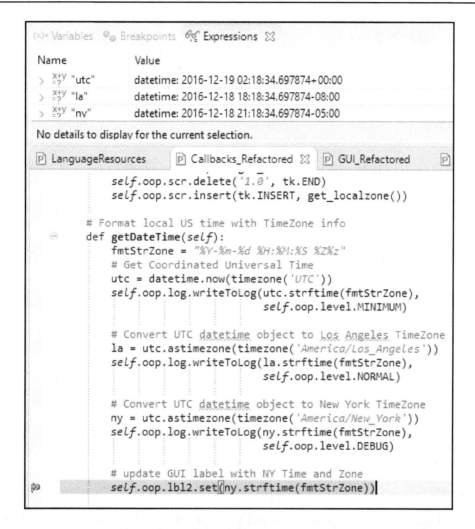

While we are printing out the values of the different time zone locations, in the long term, it is much more convenient and efficient to set debug watches. We do not have to clutter our code with old-fashioned C-style `printf()` statements.

If you are interested in learning how to install Eclipse with the PyDev plugin for Python, there is a great tutorial that will get you started with installing all the necessary free software and then introduce you to PyDev within Eclipse by creating a simple, working Python program: `http://www.vogella.com/tutorials/Python/article.html`

How it works...

We use modern Integrated Development Environments (IDEs) in the 21st century that are freely available to help us to create solid code.

This recipe showed how to set debug watches, which is a fundamental tool in every developer's skill set. Stepping through our own code even when not hunting down bugs ensures that we understand our code, and it can lead to improving our code via refactoring.

The following is a quote from the first programming book I read, *Thinking in Java*, written by Bruce Eckel.

> *"Resist the Urge to Hurry, it will only slow you down."*
> *- Bruce Eckel*

Almost two decades later, this advice has passed the test of time.

 Debug watches help us create solid code and is not a waste of time.

Configuring different debug output levels

In this recipe, we will configure different debug levels, which we can select and change at runtime. This allows us to control how much we want to drill down into our code when debugging our code.

We will create two new Python classes and place both of them into the same module.

We will use four different logging levels and write our debugging output to a log file we will create. If the `logs` folder does not exist, we will create it automatically as well.

The name of the log file is the name of the executing script, which is our refactored `GUI.py`. We can also choose other names for our log files by passing in the full path to the initializer of our `Logger` class.

Getting ready

We will continue using our refactored `GUI.py` code from the previous recipe.

How to do it…

First, we create a new Python module into which we place two new classes. The first class is very simple and defines the logging levels. This is basically an enumeration:

```
class LogLevel:
'''Define logging levels.'''
    OFF     = 0
    MINIMUM = 1
    NORMAL  = 2
    DEBUG   = 3
```

The second class creates a log file by using the passed-in full path of the file name and places this into a `logs` folder. On the first run, the `logs` folder might not exist, so the code automatically creates the folder:

```
import os, time
from datetime import datetime
class Logger:
    ''' Create a test log and write to it. '''
    #------------------------------------------------------
    def __init__(self, fullTestName, loglevel=LogLevel.DEBUG):
        testName = os.path.splitext(os.path.basename(fullTestName))[0]
        logName  = testName  + '.log'

        logsFolder = 'logs'
        if not os.path.exists(logsFolder):
            os.makedirs(logsFolder, exist_ok = True)

        self.log = os.path.join(logsFolder, logName)
        self.createLog()

        self.loggingLevel = loglevel
        self.startTime    = time.perf_counter()

    #------------------------------------------------------
    def createLog(self):
        with open(self.log, mode='w', encoding='utf-8') as logFile:
            logFile.write(self.getDateTime() +
                          '\t\t*** Starting Test ***\n')
        logFile.close()
```

In order to write to our log file, we use the `writeToLog()` method. Inside the method, the first thing we do is check whether the message has a logging level higher than the limit we set our desired logging output to. If the message has a lower level, we discard it and immediately return from the method.

If the message has the logging level that we want to display, we then check whether it starts with a newline character, and if it does, we discard the newline by slicing the method starting at index 1, using Python's slice operator (`msg = msg[1:]`).

We then write one line to our log file consisting of the current date timestamp, two tab spaces, our message, and ending in a newline character:

```
#-------------------------------------------------------
def writeToLog(self, msg='', loglevel=LogLevel.DEBUG):
    # control how much gets logged
    if loglevel > self.loggingLevel:
        return

    # open log file in append mode
    with open(self.log, mode='a', encoding='utf-8') as logFile:
        msg = str(msg)
        if msg.startswith('\n'):
            msg = msg[1:]
        logFile.write(self.getDateTime() + '\t\t' + msg + '\n')

    logFile.close()
```

We can now import our new Python module and, inside the __init__ section of our GUI code, can create an instance of the `Logger` class:

```
from os import path
from Ch08_Code.Logger import Logger
class OOP():
    def __init__(self):
        # create Logger instance
        fullPath = path.realpath(__file__)
        self.log = Logger(fullPath)
        print(self.log)
```

We are retrieving the full path to our running GUI script via `path.realpath(__file__)` and passing this into the initializer of the `Logger` class. If the `logs` folder does not exist, it will automatically be created by our Python code.

This creates the following results:

`Callbacks_Refactored.py` with `print(self.log)` uncommented

```
# create Logger instance
fullPath = path.realpath(__file__)
self.log = Logger(fullPath)
print(self.log)
```

Console ⊠   Bookmarks

\<terminated\> C:\Eclipse_NEON_workspace\2nd Edition Python GUI Programming
\<Ch08_Code.Logger.Logger object at 0x000001FFAD0C5CF8\>

The preceding screenshot shows that we created an instance of our new `Logger` class and the following screenshot shows that both the `logs` folder as well as the log were created:

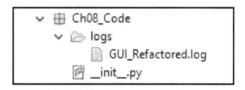

When we open up the log, we can see that the current date and time as well as a default string have been written into the log:

GUI_Refactored.log ⊠

2016-12-19 18:09:14   *** Starting Test ***

How it works...

In this recipe, we created our own logging class. While Python ships with a `Logging` module, it is very easy to create our own, which gives us absolute control over our logging format. This is very useful when we combine our own logging output with MS Excel or the `Matplotlib` we explored in the recipes of a previous chapter.

In the next recipe, we will use Python's built-in __main__ functionality to use the four different logging levels we just created.

Creating self-testing code using Python's __main__ section

Python comes with a very nice feature that enables each module to self-test. Making use of this feature is a great way of making sure that the changes to our code do not break the existing code and, additionally, the __main__ self-testing section can serve as documentation for how each module works.

 After a few months or years, we sometimes forget what our code is doing, so having an explanation written in the code itself is indeed of great benefit.

It is a good idea to always add a self-testing section to every Python module, when possible. It is sometimes not possible but, in most modules, it is possible to do so.

Getting ready

We will extend the previous recipe, so in order to understand what the code in this recipe is doing, we have to first read and understand the code of the previous recipe.

How to do it...

First, we will explore the power of the Python __main__ self-testing section by adding this self-testing section to our `LanguageResources.py` module. Whenever we run a module that has this self-testing section located at the bottom of the module, when the module is executed by itself, this code will run.

When the module is imported and used from other modules, the code in the __main__ self-testing section will not be executed.

This is the code which is also shown in the screenshot that follows:

```python
if __name__ == '__main__':
    language = 'en'
    inst = I18N(language)
    print(inst.title)

    language = 'de'
    inst = I18N(language)
    print(inst.title)
```

After adding the self-testing section can we now run this module by itself and it creates a useful output while at the same time showing us that our code works as intended:

`LanguageResources.py`

```
#====================================================
if __name__ == '__main__':
    language = 'en'
    inst = I18N(language)
    print(inst.title)

    language = 'de'
    inst = I18N(language)
    print(inst.title)
```

```
Console 23    Bookmarks
<terminated> C:\Eclipse_NEON_workspace\2nd Edition Python GUI Programming
Python Graphical User Interface
Python Grafische Benutzeroberfläche
```

We first pass English as the language to be displayed in our GUI and then we'll pass German as the language our GUI will display.

We print out the title of our GUI to show that our Python module works as we intended it to work.

The next step is to use our logging capabilities, which we created in the previous recipe.

We do this by first adding a `__main__` self-testing section to our refactored `GUI_Refactored.py` module, and we then verify that we created an instance of our `Logger` class:

`GUI_Refactored.py` with `print(oop.log)` uncommented

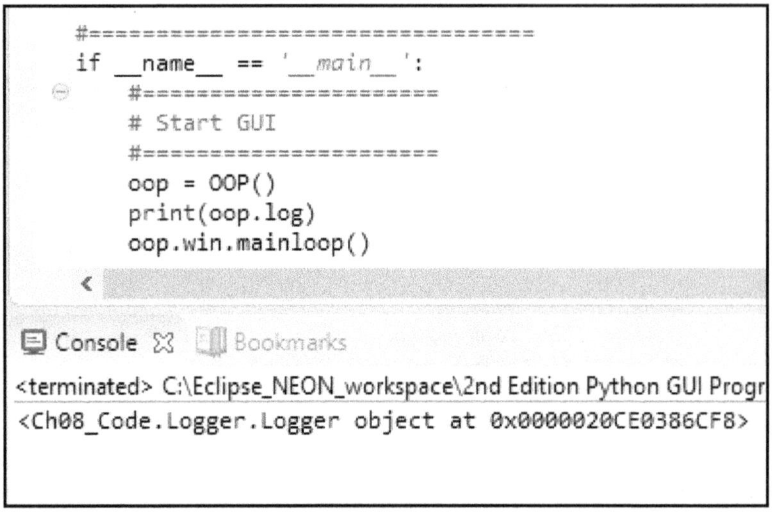

```
#===================================
if __name__ == '__main__':
    #=======================
    # Start GUI
    #=======================
    oop = OOP()
    print(oop.log)
    oop.win.mainloop()
```

🖥 Console ⊠ 📖 Bookmarks

<terminated> C:\Eclipse_NEON_workspace\2nd Edition Python GUI Progr
<Ch08_Code.Logger.Logger object at 0x0000020CE0386CF8>

We next write to our log file by using the command shown. We have designed our logging level to default to log every message, which is the DEBUG level, and because of this we do not have to change anything. We just pass the message to be logged to the `writeToLog` method:

```
if __name__ == '__main__':
#=======================
# Start GUI
#=======================
oop = OOP()
    print(oop.log)
    oop.log.writeToLog('Test message')
    oop.win.mainloop()
```

This gets written to our log file, as can be seen in the following screenshot of the log:

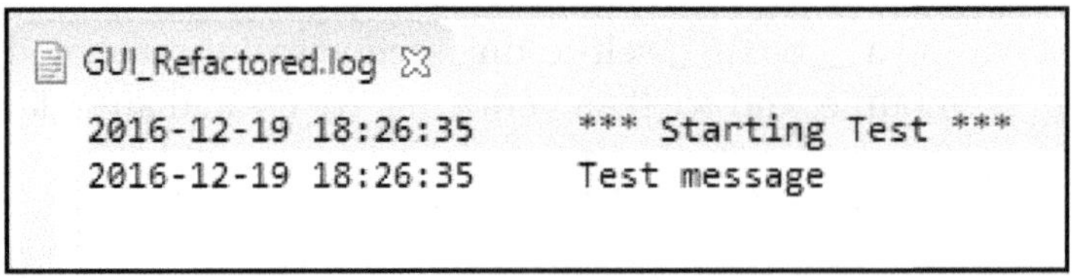

📄 GUI_Refactored.log ⊠

```
2016-12-19 18:26:35      *** Starting Test ***
2016-12-19 18:26:35      Test message
```

Now, we can control the logging by adding logging levels to our logging statements and setting the level we wish to output. Let's add this capability to our **New York** button callback method in the `Callbacks_Refactored.py` module, which is the `getDateTime` method.

We change the previous `print` statements to `log` statements using different debug levels.

In the `GUI_Refactored.py`, we import both the new classes from our `Logger` module:

```
from Ch08_Code.Logger import Logger, LogLevel
```

Next, we create local instances of those classes:

```
# create Logger instance
fullPath = path.realpath(__file__)
self.log = Logger(fullPath)

# create Log Level instance
self.level = LogLevel()
```

As we are passing an instance of the GUI class to the `Callbacks_Refactored.py` initializer, we can use logging level constraints according to the `LogLevel` class we created:

```
        # Format local US time with TimeZone info
        def getDateTime(self):
            fmtStrZone = "%Y-%m-%d %H:%M:%S %Z%z"
            # Get Coordinated Universal Time
            utc = datetime.now(timezone('UTC'))
            self.oop.log.writeToLog(utc.strftime(fmtStrZone),
                                self.oop.level.MINIMUM)

            # Convert UTC datetime object to Los Angeles TimeZone
            la = utc.astimezone(timezone('America/Los_Angeles'))
            self.oop.log.writeToLog(la.strftime(fmtStrZone),
                                self.oop.level.NORMAL)

            # Convert UTC datetime object to New York TimeZone
            ny = utc.astimezone(timezone('America/New_York'))
            self.oop.log.writeToLog(ny.strftime(fmtStrZone),
                                self.oop.level.DEBUG)

            # update GUI label with NY Time and Zone
            self.oop.lbl2.set(ny.strftime(fmtStrZone))
```

When we now click our **New York** button, depending upon the selected logging level, we get different output written to our log file. The default logging level is DEBUG, which means that everything gets written to our log:

```
GUI_Refactored.log  ⊠
    2016-12-19 18:30:40        *** Starting Test ***
    2016-12-19 18:30:40        Test message
    2016-12-19 18:30:42        2016-12-20 02:30:42 UTC+0000
    2016-12-19 18:30:42        2016-12-19 18:30:42 PST-0800
    2016-12-19 18:30:42        2016-12-19 21:30:42 EST-0500
```

When we change the logging level, we control what gets written to our log. We do this by calling the setLoggingLevel method of the Logger class:

```
#------------------------------------------------------------------
def setLoggingLevel(self, level):
    '''change logging level in the middle of a test.'''
    self.loggingLevel = level
```

In the __main__ section of our GUI, we change the logging level to MINIMU, which results in a reduced output written to our log file:

```
if __name__ == '__main__':
#=======================
# Start GUI
#=======================
oop = OOP()
    oop.log.setLoggingLevel(oop.level.MINIMUM)
    oop.log.writeToLog('Test message')
    oop.win.mainloop()
```

Now, our log file no longer shows the Test Message and only shows messages that meet the set logging level:

```
GUI_Refactored.log  ⊠
    2016-12-19 18:34:42        *** Starting Test ***
    2016-12-19 18:34:43        2016-12-20 02:34:43 UTC+0000
```

How it works...

In this recipe, we made good use of Python's built-in __main__ self-testing section. We introduced our own logging file and, at the same time, learned how to create different logging levels. By doing this, we have full control over what gets written to our log files.

Creating robust GUIs using unit tests

Python comes with a built-in unit testing framework and, in this recipe, we will start using this framework to test our Python GUI code.

Before we start writing unit tests, we want to design our testing strategy. We could easily intermix the unit tests with the code they are testing but a better strategy is to separate the application code from the unit test code.

 PyUnit has been designed according to the principles of all the other xUnit testing Frameworks.

Getting ready

We will test the internationalized GUI we created earlier in this chapter.

How to do it...

In order to use Python's built-in unit testing framework, we have to import the Python unittest module. Let's create a new module and name it UnitTests.py.

We first import the unittest module, then we create our own class and, within this class, we inherit and extend the unittest.TestCase class.

The simplest code to do it looks as follows:

```
import unittest

class GuiUnitTests(unittest.TestCase):
    pass

if __name__ == '__main__':
```

```
unittest.main()
```

The code isn't doing much yet, but when we run it, we do not get any errors, which is a good sign:

UnitTestsMinimum.py

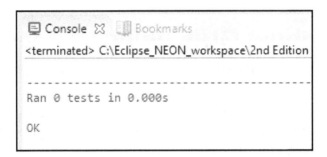

We actually do get an output written to the console stating that we successfully ran zero tests…

That output is a bit misleading, as all we have done so far is create a class that contains no actual testing methods.

We add testing methods that do the actual unit testing by following the default naming for all the test methods to start with the word test. This is an option that can be changed, but it is much easier and clearer to follow this naming convention.

Let's add a test method that will test the title of our GUI. This will verify that, by passing the expected arguments, we get the expected result:

```python
import unittest
from Ch08_Code.LanguageResources import I18N

class GuiUnitTests(unittest.TestCase):

    def test_TitleIsEnglish(self):
        i18n = I18N('en')
        self.assertEqual(i18n.title, "Python Graphical User Interface")
```

We are importing our `I18N` class from our `Resources.py` module, passing English as the language to be displayed in our GUI. As this is our first unit test, we will print out the Title result as well, just to make sure we know what we are getting back. We next use the `unittest assertEqual` method to verify that our title is correct.

Running this code gives us an **OK**, which means that the unit test passed:

`UnitTests_One.py`

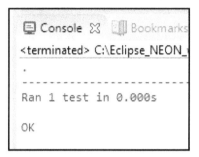

The unit test runs and succeeds, which is indicated by one dot and the word **OK**. If it had failed or got an error, we would not have got the dot but an **F** or **E** as the output.

We can now do the same automated unit testing check by verifying the title for the German version of our GUI. We simply copy, paste, and modify our code:

```
import unittest
from Ch08_Code.LanguageResources import I18N

class GuiUnitTests(unittest.TestCase):

    def test_TitleIsEnglish(self):
        i18n = I18N('en')
        self.assertEqual(i18n.title, "Python Graphical User Interface")

    def test_TitleIsGerman(self):
        i18n = I18N('en')
        self.assertEqual(i18n.title,
                'Python Grafische Benutzeroberfl' + "u00E4" + 'che')
```

Now, we test our internationalized GUI title in two languages and get the following result on running the code:

```
Console 23  Bookmarks
<terminated> C:\Eclipse_NEON_workspace\2nd Edition Python GUI Programming Cookbook\Ch08_Code\UnitTestsFail.py
.F
======================================================================
FAIL: test_TitleIsGerman (__main__.GuiUnitTests)
----------------------------------------------------------------------
Traceback (most recent call last):
  File "C:\Eclipse_NEON_workspace\2nd Edition Python GUI Programming Cookbook\Ch08_Code\UnitTestsFail.py", line 23, in test_TitleIsGerman
    + "\u00E4" + 'che')
AssertionError: 'Python Graphical User Interface' != 'Python Grafische Benutzeroberfläche'
- Python Graphical User Interface
+ Python Grafische Benutzeroberfläche


----------------------------------------------------------------------
Ran 2 tests in 0.001s

FAILED (failures=1)
```

We ran two unit tests but, instead of an OK, we got a failure. What happened?

Our `assertion` failed for the German version of our GUI...

While debugging our code, it turns out that in the copy, paste, and modify approach of our unit test code, we forgot to pass German as the language. We can easily fix this:

```
def test_TitleIsGerman(self):
    # i18n = I18N('en')              # <= Bug in Unit Test
    i18n = I18N('de')
    self.assertEqual(i18n.title,
            'Python Grafische Benutzeroberfl' + "u00E4" + 'che')
```

When we rerun our unit tests, we get the expected result of all our tests passing:

`UnitTestsFail.py` with failure corrected

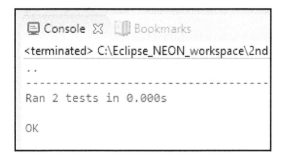

Unit testing code is code and can have bugs too.

While the purpose of writing unit tests is really to test our application code, we have to make sure that our tests are written correctly. One approach from the **Test-Driven-Development** (**TDD**) methodology might help us.

 In TDD, we develop the unit tests before we actually write the application code. Now, if a test passes for a method that does not even exist, something is wrong. The next step is to create the non-existing method and make sure it will fail. After that, we can write the minimum amount of code necessary to make the unit test pass.

How it works...

In this recipe we started testing our Python GUI, writing unit tests in Python. We saw that Python unit test code is just code and can contain mistakes that need to be corrected. In the next recipe, we will extend this recipe's code and use the graphical unit test runner that comes with the PyDev plugin for the Eclipse IDE.

How to write unit tests using the Eclipse PyDev IDE

In the previous recipe, we started using Python's unit testing capabilities, and in this recipe, we will ensure the quality of our GUI code by further using this capability.

We will unit test our GUI in order to make sure that the internationalized strings our GUI displays are as expected.

In the previous recipe, we encountered some bugs in our unit testing code but, typically, our unit tests will find regression bugs that are caused by modifying the existing application code, not the unit test code. Once we have verified that our unit testing code is correct, we do not usually change it.

Our unit tests also serve as a documentation of what we expect our code to do.

By default, Python's unit tests are executed with a textual unit test runner, and we can run this in the PyDev plugin from within the Eclipse IDE. We can also run the very same unit tests from a console window.

In addition to the text runner in this recipe, we will explore PyDev's graphical unit test feature, which can be used from within the Eclipse IDE.

Getting ready

We will extend the previous recipe in which we began using Python unit tests.

How to do it...

The Python unit testing framework comes with what are called **Fixtures**.

Refer to the following URLs for a description of what a test fixture is:

- https://docs.python.org/3.6/library/unittest.html
- https://en.wikipedia.org/wiki/Test_fixture
- http://www.boost.org/doc/libs/1_51_0/libs/test/doc/html/utf/user-guide /fixture.html

What this means is that we can create `setup()` and `teardown()` unit testing methods so that the `setup()` method is called at the beginning before any single test is executed, and at the end of every single unit test, the `teardown()` method is called.

 This fixture capability provides us with a very controlled environment in which we can run our unit tests. It is similar to using pre- and post-conditions.

Let's set up our unit testing environment. We will create a new testing class which focuses on the aforementioned correctness of code:

```
import unittest
from Ch08_Code.LanguageResources import I18N
```

```
from Ch08_Code.GUI_Refactored import OOP as GUI

class GuiUnitTests(unittest.TestCase):
    def test_TitleIsEnglish(self):
        i18n = I18N('en')
        self.assertEqual(i18n.title, "Python Graphical User Interface")

    def test_TitleIsGerman(self):
        # i18n = I18N('en') # <= Bug in Unit Test
        i18n = I18N('de')
        self.assertEqual(i18n.title,
                    'Python Grafische Benutzeroberfl' + "u00E4" + 'che')

class WidgetsTestsEnglish(unittest.TestCase):
    def setUp(self):
        self.gui = GUI('en')

    def tearDown(self):
        self.gui = None

    def test_WidgetLabels(self):
        self.assertEqual(self.gui.i18n.file, "File")
        self.assertEqual(self.gui.i18n.mgrFiles, ' Manage Files ')
        self.assertEqual(self.gui.i18n.browseTo, "Browse to File...")

#===========================
if __name__ == '__main__':
 unittest.main()
```

unittest.main() runs any method that starts with the prefix test, no matter how many classes we create within a given Python module.

This gives the following output:

UnitTestsEnglish.py

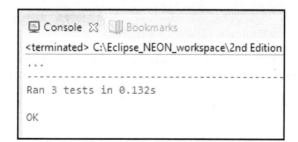

The above unit testing code shows that we can create several unit testing classes and they can all be run in the same module by calling `unittest.main()`.

It also shows that the `setup()` method does not count as a test in the output of the unit test report (the count of tests is 3) while, at the same time, it did its intended job as we can now access our class instance variable `self.gui` from within the unit test method.

We are interested in testing the correctness of all of our labels and, especially, catching bugs when we make changes to our code.

If we have copied and pasted strings from our application code to the testing code, it will catch any unintended changes with the click of a unit testing framework button.

We also want to test that invoking any of our `Radiobutton` widgets in any language results in the `LabelFrame` widget `text` being updated. In order to automatically test this, we have to do two things.

First, we have to retrieve the value of the `LabelFrame` widget and assign the value to a variable we name `labelFrameText`. We have to use the following syntax because the properties of this widget are being passed and retrieved via a dictionary data type:

```
self.gui.widgetFrame['text']
```

We can now verify the default text and then the internationalized versions after clicking one of the Radio button widgets programmatically:

```
class WidgetsTestsGerman(unittest.TestCase):
    def setUp(self):
        self.gui = GUI('de')

    def test_WidgetLabels(self):
        self.assertEqual(self.gui.i18n.file, "Datei")
        self.assertEqual(self.gui.i18n.mgrFiles, ' Dateien Organisieren ')
        self.assertEqual(self.gui.i18n.browseTo, "Waehle eine Datei... ")

    def test_LabelFrameText(self):
        labelFrameText = self.gui.widgetFrame['text']
        self.assertEqual(labelFrameText, " Widgets Rahmen ")
        self.gui.radVar.set(1)
        self.gui.callBacks.radCall()
        labelFrameText = self.gui.widgetFrame['text']
        self.assertEqual(labelFrameText, " Widgets Rahmen in Gold")
```

After verifying the default `labelFrameText`, we programmatically set the radio button to index 1 and then invoke the radio button's callback method:

```
self.gui.radVar.set(1)
self.gui.callBacks.radCall()
```

 This is basically the same action as clicking the radio button in the GUI, but we do this button click event via code in the unit tests.

Then we verify that our text in the `LabelFrame` widget has changed as intended.

When we run the unit tests from within Eclipse with the Python PyDev plugin, we get the following output written to the Eclipse console:

`UnitTests.py`

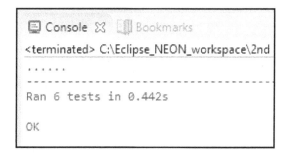

Run from a Command Prompt, we get a similar output once we navigate to the folder where our code resides:

```
C:\WINDOWS\system32\cmd.exe                                          —    □    ×

C:\Eclipse_NEON_workspace\2nd Edition Python GUI Programming Cookbook\Ch08_Code>UnitTests.py
......
--------------------------------------------------------------------------
Ran 6 tests in 0.376s

OK

C:\Eclipse_NEON_workspace\2nd Edition Python GUI Programming Cookbook\Ch08_Code>
```

If you get a `ModuleNotFoundError`, simply add the directory where your Python code lives to the Windows PYTHONPATH environmental variable, as shown in the following screenshots:

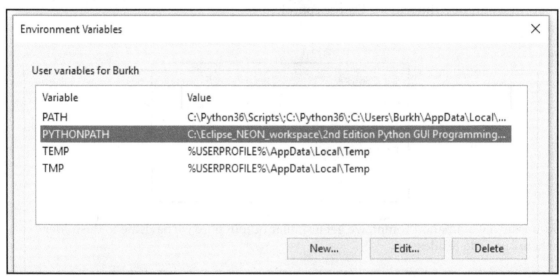

For example, `C:\Eclipse_NEON_workspace\2nd Edition Python GUI Programming Cookbook`:

Name	Date modified	Type	Size
.settings	12/18/2016 4:27 PM	File folder	
Ch01_Code	11/24/2016 11:31 AM	File folder	
Ch02_Code	11/26/2016 8:34 PM	File folder	
Ch03_Code	11/29/2016 10:41 PM	File folder	
Ch04_Code	12/4/2016 12:54 PM	File folder	
Ch05_Code	12/6/2016 11:02 PM	File folder	
Ch06_Code	12/12/2016 1:39 AM	File folder	
Ch07_Code	12/14/2016 8:40 PM	File folder	
Ch08_Code	12/19/2016 7:37 PM	File folder	

This PC > OS (C:) > Eclipse_NEON_workspace > 2nd Edition Python GUI Programming Cookbook

This will recognize the Ch08_Code folder as a Python package and the code will run.

Using Eclipse, we can also choose to run our unit tests, not as a simple Python script, but as a *Python unit-test* script, which gives us some colorful output instead of the black and white world of the DOS prompt:

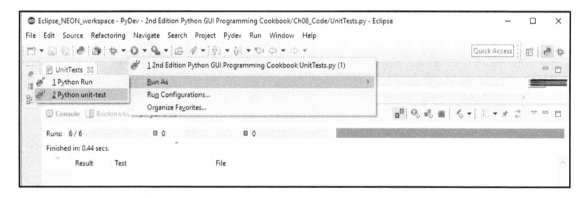

The unit testing result bar is green, which means that all our unit tests have passed. The preceding screenshot also shows that the GUI test runner is slower than the textual test runner: 0.44 seconds compared to 0.376 seconds in Eclipse.

How it works...

We extended our unit testing code by testing `labels`, programmatically invoking a `Radiobutton`, and then verifying in our unit tests that the corresponding `text` property of the `LabelFrame` widget has changed as expected. We tested two different languages. We then moved on to use the built-in Eclipse/PyDev graphical unit test runner.

9
Extending Our GUI with the wxPython Library

In this chapter, we will enhance our Python GUI by using the `wxPython` library. We will cover the following recipes:

- Installing the `wxPython` library
- Creating our GUI in wxPython
- Quickly adding controls using wxPython
- Trying to embed a main wxPython app in a main tkinter app
- Trying to embed our tkinter GUI code into wxPython
- Using Python to control two different GUI frameworks
- Communicating between two connected GUIs

Introduction

In this chapter, we will introduce another Python GUI toolkit that currently does not ship with Python. It is called `wxPython`.

There are two versions of this library. The original is called Classic, while the newest is called by its development project code name, which is Phoenix.

In this book, we are solely programming using Python 3.6 and above, and because the new Phoenix project is aimed at supporting Python 3.6 and above, this is the version of wxPython we will use in this chapter.

First, we will create a simple wxPython GUI, and then we will try to connect both of the tkinter-based GUIs we developed in this book with the new `wxPython` library.

wxPython is a Python binding to wxWidgets. The w in wxPython stands for the Windows OS and the x stands for Unix-based operating systems, such as Linux and Apple's OS X (now renamed Mac OS).

If things don't work out using these two GUI toolkits in unison, we will attempt to use Python to solve any problems and, if necessary, we will use **Inter Process Communication** (**IPC**) within Python to make sure that our Python code works as we want it to work.

Here is the overview of Python modules for this chapter:

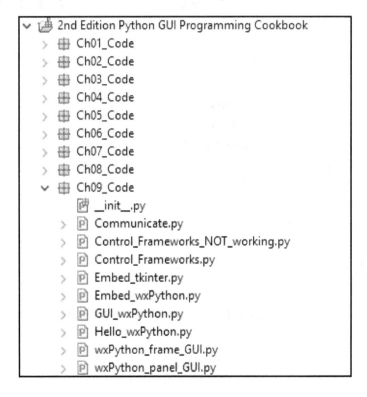

Installing the wxPython library

The wxPython library does not ship with Python, so in order to use it, we first have to install it.

This recipe will show us where and how to find the right version to install in order to match both the installed version of Python and the operating system we are running.

 The wxPython third-party library has been around for more than 18 years, which indicates that it is a robust library.

Getting ready

In order to use wxPython with Python 3.6 and above, we have to install the wxPython **Phoenix** version.

How to do it...

When searching online for wxPython, you will probably find the official website at `www.wxpython.org`:

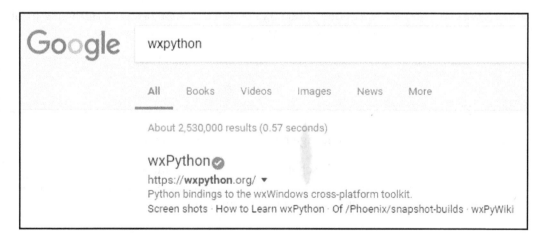

If you click on the download link for MS Windows, you will see several Windows installers, all of which are for Python 2.x only:

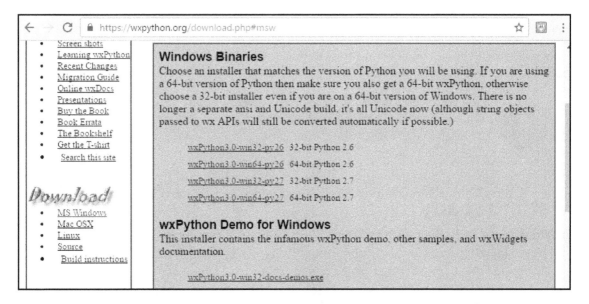

To use wxPython with Python 3.6, we have to install the wxPython/Phoenix library. We can find the installer at the snapshot-builds
link: `http://wxpython.org/Phoenix/snapshot-builds/`

From here, we can select the wxPython/Phoenix version that matches both our versions of Python and our OS. I am using Python 3.6 running on a 64-bit Windows 10 OS.

The Python wheel (`.whl`) installer package has a numbering scheme.

For us, the most important part of this scheme is that we are installing the wxPython/Phoenix build that is for Python 3.6 (the *cp36* in the installer name) and for the Windows 64-bit OS (the *win_amd64* part of the installer name).

After successfully downloading the wxPython/Phoenix package, we can now navigate to the directory where it resides and install this package using `pip`:

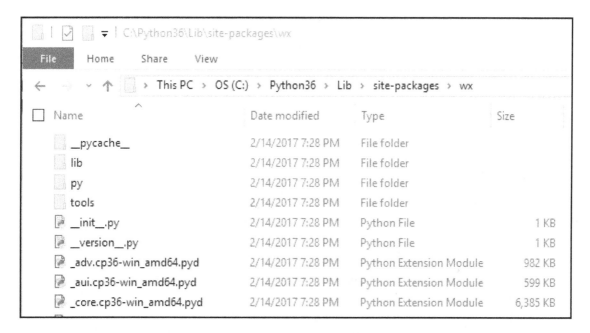

We have a new folder named `wx` in our Python `site-packages` folder:

 `wx` is the folder name, which the wxPython Phoenix library was installed into. We will import this module into our Python code.

We can verify that our installation worked by executing this simple demo script from the official wxPython/Phoenix website. The link to the official website is `http://wxpython.org/Phoenix/docs/html/`.

Consider the following code:

```
import wx
app = wx.App()
frame = wx.Frame(None, -1, "Hello World")
frame.Show()
app.MainLoop()
```

Running the preceding Python 3.6 script creates the following GUI using wxPython/Phoenix:

Hello_wxPython.py

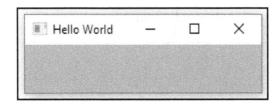

How it works...

In this recipe, we successfully installed the correct version of the wxPython toolkit that we can use with Python 3.6. We found the Phoenix project for this GUI toolkit, which is the current and active development line. Phoenix will replace the classic wxPython toolkit in time and is especially aimed at working well with Python 3.6.

After successfully installing the wxPython/Phoenix toolkit, we then created a GUI using this toolkit in only five lines of code.

 We previously achieved the same results by using tkinter.

Creating our GUI in wxPython

In this recipe, we will start creating our Python GUIs using the wxPython GUI toolkit.

We will first recreate several of the widgets we previously created using tkinter, which ships with Python.

Then, we will explore some of the widgets the wxPython GUI toolkit offers, which are not that easy to create by using tkinter.

Getting ready

The previous recipe showed you how to install the correct version of wxPython that matches both your version of Python and the OS you are running.

How to do it...

A good place to start exploring the wxPython GUI toolkit is by going to the following URL:
`http://wxpython.org/Phoenix/docs/html/gallery.html`

This web page displays many wxPython widgets and, by clicking on any of them, we are taken to their documentation, which is a very helpful feature to quickly learn about a wxPython control:

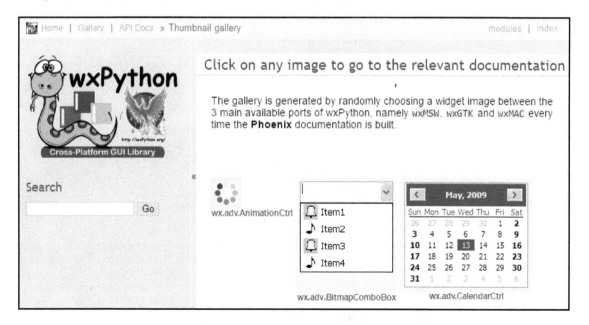

The following screenshot shows the documentation for a wxPython button widget:

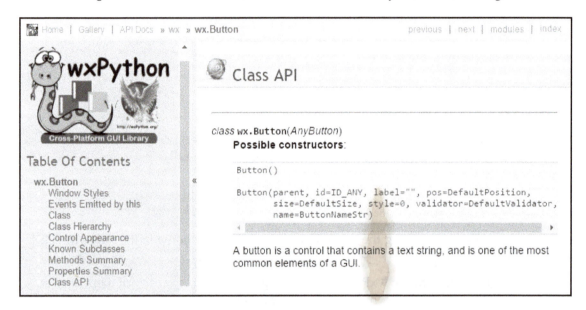

We can very quickly create a working window that comes with a title, a menu bar, and also a status bar. This status bar displays the text of a menu item when hovering the mouse over it. This can be achieved by writing the following code:

```python
# Import wxPython GUI toolkit
import wx

# Subclass wxPython frame
class GUI(wx.Frame):
    def __init__(self, parent, title, size=(200,100)):
        # Initialize super class
        wx.Frame.__init__(self, parent, title=title, size=size)

        # Change the frame background color
        self.SetBackgroundColour('white')

        # Create Status Bar
        self.CreateStatusBar()

        # Create the Menu
        menu= wx.Menu()

        # Add Menu Items to the Menu
        menu.Append(wx.ID_ABOUT, "About", "wxPython GUI")
        menu.AppendSeparator()
```

```
            menu.Append(wx.ID_EXIT,"Exit"," Exit the GUI")

            # Create the MenuBar
            menuBar = wx.MenuBar()

            # Give the Menu a Title
            menuBar.Append(menu,"File")

            # Connect the MenuBar to the frame
            self.SetMenuBar(menuBar)

            # Display the frame
            self.Show()

    # Create instance of wxPython application
    app = wx.App()

    # Call sub-classed wxPython GUI increasing default Window size
    GUI(None, "Python GUI using wxPython", (300,150))

    # Run the main GUI event loop
    app.MainLoop()
```

This creates the following GUI, which is written in Python using the `wxPython` library:

`GUI_wxPython.py`

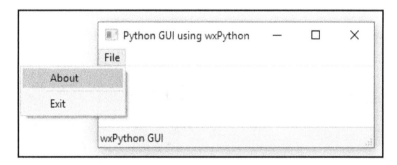

In the previous code, we inherited from `wx.Frame`. In the next code, we inherit from `wx.Panel` and we pass in `wx.Frame` to the `__init__()` method of our class.

> In `wxPython`, the top-level GUI window is called a frame. There cannot be a wxPython GUI without a frame, and the frame has to be created as part of a wxPython application. We create both the application and the frame at the bottom of our code.

In order to add widgets to our GUI, we have to attach them to a panel. The parent of the panel is the frame (our top-level window), and the parent of the widgets we place into the panel is the panel.

The following code adds a multiline `textbox` widget to a panel whose parent is a frame. We also add a button widget to the panel widget, which, when clicked, prints out some text to the `textbox`.

Here is the complete code:

```python
import wx                                  # Import wxPython GUI toolkit
class GUI(wx.Panel):                        # Subclass wxPython Panel
    def __init__(self, parent):

        # Initialize super class
        wx.Panel.__init__(self, parent)

        # Create Status Bar
        parent.CreateStatusBar()

        # Create the Menu
        menu= wx.Menu()

        # Add Menu Items to the Menu
        menu.Append(wx.ID_ABOUT, "About", "wxPython GUI")
        menu.AppendSeparator()
        menu.Append(wx.ID_EXIT,"Exit"," Exit the GUI")

        # Create the MenuBar
        menuBar = wx.MenuBar()

        # Give the Menu a Title
        menuBar.Append(menu,"File")

        # Connect the MenuBar to the frame
        parent.SetMenuBar(menuBar)

        # Create a Print Button
        button = wx.Button(self, label="Print", pos=(0,60))

        # Connect Button to Click Event method
        self.Bind(wx.EVT_BUTTON, self.printButton, button)

        # Create a Text Control widget
        self.textBox = wx.TextCtrl(self, size=(280,50),
                                   style=wx.TE_MULTILINE)
```

```
        # callback event handler
        def printButton(self, event):
            self.textBox.AppendText("The Print Button has been clicked!")

app = wx.App()       # Create instance of wxPython application
                     # Create frame
frame = wx.Frame(None, , size=(300,180))
GUI(frame)           # Pass frame into GUI
frame.Show()         # Display the frame
app.MainLoop()       # Run the main GUI event loop
```

In the preceding code, `parent` is a `wx.Frame` we are passing into the GUI initializer.

Running the preceding code and clicking our wxPython button widget results in the following GUI output:

`wxPython_panel_GUI.py`

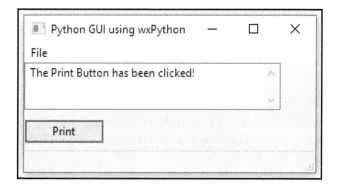

How it works...

We have created our own GUI in this recipe using the mature wxPython GUI toolkit. In only a few lines of Python code, we were able to create a fully functional GUI that comes with `Minimize`, `Maximize`, and `Exit` buttons. We added a menu bar, a multiline text control, and a button. We also created a status bar that displays text when we select a menu item. We placed all these widgets into a Panel container widget.

We hooked up the button to print to the text control.

When hovering over a menu item, some text gets displayed in the status bar.

Quickly adding controls using wxPython

In this recipe, we will recreate the GUI we originally created earlier in this book with tkinter, but this time, we will be using the wxPython library. We will see how easy and quick it is to use the wxPython GUI toolkit to create our own Python GUIs.

We will not recreate the entire functionality we created in the previous chapters. For example, we will not internationalize our wxPython GUI, nor connect it to a MySQL database. We will recreate the visual aspects of the GUI and add some functionality.

Comparing different libraries gives us the choice of which toolkits to use for our own Python GUI development, and we can combine several of those toolkits in our own Python code.

Getting ready

Ensure you have the wxPython module installed to follow this recipe.

How to do it…

First, we create our Python OOP class as we did before, using tkinter, but this time we inherit from and extend the wx.Frame class. For reasons of clarity, we no longer call our class OOP but, instead, rename it as MainFrame.

In wxPython, the main GUI window is called a Frame.

We also create a callback method that closes the GUI when we click the **Exit** menu item and declare a light-grey tuple as the background color for our GUI:

```python
import wx
BACKGROUNDCOLOR = (240, 240, 240, 255)

class MainFrame(wx.Frame):
    def __init__(self, *args, **kwargs):
        wx.Frame.__init__(self, *args, **kwargs)
        self.createWidgets()
        self.Show()
```

```
    def exitGUI(self, event):        # callback
        self.Destroy()

    def createWidgets(self):
        self.CreateStatusBar()        # wxPython built-in method
        self.createMenu()
        self.createNotebook()
```

We then add a tabbed control to our GUI by creating an instance of the wxPython `Notebook` class and assign it as the parent of our own custom class named `Widgets`.

The `notebook` class instance variable has `wx.Panel` as its parent:

```
    #-----------------------------------------------------------
    def createNotebook(self):
        panel = wx.Panel(self)
        notebook = wx.Notebook(panel)
        widgets = Widgets(notebook) # Custom class explained below
        notebook.AddPage(widgets, "Widgets")
        notebook.SetBackgroundColour(BACKGROUNDCOLOR)
        # layout
        boxSizer = wx.BoxSizer()
        boxSizer.Add(notebook, 1, wx.EXPAND)
        panel.SetSizerAndFit(boxSizer)
```

 In wxPython, the tabbed widget is named `Notebook`, just as in tkinter.

Every `Notebook` widget needs to have a parent and, in order to lay out widgets in the `Notebook` in wxPython, we use different kinds of `sizers`.

 wxPython `sizers` are layout managers, similar to tkinter's grid layout manager.

Next, we add controls to our Notebook page, and we do this by creating a separate class that inherits from `wx.Panel`:

```
class Widgets(wx.Panel):
    def __init__(self, parent):
        wx.Panel.__init__(self, parent)
        self.createWidgetsFrame()
        self.addWidgets()
        self.layoutWidgets()
```

We modularize our GUI code by breaking it into small methods, following Python OOP programming protocol, which keeps our code manageable and understandable:

```
#--------------------------------------------------------
def createWidgetsFrame(self):
    self.panel = wx.Panel(self)
    staticBox = wx.StaticBox(self.panel, -1, "Widgets Frame")
    self.statBoxSizerV = wx.StaticBoxSizer(staticBox, wx.VERTICAL)
#--------------------------------------------------------
def layoutWidgets(self):
    boxSizerV = wx.BoxSizer(wx.VERTICAL)
    boxSizerV.Add(self.statBoxSizerV, 1, wx.ALL)
    self.panel.SetSizer(boxSizerV)
    boxSizerV.SetSizeHints(self.panel)
#--------------------------------------------------------
def addWidgets(self):
    self.addCheckBoxes()
    self.addRadioButtons()
    self.addStaticBoxWithLabels()
```

 When using wxPython `StaticBox` widgets, in order to successfully lay them out, we use a combination of `StaticBoxSizer` and a regular `BoxSizer`. The wxPython `StaticBox` is very similar to the tkinter `LabelFrame` widget.

Embedding a `StaticBox` within another `StaticBox` is straightforward in tkinter, but using wxPython is a little non-intuitive. One way to make it work is shown in the following code snippet:

```
def addStaticBoxWithLabels(self):
    boxSizerH = wx.BoxSizer(wx.HORIZONTAL)
    staticBox = wx.StaticBox(self.panel, -1, "Labels within a Frame")
    staticBoxSizerV = wx.StaticBoxSizer(staticBox, wx.VERTICAL)
    boxSizerV = wx.BoxSizer( wx.VERTICAL )
    staticText1 = wx.StaticText(self.panel, -1, "Choose a number:")
    boxSizerV.Add(staticText1, 0, wx.ALL)
    staticText2 = wx.StaticText(self.panel, -1,"Label 2")
    boxSizerV.Add(staticText2, 0, wx.ALL)
    #-------------------------------------------------------
    staticBoxSizerV.Add(boxSizerV, 0, wx.ALL)
    boxSizerH.Add(staticBoxSizerV)
    #-------------------------------------------------------
    boxSizerH.Add(wx.TextCtrl(self.panel))
    # Add local boxSizer to main frame
    self.statBoxSizerV.Add(boxSizerH, 1, wx.ALL)
```

First, we create a horizontal `BoxSizer`. Next, we create a vertical `StaticBoxSizer` because we want to arrange two labels in a vertical layout in this frame.

In order to arrange another widget to the right of the embedded `StaticBox`, we have to assign both the embedded `StaticBox` with its children controls and the next widget to the horizontal `BoxSizer` and then assign this `BoxSizer`, which now contains both our embedded `StaticBox` and our other widgets, to the main `StaticBox`.

Does this sound confusing?

You just have to experiment with these `sizers` to get a feel of how to use them. Start with the code for this recipe and comment out some code or modify some *x* and *y* coordinates to see the effects.

It is also good to read the official wxPython documentation to learn more.

 The important thing is knowing where to add to the different `sizers` in the code in order to achieve the layout we wish.

In order to create the second `StaticBox` below the first, we create separate `StaticBoxSizers` and assign them to the same panel:

```
class Widgets(wx.Panel):
    def __init__(self, parent):
        wx.Panel.__init__(self, parent)
        self.panel = wx.Panel(self)
        self.createWidgetsFrame()
        self.createManageFilesFrame()
        self.addWidgets()
        self.addFileWidgets()
        self.layoutWidgets()
    #-------------------------------------------------------------
    def createWidgetsFrame(self):
        staticBox = wx.StaticBox(self.panel, -1, "Widgets Frame",
                                 size=(285, -1))
        self.statBoxSizerV = wx.StaticBoxSizer(staticBox, wx.VERTICAL)
    #-------------------------------------------------------------
    def createManageFilesFrame(self):
        staticBox = wx.StaticBox(self.panel, -1, "Manage Files",
                                 size=(285, -1))
        self.statBoxSizerMgrV = wx.StaticBoxSizer(staticBox, wx.VERTICAL)
    #-------------------------------------------------------------
    def layoutWidgets(self):
        boxSizerV = wx.BoxSizer( wx.VERTICAL )
```

```
        boxSizerV.Add( self.statBoxSizerV, 1, wx.ALL )
        boxSizerV.Add( self.statBoxSizerMgrV, 1, wx.ALL )

        self.panel.SetSizer( boxSizerV )
        boxSizerV.SetSizeHints( self.panel )
    #-------------------------------------------------------
    def addFileWidgets(self):
        boxSizerH = wx.BoxSizer(wx.HORIZONTAL)
        boxSizerH.Add(wx.Button(self.panel, label='Browse to File...'))
        boxSizerH.Add(wx.TextCtrl(self.panel, size=(174, -1),
                                  value= "Z:" ))

        boxSizerH1 = wx.BoxSizer(wx.HORIZONTAL)
        boxSizerH1.Add(wx.Button(self.panel, label='Copy File To:    '))
        boxSizerH1.Add(wx.TextCtrl(self.panel, size=(174, -1),
                                   value="Z:Backup" ))

        boxSizerV = wx.BoxSizer(wx.VERTICAL)
        boxSizerV.Add(boxSizerH)
        boxSizerV.Add(boxSizerH1)

        self.statBoxSizerMgrV.Add( boxSizerV, 1, wx.ALL )
```

The following code instantiates the main event loop, which runs our wxPython GUI program:

```
#=======================
# Start GUI
#=======================
app = wx.App()
MainFrame(None, , size=(350,450))
app.MainLoop()
```

The final result of our wxPython GUI looks as follows:

```
GUI_wxPython.py
```

How it works...

We design and lay out our wxPython GUI in several classes.

Once we have done this, in the bottom section of our Python module, we create an instance of the wxPython application. Next, we instantiate our wxPython GUI code.

After that, we call the main GUI event loop, which executes all of our Python code running within this application process. This displays our wxPython GUI.

Whatever code we place between the creation of the app and calling its main event loop, becomes our wxPython GUI. It might take some time to really get used to the wxPython library and its API, but once we understand how to use it, this library is really fun and a powerful tool to build our own Python GUIs. There is also a visual designer tool that can be used with wxPython:
`http://www.cae.tntech.edu/help/programming/wxdesigner-getting-started/view`

This recipe used OOP to learn how to use the wxPython GUI toolkit.

Trying to embed a main wxPython app in a main tkinter app

Now that we have created the same GUI using both Python's built-in tkinter library as well as the wxPython wrapper of the `wxWidgets` library, we really do need to combine the GUIs we created using these technologies.

Both the wxPython and the tkinter libraries have their own advantages. In online forums such as `http://stackoverflow.com/`, we often see questions, such as which one is better, which GUI toolkit should I use, and so on. This suggests that we have to make an either-or decision. We do not have to make such a decision.

One of the main challenges in doing so is that each GUI toolkit must have its own event loop.

In this recipe, we will try to embed a simple wxPython GUI by calling it from our tkinter GUI.

Getting ready

We will reuse the tkinter GUI we built in the recipe *Combo Box Widgets*, in `Chapter 1`, *Creating the GUI Form and Adding Widgets*.

How to do it...

We will start from a simple tkinter GUI, which looks as follows:

`Embed_wxPython.py`

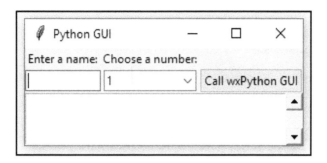

Next, we will try to invoke a simple wxPython GUI, which we created in a previous recipe in this chapter.

The following is the entire code to do this in a simple, non-OOP way:

```
#===========================================================
import tkinter as tk
from tkinter import ttk, scrolledtext

win = tk.Tk()
win.title("Python GUI")
aLabel = ttk.Label(win, text="A Label")
aLabel.grid(column=0, row=0)
ttk.Label(win, text="Enter a name:").grid(column=0, row=0)
name = tk.StringVar()
nameEntered = ttk.Entry(win, width=12, textvariable=name)
nameEntered.grid(column=0, row=1)
ttk.Label(win, text="Choose a number:").grid(column=1, row=0)
number = tk.StringVar()
numberChosen = ttk.Combobox(win, width=12, textvariable=number)
numberChosen['values'] = (1, 2, 4, 42, 100)
numberChosen.grid(column=1, row=1)
numberChosen.current(0)
scrolW = 30
scrolH =  3
scr = scrolledtext.ScrolledText(win, width=scrolW, height=scrolH,
wrap=tk.WORD)
scr.grid(column=0, sticky='WE', columnspan=3)
nameEntered.focus()
```

```
#==============================================================
def wxPythonApp():
    import wx
    app = wx.App()
    frame = wx.Frame(None, -1, "wxPython GUI", size=(200,150))
    frame.SetBackgroundColour('white')
    frame.CreateStatusBar()
    menu= wx.Menu()
    menu.Append(wx.ID_ABOUT, "About", "wxPython GUI")
    menuBar = wx.MenuBar()
    menuBar.Append(menu,"File")
    frame.SetMenuBar(menuBar)
    frame.Show()
    app.MainLoop()

action = ttk.Button(win, text="Call wxPython GUI", command=wxPythonApp)
action.grid(column=2, row=1)


#=======================
# Start GUI
#=======================
win.mainloop()
```

Running the preceding code starts a wxPython GUI from our tkinter GUI after clicking the tkinter button control:

`Embed_wxPython.py`

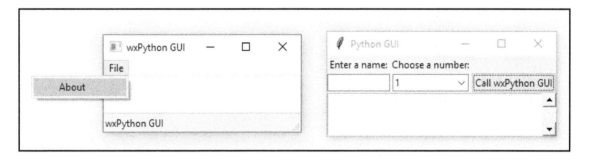

How it works...

The important part is that we placed the entire wxPython code into its own function, which we named def wxPythonApp().

In the callback function for the button click-event, we simply call this code.

One thing to note is that we have to close the wxPython GUI before we can continue using the tkinter GUI.

Trying to embed our tkinter GUI code into wxPython

In this recipe, we will go in the opposite direction of the previous recipe and try to call our tkinter GUI code from within a wxPython GUI.

Getting ready

We will reuse some of the wxPython GUI code we created in a previous recipe in this chapter.

How to do it...

We will start from a simple wxPython GUI, which looks as follows:

`Embed_tkinter.py`

Next, we will try to invoke a simple tkinter GUI.

The following is the entire code to do this in a simple, non-OOP way:

```
#================================================================
def tkinterApp():
    import tkinter as tk
    from tkinter import ttk
    win = tk.Tk()
    win.title("Python GUI")
    aLabel = ttk.Label(win, text="A Label")
    aLabel.grid(column=0, row=0)
    ttk.Label(win, text="Enter a name:").grid(column=0, row=0)
    name = tk.StringVar()
    nameEntered = ttk.Entry(win, width=12, textvariable=name)
    nameEntered.grid(column=0, row=1)
    nameEntered.focus()

    def buttonCallback():
        action.configure(text='Hello ' + name.get())
    action = ttk.Button(win, text="Print", command=buttonCallback)
    action.grid(column=2, row=1)
    win.mainloop()

#================================================================
import wx
app = wx.App()
frame = wx.Frame(None, -1, "wxPython GUI", size=(270,180))
frame.SetBackgroundColour('white')
frame.CreateStatusBar()
menu= wx.Menu()
menu.Append(wx.ID_ABOUT, "About", "wxPython GUI")
menuBar = wx.MenuBar()
menuBar.Append(menu, "File")
frame.SetMenuBar(menuBar)
textBox = wx.TextCtrl(frame, size=(250,50), style=wx.TE_MULTILINE)

def tkinterEmbed(event):
    tkinterApp()

button = wx.Button(frame, label="Call tkinter GUI", pos=(0,60))
frame.Bind(wx.EVT_BUTTON, tkinterEmbed, button)
frame.Show()

#=====================
# Start wxPython GUI
#=====================
app.MainLoop()
```

Running the preceding code starts a tkinter GUI from our wxPython GUI after clicking the wxPython button widget. We can then enter text into the tkinter textbox and, by clicking its button, the button text gets updated with the name:

`Embed_tkinter.py`

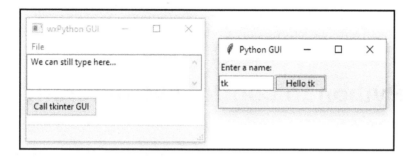

After starting the tkinter event loop, the wxPython GUI is still responsive because we can type into the `TextCtrl` widget while the tkinter GUI is up and running.

 In the previous recipe, we could not use our tkinter GUI until we had closed the wxPython GUI. Being aware of this difference can help our design decisions if we want to combine the two Python GUI technologies.

We can also create several tkinter GUI instances by clicking the wxPython GUI button several times. We cannot, however, close the wxPython GUI while any tkinter GUIs are still running. We have to close them first:

`Embed_tkinter.py`

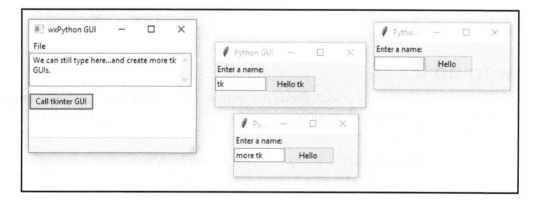

How it works...

In this recipe, we went in the opposite direction of the previous recipe by first creating a GUI using wxPython and then, from within it, creating several GUI instances built using tkinter.

The wxPython GUI remained responsive while one or more `tkinter` GUIs were running. However, clicking the tkinter button only updated its button text in the first instance.

Using Python to control two different GUI frameworks

In this recipe, we will explore ways to control the tkinter and wxPython GUI frameworks from Python. We have already used the Python threading module to keep our GUI responsive in a previous chapter, *Threads and Networking*, so here we will attempt to use the same approach.

We will see that things don't always work in a way that would be intuitive.

However, we will improve our tkinter GUI from being unresponsive while we invoke an instance of the wxPython GUI from within it.

Getting ready

This recipe will extend a previous recipe from this chapter, *Trying to embed a main wxPython app in a main tkinter app*, in which we tried to embed a main wxPython GUI into our tkinter GUI.

How to do it...

When we created an instance of a wxPython GUI from our tkinter GUI, we could no longer use the tkinter GUI controls until we closed the one instance of the wxPython GUI. Let's improve on this now.

Our first attempt might be to use threading from the tkinter button callback function.

For example, our code might look as follows:

```
def wxPythonApp():
    import wx
    app = wx.App()
    frame = wx.Frame(None, -1, "wxPython GUI", size=(200,150))
    frame.SetBackgroundColour('white')
    frame.CreateStatusBar()
    menu= wx.Menu()
    menu.Append(wx.ID_ABOUT, "About", "wxPython GUI")
    menuBar = wx.MenuBar()
    menuBar.Append(menu,"File")
    frame.SetMenuBar(menuBar)
    frame.Show()
    app.MainLoop()

def tryRunInThread():
    runT = Thread(target=wxPythonApp)
    runT.setDaemon(True)
    runT.start()
    print(runT)
    print('createThread():', runT.isAlive())

action = ttk.Button(win, text="Call wxPython GUI", command=tryRunInThread)
```

At first, this seems to be working, which would be intuitive, as the tkinter controls are no longer disabled and we can create several instances of the wxPython GUI by clicking the button. We can also type into the wxPython GUI and select the other tkinter widgets:

```
Control_Frameworks_NOT_working.py
```

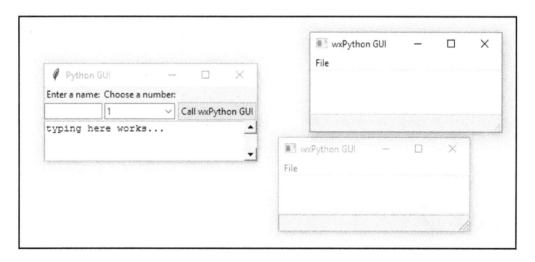

However, once we try to close the GUIs, we get an error from `wxWidgets`, and our Python executable crashes:

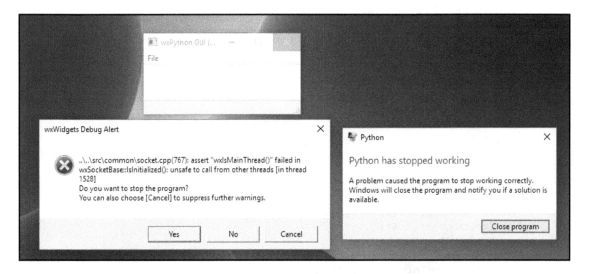

In order to avoid this, instead of trying to run the entire wxPython application in a thread, we can change the code to make only the `wxPython app.MainLoop` run in a thread:

```python
def wxPythonApp():
    import wx
    app = wx.App()
    frame = wx.Frame(None, -1, "wxPython GUI", size=(200,150))
    frame.SetBackgroundColour('white')
    frame.CreateStatusBar()
    menu= wx.Menu()
    menu.Append(wx.ID_ABOUT, "About", "wxPython GUI")
    menuBar = wx.MenuBar()
    menuBar.Append(menu,"File")
    frame.SetMenuBar(menuBar)
    frame.Show()

    runT = Thread(target=app.MainLoop)
    runT.setDaemon(True)
    runT.start()
    print(runT)
    print('createThread():', runT.isAlive())

action = ttk.Button(win, text="Call wxPython GUI", command=wxPythonApp)
action.grid(column=2, row=1)
```

How it works...

We first tried to run the entire wxPython GUI application in a thread, but this did not work because the wxPython main event loop expects to be the main thread of the application.

We found a workaround for this by only running the wxPython `app.MainLoop` in a thread that tricks it into believing it is the main thread.

One side-effect of this approach is that we can no longer individually close all of the wxPython GUI instances. At least one of them only closes when we close the wxPython GUI that created the threads as daemons. You can test this out by clicking the **Call wxPython GUI** button once or several times and then try to close all the created wxPython window forms. We cannot close the last one until we close the calling tkinter GUI!

I am not quite sure why this is. Intuitively, one might expect to be able to close all daemon threads without having to wait for the main thread that created them to close first.

It possibly has to do with a reference counter not having been set to zero while our main thread is still running.

On a pragmatic level, this is how it currently works.

Communicating between the two connected GUIs

In the previous recipes, we found ways to connect a wxPython GUI with a tkinter GUI, invoking one from the other and vice versa.

While both GUIs were successfully running at the same time, they did not really communicate with each other, as they were only launching one another.

In this recipe, we will explore ways to make the two GUIs talk to each other.

Getting ready

Reading one of the previous recipes might be good preparation for this recipe.

In this recipe, we will use slightly modified GUI code with respect to the previous recipe, but most of the basic GUI-building code is the same.

How to do it...

In the previous recipes, one of our main challenges was how to combine two GUI technologies that were designed to be the one-and-only GUI toolkit for an application. We found various simple ways to combine them.

We will again launch the wxPython GUI from a tkinter GUI main event loop and start the wxPython GUI in its own thread, which runs within the Python.exe process.

In order to do this, we will use a shared global multiprocessing Python Queue.

 While it is often best to avoid global data, in this recipe it is a practical solution and Python globals are really only global in the module they have been declared.

Here is the Python code that makes the two GUIs communicate with each other to a certain degree. In order to save space, this is not pure OOP code. Neither are we showing the creation code for all widgets. That code is the same as in the previous recipes:

```python
# Communicate.py
import tkinter as tk
from tkinter import ttk
from threading import Thread

win = tk.Tk()
win.title("Python GUI")

from queue import Queue
sharedQueue = Queue()
dataInQueue = False

def putDataIntoQueue(data):
    global dataInQueue
    dataInQueue =  True
    sharedQueue.put(data)

def readDataFromQueue():
```

```
        global dataInQueue
        dataInQueue = False
        return sharedQueue.get()
#============================================================
import wx
class GUI(wx.Panel):
    def __init__(self, parent):
        wx.Panel.__init__(self, parent)
        parent.CreateStatusBar()
        button = wx.Button(self, label="Print", pos=(0,60))
        self.Bind(wx.EVT_BUTTON, self.writeToSharedQueue, button)

        #-----------------------------------------------------
    def writeToSharedQueue(self, event):
        self.textBox.AppendText("The Print Button has been clicked!n")
        putDataIntoQueue('Hi from wxPython via Shared Queue.n')
        if dataInQueue:
            data = readDataFromQueue()
            self.textBox.AppendText(data)
            text.insert('0.0', data) # insert data into tkinter GUI


#============================================================
def wxPythonApp():
    app = wx.App()
    frame = wx.Frame(None, ,
                     size=(300,180))
    GUI(frame)
    frame.Show()
    runT = Thread(target=app.MainLoop)
    runT.setDaemon(True)
    runT.start()
    print(runT)
    print('createThread():', runT.isAlive())
#============================================================
action = ttk.Button(win, text="Call wxPython GUI", command=wxPythonApp)
action.grid(column=2, row=1)


#======================
# Start GUI
#======================
win.mainloop()
```

Running the preceding code first creates the tkinter part of the program and, when we click the button in this GUI, it runs the wxPython GUI. Both are running at the same time as before but, this time, there is an extra level of communication between the two GUIs:

`Communicate.py`

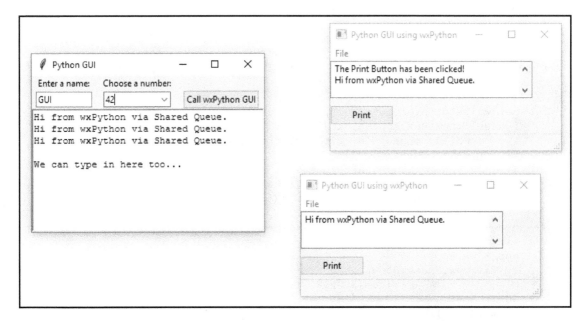

The tkinter GUI is shown on the left-hand side in the preceding screenshot, and by clicking the **Call wxPython GUI** button, we invoke an instance of the wxPython GUI. We can create several instances by clicking the button several times.

 All of the created GUIs remain responsive. They do not crash nor freeze.

Clicking the **Print** button on any of the wxPython GUI instances writes one sentence to its own `TextCtrl` widget and then writes another line to itself, as well as to the tkinter GUI. You will have to scroll up to see the first sentence in the wxPython GUI.

 The way this works is by using a module-level `queue` and a tkinter `Text` widget.

One important element to note is that we create a thread to run the wxPython `app.MainLoop`, as we did in the previous recipe:

```
def wxPythonApp():
    app = wx.App()
    frame = wx.Frame(None, ,
                        size=(300,180))
    GUI(frame)
    frame.Show()
    runT = Thread(target=app.MainLoop)
    runT.setDaemon(True)
    runT.start()
```

We create a class which inherits from `wx.Panel` and name it `GUI` and then instantiate an instance of this class in the preceding code.

We create a button-click event callback method in this class, which then calls the procedural code that was written above it. Because of this, the class has access to the functions and can write to the shared queue:

```
#---------------------------------------------------
def writeToSharedQueue(self, event):
    self.textBox.AppendText("The Print Button has been clicked!n")
    putDataIntoQueue('Hi from wxPython via Shared Queue.n')
    if dataInQueue:
        data = readDataFromQueue()
        self.textBox.AppendText(data)
        text.insert('0.0', data) # insert data into tkinter
```

We first check whether the data has been placed in the shared queue in the preceding method and, if that is the case, print the common data to both GUIs.

The `putDataIntoQueue()` line places data into the queue and `readDataFromQueue()` reads it back out, saving it in the `data` variable. `text.insert('0.0', data)` is the line that writes this data into the tkinter GUI from the **Print** button's wxPython callback method.

The following are the procedural functions (not methods, for they are not bound) which are being called in the code and make it work:

```
from multiprocessing import Queue
sharedQueue = Queue()
dataInQueue = False

def putDataIntoQueue(data):
    global dataInQueue
    dataInQueue =  True
```

```
            sharedQueue.put(data)

    def readDataFromQueue():
        global dataInQueue
        dataInQueue = False
        return sharedQueue.get()
```

We used a simple Boolean flag named `dataInQueue` to communicate when the data is available in the queue.

How it works...

In this recipe, we have successfully combined the two GUIs we created in a similar fashion, but which were previously standalone and not talking to each other. However, in this recipe, we connected them further by making one GUI launch another, and, via a simple multiprocessing Python queue mechanism, we were able to make them communicate with each other, writing data from a shared queue into both GUIs.

There are many more advanced and complicated technologies available to connect different processes, threads, pools, locks, pipes, TCP/IP connections, and so on.

In the Pythonic spirit, we found a simple solution that works for us. Once our code becomes more complicated, we might have to refactor it, but this is a good beginning.

10

Creating Amazing 3D GUIs with PyOpenGL and PyGLet

In this chapter, we will create amazing Python GUIs that display true three-dimensional images that can be rotated around themselves so that we can look at them from all sides. We will cover the following recipes:

- PyOpenGL transforms our GUI
- Our GUI in 3D!
- Using bitmaps to make our GUI pretty
- PyGLet transforms our GUI easier than PyOpenGL
- Our GUI in amazing colors
- OpenGL animation
- Creating a slide show using tkinter

Introduction

In this chapter, we will transform our GUI by giving it true three-dimensional capabilities. We will use two Python third-party packages. **PyOpenGL** is a Python binding to the OpenGL standard, which is a graphics library that comes built in with all major operating systems. This gives the resulting widgets a native look and feel.

PyGLet is another Python binding to the `OpenGL` library, but it can also create GUI applications, which can make coding using PyGLet easier than using PyOpenGL.

Here is the overview of Python modules for this chapter:

```
∨ 🗃 2nd Edition Python GUI Programming Cookbook
  > ⊞ Ch01_Code
  > ⊞ Ch02_Code
  > ⊞ Ch03_Code
  > ⊞ Ch04_Code
  > ⊞ Ch05_Code
  > ⊞ Ch06_Code
  > ⊞ Ch07_Code
  > ⊞ Ch08_Code
  > ⊞ Ch09_Code
  ∨ ⊞ Ch10_Code
    > 📂 Resources
      📄 _init_.py
    > 📄 import_OpenGL_cube_and_cone.py
    > 📄 import_OpenGL.py
    > 📄 OpenGL_SuperBible_Animation_with_stencil_NOT_working.py
    > 📄 OpenGL_SuperBible_Animation.py
    > 📄 OpenGL_SuperBible_Simple_Rectangle.py
    > 📄 OpenGL_SuperBible_Simple.py
    > 📄 pyglet_GUI_Simple.py
    > 📄 pyglet_GUI.py
    > 📄 SlideShow_Pillow.py
    > 📄 SlideShow_try_jpg.py
    > 📄 SlideShow.py
      🌐 Tile.bmp
    > 📄 wxPython_OpenGL_GUI.py
    > 📄 wxPython_Wallpaper_simple.py
    > 📄 wxPython_Wallpaper.py
```

PyOpenGL transforms our GUI

In this recipe, we will successfully create a Python GUI that imports PyOpenGL modules and does actually work! In order to do so, we will overcome some initial challenges.

This recipe will show one proven way that does work. If you experiment on your own and get stuck, remember the famous words from Thomas A. Edison.

 Thomas Edison, inventor of the light bulb, answered a question from a reporter who talked about Edison's failures. Edison replied, *"I have not failed. I've just found 10,000 ways that won't work."*

First, we have to install the PyOpenGL extension module. After successfully installing the PyOpenGL modules that match our OS architecture, we will create some example code.

Getting ready

We will install the PyOpenGL package. In this book, we are using Windows 10 64-bit OS and Python 3.6. The screenshot of downloads that follows is for this configuration.

We will also be using wxPython. If you do not have wxPython installed, you can read some recipes from the previous chapter about how to install wxPython and how to use this GUI framework.

 We are using the wxPython Phoenix release, which is the newest release and is intended to replace the original classic wxPython release in the future.

How to do it…

In order to use PyOpenGL, we have to first install it. The following URL is the official Python package installer website:

```
https://pypi.python.org/pypi/PyOpenGL/3.0.2.
```

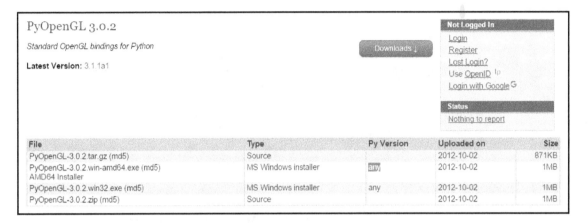

This seems to be the correct installation but, as it turns out, it doesn't work with Windows 10 64-bit OS with Python 3.6 64-bit.

A better place to look for Python installation packages was mentioned in a recipe in the previous chapter. You are probably already familiar with it. The URL is `http://www.lf d.uci.edu/~gohlke/pythonlibs/`.

We have to download the package that matches both our OS and our Python version. It comes with the new `.whl` format. If you are using an older version of Python, you have to install the Python `wheel` package first:

 How to install the Python `wheel` package is described in a recipe, *Installing Matplotlib using pip with whl extension*, in `Chapter 5`, *Matplotlib Charts*.

Installing `PyOpenGL` via the `PyOpenGL-3.1.1-cp36-cp36m-win_amd64.whl` file using the `pip` command is both successful and installs all the 64-bit modules we require.

Replace `<your full path>` with the full path you downloaded the `.whl` installer to:

> **pip install <your full path> PyOpenGL-3.1.1-cp36-cp36m-win_amd64.whl**

When we now try to import some `PyOpenGL` modules, it works, as can be seen in this code example:

```
import wx
from wx import glcanvas
from OpenGL.GL import *
from OpenGL.GLUT import *
```

All this code is doing is importing several `OpenGL` Python modules, in addition to importing wxPython. It does not do anything else but, when we run our Python module, we do not get any errors.

This proves that we have successfully installed the `OpenGL` bindings to Python.

Now that our development environment has been successfully set up, we can try it out using wxPython.

 Many online examples are restricted to using Python 2 as well as using the classic version of wxPython. We are using Python 3.6 and Phoenix.

Using the code based on the wxPython demo examples creates a working 3D cube. In contrast, running the cone example did not work, but this example got us started on the right track.

Here is the URL: `http://wiki.wxpython.org/GLCanvas%20update`

Here are some modifications to the code:

```
import wx
from wx import glcanvas
from OpenGL.GL import *
from OpenGL.GLUT import *

class MyCanvasBase(glcanvas.GLCanvas):
    def __init__(self, parent):
        glcanvas.GLCanvas.__init__(self, parent, -1)
        # This context was missing from the original code
```

```
        self.context = glcanvas.GLContext(self)

    def OnPaint(self, event):
        dc = wx.PaintDC(self)
        # self.SetCurrent()              # commented out because:
        self.SetCurrent(self.context)    # We have to pass in a context
```

We now can create the following GUI:

`import_OpenGL_cube_and_cone.py`

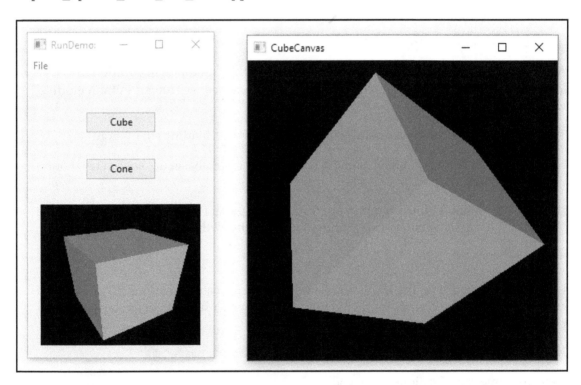

In the classic version of wxPython, `SetCurrent()` did not require a context. Here is some code we might find when searching online:

```
    def OnPaint(self, event):
        dc = wx.PaintDC(self)
        self.SetCurrent()
        if not self.init:
            self.InitGL()
            self.init = True
        self.OnDraw()
```

The preceding code does not work when using wxPython Phoenix. We can look up the correct syntax for Phoenix online:

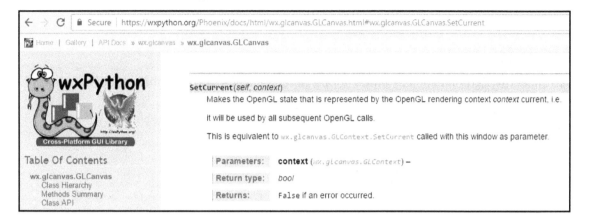

How it works...

In this recipe, we had our first experiences of OpenGL with PyOpenGL Python bindings. While OpenGL can create truly amazing images in true 3D, we ran into some challenges along the way and then found solutions to these challenges that made it work.

We are coding in Python, creating 3D images!

Our GUI in 3D!

In this recipe, we will create our own GUI using wxPython. We will reuse some code from the wxPython demo examples, which we have reduced to the minimum code required to display `OpenGL` in 3D.

OpenGL is a very large library. We will not go into detailed explanations of this library. There are a lot of books and online documentation available if you want to study `OpenGL` further. It has its own shading language.

Getting ready

Reading the previous recipe is probably a good preparation for this recipe.

How to do it...

As the entire Python code is a little bit long here, we will show just a little bit of the code.

The entire code is available online and this Python module is called `wxPython_OpenGL_GUI.py`:

```python
import wx
from wx import glcanvas
from OpenGL.GL import *
from OpenGL.GLUT import *

#-----------------------------------------------------
class CanvasBase(glcanvas.GLCanvas):
    def __init__(self, parent):
        glcanvas.GLCanvas.__init__(self, parent, -1)
        self.context = glcanvas.GLContext(self)
        self.init = False

        # Cube 3D start rotation
        self.last_X = self.x = 30
        self.last_Y = self.y = 30

        self.Bind(wx.EVT_SIZE, self.sizeCallback)
        self.Bind(wx.EVT_PAINT, self.paintCallback)
        self.Bind(wx.EVT_LEFT_DOWN, self.mouseDownCallback)
        self.Bind(wx.EVT_LEFT_UP, self.mouseUpCallback)
        self.Bind(wx.EVT_MOTION, self.mouseMotionCallback)

    def sizeCallback(self, event):
        wx.CallAfter(self.setViewport)
        event.Skip()

    def setViewport(self):
        self.size = self.GetClientSize()
        self.SetCurrent(self.context)
        glViewport(0, 0, self.size.width, self.size.height)

    def paintCallback(self, event):
        wx.PaintDC(self)
        self.SetCurrent(self.context)
        if not self.init:
```

```
        self.initGL()
        self.init = True
    self.onDraw()

def mouseDownCallback(self, event):
    self.CaptureMouse()
    self.x, self.y = self.last_X, self.last_Y = event.GetPosition()

def mouseUpCallback(self, evt):
    self.ReleaseMouse()

def mouseMotionCallback(self, evt):
    if evt.Dragging() and evt.LeftIsDown():
        self.last_X, self.last_Y = self.x, self.y
        self.x, self.y = evt.GetPosition()
        self.Refresh(False)

#-----------------------------------------------------
class CubeCanvas(CanvasBase):
    def initGL(self):
        # set viewing projection
        glMatrixMode(GL_PROJECTION)
        glFrustum(-0.5, 0.5, -0.5, 0.5, 1.0, 3.0)

        # position viewer
        glMatrixMode(GL_MODELVIEW)
        glTranslatef(0.0, 0.0, -2.0)

        # position object
        glRotatef(self.y, 1.0, 0.0, 0.0)
        glRotatef(self.x, 0.0, 1.0, 0.0)

        glEnable(GL_DEPTH_TEST)
        glEnable(GL_LIGHTING)
        glEnable(GL_LIGHT0)

    def onDraw(self):
        # clear color and depth buffers
        glClear(GL_COLOR_BUFFER_BIT | GL_DEPTH_BUFFER_BIT)

        # draw six faces of a cube
        glBegin(GL_QUADS)
        glNormal3f( 0.0, 0.0, 1.0)
        glVertex3f( 0.5, 0.5, 0.5)
        glVertex3f(-0.5, 0.5, 0.5)
        glVertex3f(-0.5,-0.5, 0.5)
        glVertex3f( 0.5,-0.5, 0.5)
```

```
        glNormal3f( 0.0, 0.0,-1.0)
        glVertex3f(-0.5,-0.5,-0.5)


    #===============================================================
app = wx.App()
frame = wx.Frame(None, , size=(300,230))
GUI(frame)
frame.Show()
app.MainLoop()
```

The following screenshot shows our wxPython GUI: `wxPython_OpenGL_GUI.py`

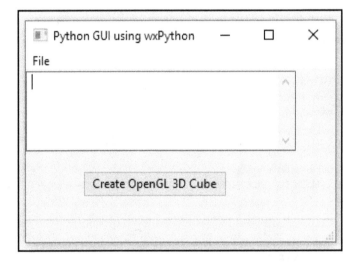

When we click the button widget, the following second window appears:

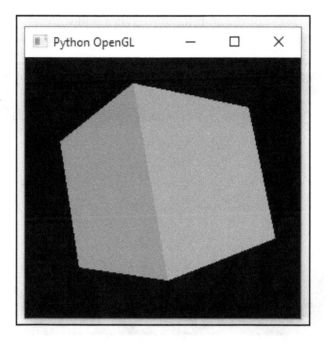

We can now use the mouse to drag the cube around to see all of its six sides:

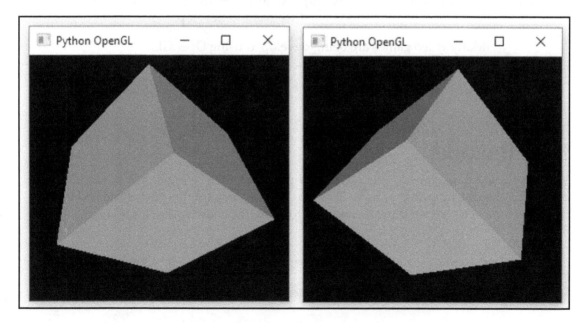

We can also maximize this window and the coordinates will scale, and we can spin this cube around in this much larger window!

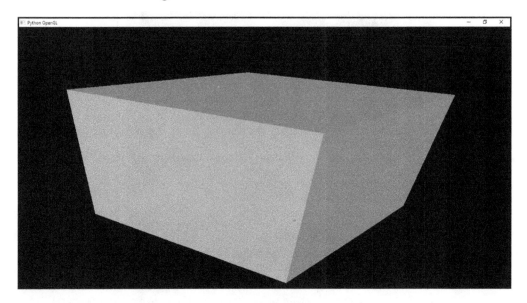

The cube could also be a Star Trek space ship! We just have to become an advanced programmer in this technology if this is what we want to develop.

Many video games are being developed using OpenGL.

How it works...

We first created a regular wxPython GUI and placed a button widget onto it. Clicking this button invokes the imported OpenGL 3D libraries. The code used is part of the wxPython demo examples, which we slightly modified to make the code work with Phoenix.

This recipe glued our own GUI to this library.

`OpenGL` is such a huge and very impressive library. This recipe gave a taste of how to create a working example in Python.

 Often, a working example is all we need to get started on our journey.

Using bitmaps to make our GUI pretty

This recipe was inspired by a wxPython IDE builder framework that, at some point in time, used to work. We will reuse a bitmap image from the large amount of code this project supplies.

The URL to the GitHub repository is `https://github.com/reingart/gui2py`.

I was not able to recreate this IDE using Python 3.6. Yet it shows what is possible. If you are interested in developing a drag and drop IDE framework, you can help the entire Python Windows developer community (and compete with MS Visual Studio...) by making this code work on Python 3.6 and beyond.

Getting ready

We will continue using wxPython in this recipe, so reading at least parts of the previous chapter might be useful as a preparation for this recipe.

How to do it...

After reverse-engineering the `gui2py` code and making other changes to this code, we may achieve the following window widget, which displays a nice, tiled background:

`wxPython_Wallpaper_simple.py`

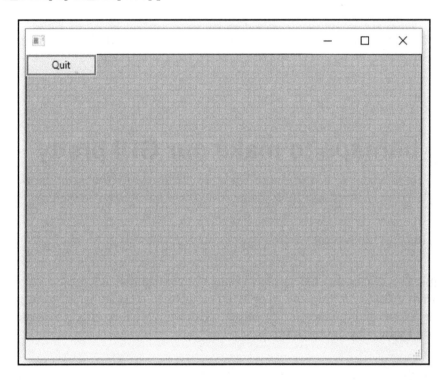

Of course, we lost a lot of widgets refactoring the code from the aforementioned website, yet it does give us a cool background, and clicking the **Quit** button still works.

The next step is to figure out how to integrate the interesting part of the code into our own GUI. We do this by adding the following code to the GUI in the previous recipe:

```
#------------------------------------------------------------
class GUI(wx.Panel):                    # Subclass wxPython Panel
    def __init__(self, parent):
        wx.Panel.__init__(self, parent)

        imageFile = 'Tile.bmp'
        self.bmp = wx.Bitmap(imageFile)
        # react to a resize event and redraw image
        parent.Bind(wx.EVT_SIZE, self.canvasCallback)
```

```
def canvasCallback(self, event=None):
    # create the device context
    dc = wx.ClientDC(self)
    brushBMP = wx.Brush(self.bmp)
    dc.SetBrush(brushBMP)
    width, height = self.GetClientSize()
    dc.DrawRectangle(0, 0, width, height)
```

 We have to bind to parent, not self; otherwise, our bitmap will not show up.

Running our improved code now tiles a bitmap as the background of our GUI:

wxPython_Wallpaper.py

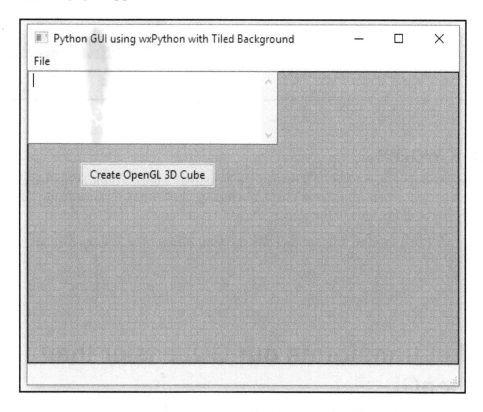

Clicking the button still invokes our `OpenGL` 3D drawing, so we did not lose any functionality:

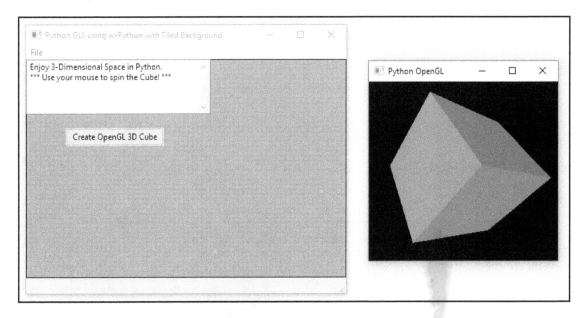

How it works...

In this recipe, we enhanced our GUI by using a bitmap as a background. We tiled the bitmap image and, when we resized the GUI window, the bitmap automatically adjusted itself to fill in the entire area of the canvas we were painting on using the device context.

 The preceding wxPython code can load different image file formats.

PyGLet transforms our GUI easier than PyOpenGL

In this recipe, we will use the PyGLet GUI development framework to create our GUIs.

PyGLet is easier to use than PyOpenGL, as it comes with its own GUI event loop, so we do not need to use tkinter or wxPython to create our GUI.

How to do it...

In order to use PyGLet, we first have to install this third-party Python plugin.

Using the `pip` command, we can easily install the library, and a successful installation looks like this in our `site-packages` Python folder:

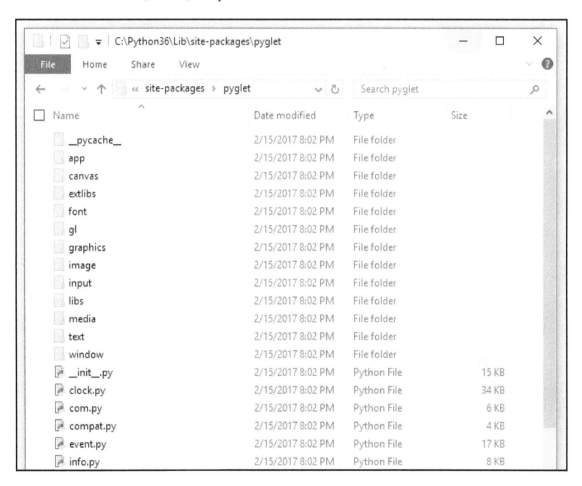

The online documentation is located at the `https://pyglet.readthedocs.org/en/pyglet-1.2-maintenance/` website for the current release:

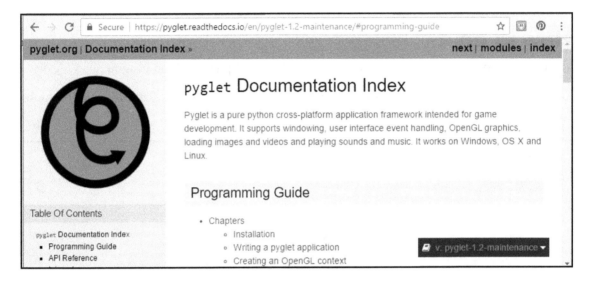

A first experience using the `pyglet` library may look as follows:

```
import pyglet
window = pyglet.window.Window()
label = pyglet.text.Label('PyGLet GUI',
                          font_size=42,
                          x=window.width//2, y=window.height//2,
                          anchor_x='center', anchor_y='center')
@window.event
def on_draw():
    window.clear()
    label.draw()

pyglet.app.run()
```

The preceding code is from the official `pyglet.org` website and results in the following fully functional GUI:

`pyglet_GUI_Simple.py`

How it works...

In this recipe, we used another third-party Python module that wraps the `OpenGL` library.

This library comes with its own event loop processing power, which enables us to avoid having to rely on yet another library to create a running Python GUI.

We have explored the official website, which shows us how to install and use this fantastic GUI library.

Our GUI in amazing colors

In this recipe, we will extend our GUI written using PyGLet from the previous recipe, *PyGLet transforms our GUI easier than PyOpenGL*, by turning it into true 3D.

We will also add some fancy colors to it. This recipe is inspired by some sample code from the *OpenGL SuperBible* book series. It creates a very colorful cube, which we can turn around in a three-dimensional space using the keyboard up, down, left, and right buttons.

We have slightly improved the sample code by making the image turn when holding down one of the keys instead of having to press and release the key.

Getting ready

The previous recipe, *PyGLet transforms our GUI easier than PyOpenGL*, explains how to install PyGLet and gives you an introduction to this library. If you have not done so, it is probably a good idea to browse through that recipe.

 In the online documentation, PyGLet is usually spelled in all lower-case. While this might be a Pythonic way, we capitalize the first letter of a class and we use lower case for variable, method, and function names to start each name.

How to do it...

The following code creates the 3D colored cube, which follows the code. This time, we will use the keyboard arrow keys to rotate the image instead of the mouse:

```python
import pyglet
from pyglet.gl import *
from pyglet.window import key
from OpenGL.GLUT import *

WINDOW    = 400
INCREMENT = 5

class Window(pyglet.window.Window):

    # Cube 3D start rotation
    xRotation = yRotation = 30

    def __init__(self, width, height, title=''):
        super(Window, self).__init__(width, height, title)
        glClearColor(0, 0, 0, 1)
        glEnable(GL_DEPTH_TEST)

    def on_draw(self):
        # Clear the current GL Window
        self.clear()

        # Push Matrix onto stack
        glPushMatrix()
```

```
    glRotatef(self.xRotation, 1, 0, 0)
    glRotatef(self.yRotation, 0, 1, 0)

    # Draw the six sides of the cube
    glBegin(GL_QUADS)

    # White
    glColor3ub(255, 255, 255)
    glVertex3f(50,50,50)

    # Yellow
    glColor3ub(255, 255, 0)
    glVertex3f(50,-50,50)

    # Red
    glColor3ub(255, 0, 0)
    glVertex3f(-50,-50,50)
    glVertex3f(-50,50,50)

    # Blue
    glColor3f(0, 0, 1)
    glVertex3f(-50,50,-50)

    # <... more color defines for cube faces>

    glEnd()

    # Pop Matrix off stack
    glPopMatrix()

def on_resize(self, width, height):
    # set the Viewport
    glViewport(0, 0, width, height)

    # using Projection mode
    glMatrixMode(GL_PROJECTION)
    glLoadIdentity()

    aspectRatio = width / height
    gluPerspective(35, aspectRatio, 1, 1000)

    glMatrixMode(GL_MODELVIEW)
    glLoadIdentity()
    glTranslatef(0, 0, -400)

def on_text_motion(self, motion):
    if motion == key.UP:
        self.xRotation -= INCREMENT
```

```
            elif motion == key.DOWN:
                self.xRotation += INCREMENT
            elif motion == key.LEFT:
                self.yRotation -= INCREMENT
            elif motion == key.RIGHT:
                self.yRotation += INCREMENT

    if __name__ == '__main__':
        Window(WINDOW, WINDOW, 'Pyglet Colored Cube')
        pyglet.app.run()
```

pyglet_GUI.py

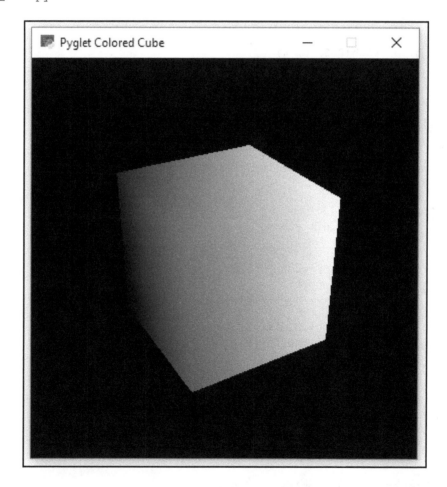

Using the keyboard arrow keys, we can spin the 3D cube around:

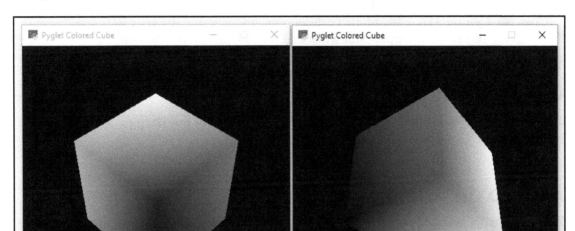

How it works...

In this recipe, we used `pyglet` to create a colorful cube, which we can rotate in 3D space using the keyboard arrow keys.

We defined several colors for the six faces of our cube, and we used `pyglet` to create our main window frame.

The code is similar to a previous recipe in this chapter, in which we used the `wxPython` library to create a cube. The reason for this is that, underneath the hood, both wxPython and PyGLet use the `OpenGL` library.

OpenGL animation

In the previous recipes, we used the wxPython and PyGLet frameworks to display `OpenGL`. In this recipe, we will use pure Python and `OpenGL` to create a red rectangle that bounces within a window that has a blue background.

The examples in this recipe have been translated from the C programming language into Python using the *OpenGL SuperBible Fourth Edition* as a guide. While the Fourth Edition was published in the year 2007, the OpenGL examples still work and we can use them with Python.

Getting ready

This recipe requires the `PyOpenGL` package. The first recipe of this chapter, *PyOpenGL transforms our GUI*, explains how to install this package.

How to do it...

First, we import several packages from `OpenGL`. In the `main()` Python function, we initialize the `GL Utility (glut)` library. Then we choose a single buffer (as opposed to double buffering) and also select the **Red, Green, Blue, Alpha** (**RGBA**) color mode.

We then create a window via GLUT. No need for tkinter, wxPython or PyGLet. We can do this directly via `OpenGL GLUT` functions.

In Python 3.6, we have to pass in the string of the window title as bytes. We do this by placing a **b** in front of the string, which encodes the string as bytes.

After this, we create and define a display function, `RenderScene()`. This function gets called when we start the glut windows event loop.

In the `SetupRC()` function, we define a color to be used for clearing the rendering/display window. Valid values are float numbers between 0.0 and 1.0. Passing different values into RGB then creates different colors. In the following example, we define the blue color.

While we have placed the `SetupRC()` function below `glutDisplayFunc()`, this function actually gets called first because `RenderScene()` only gets called once we call the `glutMainLoop()` function.

Here is the code:

`OpenGL_SuperBible_Simple.py`

```
from OpenGL.GLUT import *
from OpenGL.GL import *
from OpenGL.GLU import *


def RenderScene():                          # display callback function
    glClear(GL_COLOR_BUFFER_BIT)            # clear window with color defined in SetupRC
    glFlush()                               # flush/execute the OpenGL drawing command(s)


def SetupRC():                              # rendering context
    glClearColor(0.0, 0.0, 1.0, 1.0)        # RGBA: R=0.0, G=0.0, B=1.0 => becomes Blue


def main():
    glutInit()
    glutInitDisplayMode(GLUT_SINGLE | GLUT_RGBA)     # single buffer; RGBA color mode
    glutCreateWindow(b"Simple")                      # Python 3: bytes instead of string for Title
    glutDisplayFunc(RenderScene)
    SetupRC()

    glutMainLoop()

    #==================
main()
```

Running the code creates the following window, using pure Python with OpenGL:

OpenGL_SuperBible_Simple.py

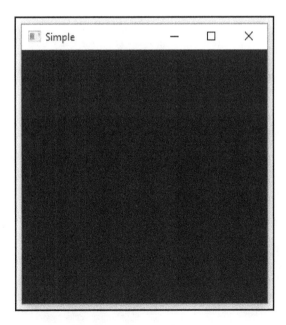

In order to display a drawing component within this OpenGL window, we enhance the RenderScene() function by creating a square rectangle with a size of 25 x 25 pixels.

We also add a new function, ChangeSize(), which gets automatically called by the GLUT library whenever the window is resized or redrawn:

OpenGL_SuperBible_Simple_Rectangle.py

```python
from OpenGL.GLUT import *
from OpenGL.GL import *
from OpenGL.GLU import *

def RenderScene():                      # display callback function
    glClear(GL_COLOR_BUFFER_BIT)        # clear window with color defined in SetupRC
    #       R    G    B                  # set drawing color to Red
    glColor3f(1.0, 0.0, 0.0)            # function expects 3 f(loats)
    glRectf(-25.0, 25.0, 25.0, -25.0)  # draw a filled rectangle with above color
    glFlush()                           # flush/execute the OpenGL drawing command(s)

def SetupRC():                          # rendering context setup
    glClearColor(0.0, 0.0, 1.0, 1.0)   # RGBA: R=0.0, G=0.0, B=1.0=white => becomes Blue

def ChangeSize(w, h):                   # callback when window size changes
    if h == 0: h =1                     # prevent divide by zero
    glViewport(0, 0, w, h)             # set Viewport to Window dimensions
    glMatrixMode(GL_PROJECTION)        # define the viewing volume
    glLoadIdentity()                    # reset coordinate system
    aspectRatio = GLfloat(w).value / GLfloat(h).value   # establish clipping volume
                                                        # GLfloat becomes ctypes.c_float
                                                        # Use the value attribute before dividing
    if w <= h: glOrtho(-100.0, 100.0, -100.0 / aspectRatio, 100.0 / aspectRatio, 1.0, -1.0)
    else:      glOrtho(-100.0 * aspectRatio, 100.0 * aspectRatio, -100.0, 100.0, 1.0, -1.0)
    glMatrixMode(GL_MODELVIEW)
    glLoadIdentity()

def main():
    glutInit()
    glutInitDisplayMode(GLUT_SINGLE | GLUT_RGBA)        # single buffer; RGBA color mode
    glutCreateWindow(b"GLRect")                          # Python 3: bytes instead of string for Title
    glutDisplayFunc(RenderScene)
    glutReshapeFunc(ChangeSize)
    SetupRC()
    glutMainLoop()
#==================
main()
```

Here is the resulting window:

OpenGL_SuperBible_Simple_Rectangle.py

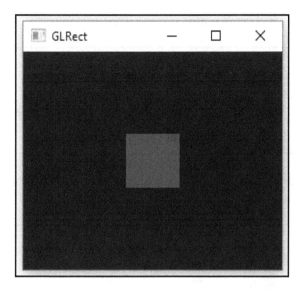

Next, we will animate our red square by having it move across the window, bouncing off each corner. In order to do so, we first create some module-level global variables:

OpenGL_SuperBible_Animation.py

```
from OpenGL.GLUT import *
from OpenGL.GL import *
from OpenGL.GLU import *

# initial position and size
x1 = GLfloat(0.0).value
y1 = GLfloat(0.0).value
rect_size = GLfloat(25.0).value

# number of pixels to move each step
xstep = GLfloat(1.0).value
ystep = GLfloat(1.0).value

# initialize bouncing window
windowWidth  = GLfloat(133).value      # 800/600 = 1.33
windowHeight = GLfloat(100).value
```

In the `RenderScene()` function, we now use double-buffering:

```python
def RenderScene():                          # display callback function
    glClear(GL_COLOR_BUFFER_BIT)            # clear window with color defined in SetupRC
    #            R    G    B                 # set drawing color to Red
    glColor3f(1.0, 0.0, 0.0)                # functions expects 3 f(loats)
    glRectf(x1, y1, x1 + rect_size, y1 - rect_size) # draw a filled rectangle with above color

    glutSwapBuffers()                       # flush and swap double buffers
```

We have to slightly change our `main()` to pass GLUT_DOUBLE into the `glutInitDisplayMode()` function:

```python
def main():
    glutInit()
    glutInitDisplayMode(GLUT_DOUBLE | GLUT_RGB)        # Double buffer
    glutInitWindowSize(800, 600)                        # window size
    glutCreateWindow(b"Bouncing Red Square")           # Python 3: bytes instead of string for Title
    glutDisplayFunc(RenderScene)
    glutReshapeFunc(ChangeSize)
    glutTimerFunc(33, TimerFunction, 1)

    SetupRC()

    glutMainLoop()

#==================
main()
```

We create the `TimerFunction()` to be passed into `glutTimerFunc()`. In this function, we do some math to position the red square and make it bounce of the window walls. At the end of the function, we recursively call this function in `glutTimerFunc()`:

```python
def TimerFunction(value):
    global x1, xstep, y1, ystep

    # reverse direction left/right
    if ((x1 > windowWidth - rect_size) or (x1 < -windowWidth)):
        xstep = -xstep

    # reverse direction top/bottom
    if ((y1 > windowHeight) or (y1 < -windowHeight + rect_size)):
        ystep = -ystep

    # move the red square
    x1 += xstep
    y1 += ystep

    # check the bounds of the clipping area
    if (x1 > (windowWidth - rect_size + xstep)):
        x1 = windowWidth - rect_size - 1
    elif (x1 < -(windowWidth + xstep)):
        x1 = -windowWidth - 1

    if (y1 > (windowHeight + ystep)):
        y1 = windowHeight - 1
    elif (y1 < -(windowHeight - rect_size + ystep)):
        y1 = -windowHeight + rect_size - 1

    # redraw the scene
    glutPostRedisplay()
    glutTimerFunc(33, TimerFunction, 1)     # recursive call
```

When we now run the program, the red square will move around inside the blue window, bouncing off each corner:

`OpenGL_SuperBible_Animation.py`

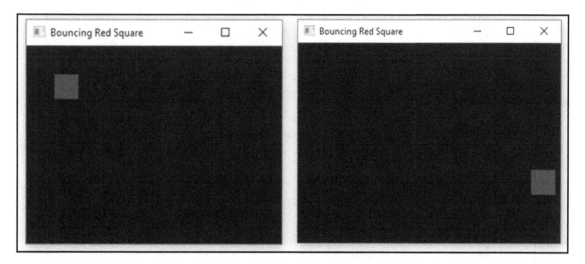

How it works...

In this recipe, we used the OpenGL library directly from Python. We created our own window without having to use any other Python GUI framework. We explored a few of the many OpenGL functions and created working programs.

 A good, short introduction to OpenGL and how to use it from Python can be found at `https://noobtuts.com/python/opengl-introduction`.

Creating a slide show using tkinter

In this recipe, we will create a nice working slide show GUI using pure Python. We will see the limitations the core Python built-ins have, and then we will explore another available third-party module called Pillow, which extends the built-in functionality of tkinter in regards to image processing.

While the name `Pillow` might sound a little bit strange at first, it actually comes with a lot of history behind it.

> We are only using Python 3.6 and above in this book. We are not going back to Python 2. Guido has expressed his decision to intentionally break backwards compatibility and decided that Python 3 is the future of Python programming.

For GUIs and images, the older line of Python 2 has a very powerful module named `PIL`, which stands for Python Image Library. This library comes with a very large amount of functionality, which, several years after the very successful creation of Python 3, has not been translated for Python 3.

Many developers still choose to use Python 2 instead of the future, as designed by the *Benevolent Dictator of Python* because Python 2 still has more libraries available.

That is a little bit sad. Fortunately, another imaging library has been created to work with Python 3.6 and it is named `PIL` plus something.

> Pillow is not compatible with the Python 2 PIL library.

Getting ready

In the first part of this recipe, we will use pure Python. In order to improve the code, we will install another Python module using the `pip` functionality, so while you are most likely familiar with `pip`, a little knowledge of how to use it might be useful.

How to do it...

First, we will create a working GUI that shuffles slides within a window frame using pure Python. Here is the working code and some screenshots of the results of running this code:

```python
from tkinter import Tk, PhotoImage, Label
from itertools import cycle
from os import listdir

class SlideShow(Tk):
    # inherit GUI framework extending tkinter
    def __init__(self, msShowTimeBetweenSlides=1500):
```

```python
        # initialize tkinter super class
        Tk.__init__(self)

        # time each slide will be shown
        self.showTime = msShowTimeBetweenSlides

        # look for images in current working directory
        listOfSlides = [slide for slide in listdir()
                        if slide.endswith('gif')]

        # cycle slides to show on the tkinter Label
        self.iterableCycle = cycle((PhotoImage(file=slide), slide)
                            for slide in listOfSlides)

        # create tkinter Label widget which can display images
        self.slidesLabel = Label(self)

        # create the Frame widget
        self.slidesLabel.pack()


    def slidesCallback(self):
        # get next slide from iterable cycle
        currentInstance, nameOfSlide = next(self.iterableCycle)

        # assign next slide to Label widget
        self.slidesLabel.config(image=currentInstance)

        # update Window title with current slide
        self.title(nameOfSlide)

        # recursively repeat the Show
        self.after(self.showTime, self.slidesCallback)



#===================================
# Start GUI
#===================================
win = SlideShow()
win.after(0, win.slidesCallback())
win.mainloop()
```

SlideShow.py

Here is another moment in time in the unfolding slide show:

While the slides sliding are truly impressive, the built-in capabilities of pure Python `tkinter` GUIs do not support the very popular `.jpg` format, so we have to reach out to another Python library. In order to use `Pillow`, we first have to install it using the `pip` command.

A successful installation looks as follows:

```
Command Prompt

Microsoft Windows [Version 10.0.14393]
(c) 2016 Microsoft Corporation. All rights reserved.

C:\Users\Burkh>pip install pillow
Collecting pillow
  Downloading Pillow-4.0.0-cp36-cp36m-win_amd64.whl (1.5MB)
    100% |                              | 1.5MB 506kB/s
Collecting olefile (from pillow)
  Downloading olefile-0.44.zip (74kB)
    100% |                              | 81kB 1.6MB/s
Installing collected packages: olefile, pillow
  Running setup.py install for olefile ... done
Successfully installed olefile-0.44 pillow-4.0.0

C:\Users\Burkh>
```

`Pillow` supports `.jpg` formats and, in order to use it, we to have to slightly change our syntax.

Without using `Pillow`, trying to display a `.jpg` image results in the following error:

`SlideShow_try_jpg.py`

```
        # try: .jpeg
        listOfSlides = [slide for slide in listdir() if slide.endswith('gif') or slide.endswith('jpg')]
```

```
Console    Bookmarks
C:\Eclipse_NEON_workspace\2nd Edition Python GUI Programming Cookbook\Ch10_Code\SlideShow_try_jpeg.py
  File "C:\Python36\lib\tkinter\__init__.py", line 3495, in __init__
    self.tk.call(('image', 'create', imgtype, name,) + options)
_tkinter.TclError: couldn't recognize data in image file "rivers expedition day.jpg"
```

Using `Pillow`, we can display both `.gif` and `.jpg` files. After a successful installation of the `Pillow` package, we only have to make a few changes:

```
# using Pillow instead of PIL (2.7) for Python 3.6
# Installation is: >pip install Pillow
from PIL import ImageTk


class SlideShow(Tk):
    # inherit GUI framework extending tkinter
    def __init__(self, msShowTimeBetweenSlides=1500):
        # initialize tkinter super class
        Tk.__init__(self)

        # time each slide will be shown
        self.showTime = msShowTimeBetweenSlides

        # look for images in current working directory where this module lives
#         listOfSlides = [slide for slide in listdir() if slide.endswith('gif')]
        listOfSlides = [slide for slide in listdir() if slide.endswith('gif') or slide.endswith('jpg')]

        # endlessly read in the slides so we can show them on the tkinter Label
#         self.iterableCycle = cycle((PhotoImage(file=slide), slide) for slide in listOfSlides)
        self.iterableCycle = cycle((ImageTk.PhotoImage(file=slide), slide) for slide in listOfSlides)
```

We search our folder for `.jpg` extensions and, instead of using the `PhotoImage()` class, we now use the `ImageTk.PhotoImage()` class. This enables us to display images with different extensions:

`SlideShow_Pillow.py`

How it works...

Python is a wonderful tool and, in this recipe, we have explored several ways to use and extend it.

11
Best Practices

In this chapter, we will explore best practices related to our Python GUI. We will cover the following recipes:

- Avoiding spaghetti code
- Using __init__ to connect modules
- Mixing fall-down and OOP coding
- Using a code naming convention
- When not to use OOP
- How to use design patterns successfully
- Avoiding complexity
- GUI design using multiple notebooks

Introduction

In this chapter, we will explore different best practices that can help us build our GUI in an efficient way and keep it both maintainable and extendable.

These best practices will also help us debug our GUI to get it just the way we want it to be.

Here is the overview of Python modules for this chapter:

```
∨ 📦 2nd Edition Python GUI Programming Cookbook
  > ⊞ Ch01_Code
  > ⊞ Ch02_Code
  > ⊞ Ch03_Code
  > ⊞ Ch04_Code
  > ⊞ Ch05_Code
  > ⊞ Ch06_Code
  > ⊞ Ch07_Code
  > ⊞ Ch08_Code
  > ⊞ Ch09_Code
  > ⊞ Ch10_Code
  ∨ ⊞ Ch11_Code
    > 📂 Folder1
    > 📄 __init__.py
    > 📄 GUI__init_import_folder_directly.py
    > 📄 GUI__init_import_folder.py
    > 📄 GUI__init.py
    > 📄 GUI_Complexity_end_tab3.py
    > 📄 GUI_Complexity_start_add_button.py
    > 📄 GUI_Complexity_start_add_three_more_buttons_add_more.py
    > 📄 GUI_Complexity_start_add_three_more_buttons.py
    > 📄 GUI_Complexity_start.py
    > 📄 GUI_DesignPattern.py
    > 📄 GUI_FallDown.py
    > 📄 GUI_Not_OOP.py
    > 📄 GUI_NOT_Spaghetti.py
    > 📄 GUI_OOP.py
    > 📄 GUI_Spaghetti.py
      🌐 pyc.ico
    > 📄 ToolTip.py
```

Avoiding spaghetti code

In this recipe, we will explore a typical way to create spaghetti code and then we will see a much better way of how to avoid such code.

Spaghetti code is code in which a lot of functionality is intertangled.

Getting ready

We will create a new, simple GUI, written in Python using the built-in Python `tkinkter` library.

How to do it...

Having searched online and read the documentation, we might start by writing the following code to create our GUI:

GUI_Spaghetti.py

```
# Spaghetti Code ############################
def PRINTME(me):print(me)
import tkinter
x=y=z=1
PRINTME(z)
from tkinter import *
scrolW=30;scrolH=6
win=tkinter.Tk()
if x:chVarUn=tkinter.IntVar()
from tkinter import ttk
WE='WE'
import tkinter.scrolledtext
outputFrame=tkinter.ttk.LabelFrame(win,text=' Type into the scrolled text
                                control: ')
scr=tkinter.scrolledtext.ScrolledText(outputFrame,width=scrolW,height=scrol
H,wrap=tkinter.WORD)
e='E'
scr.grid(column=1,row=1,sticky=WE)
outputFrame.grid(column=0,row=2,sticky=e,padx=8)
lFrame=None
if y:chck2=tkinter.Checkbutton(lFrame,text="Enabled",variable=chVarUn)
wE='WE'
if y==x:PRINTME(x)
lFrame=tkinter.ttk.LabelFrame(win,text="Spaghetti")
chck2.grid(column=1,row=4,sticky=tkinter.W,columnspan=3)
PRINTME(z)
lFrame.grid(column=0,row=0,sticky=wE,padx=10,pady=10)
```

```
chck2.select()
try: win.mainloop()
except:PRINTME(x)
chck2.deselect()
if y==x:PRINTME(x)
# End Pasta ############################
```

Running the preceding code results in the following GUI:

This is not quite the GUI we intended. We wanted it to look something more like this:

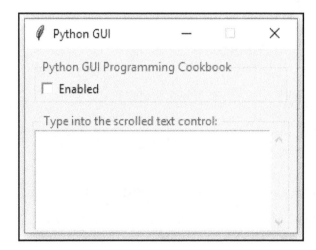

While the spaghetti code created a GUI, the code is very hard to debug because there is so much confusion in the code.

The following is the code that produces the desired GUI:

GUI_NOT_Spaghetti.py

```
#=======================
# imports
#=======================
import tkinter as tk
from tkinter import ttk
from tkinter import scrolledtext

#=======================
# Create instance
#=======================
win = tk.Tk()

#=======================
# Add a title
#=======================
win.title("Python GUI")

#=========================
# Disable resizing the GUI
#=========================
win.resizable(0,0)

#===============================================================
# Adding a LabelFrame, Textbox (Entry) and Combobox
#===============================================================
lFrame = ttk.LabelFrame(win, text="Python GUI Programming Cookbook")
lFrame.grid(column=0, row=0, sticky='WE', padx=10, pady=10)

#===============================================================
# Using a scrolled Text control
#===============================================================
outputFrame = ttk.LabelFrame(win, text=' Type into the scrolled text
                                    control: ')
outputFrame.grid(column=0, row=2, sticky='E', padx=8)
scrolW = 30
scrolH =  6
scr = scrolledtext.ScrolledText(outputFrame, width=scrolW,
                                    height=scrolH, wrap=tk.WORD)
scr.grid(column=1, row=0, sticky='WE')

#===============================================================
# Creating a checkbutton
#===============================================================
chVarUn = tk.IntVar()
```

```
check2 = tk.Checkbutton(lFrame, text="Enabled", variable=chVarUn)
check2.deselect()
check2.grid(column=1, row=4, sticky=tk.W, columnspan=3)

#=======================
# Start GUI
#=======================
win.mainloop()
```

How it works...

In this recipe, we compared spaghetti code to good code. Good code has many advantages over spaghetti code.

It has clearly commented sections.

The following is an example of spaghetti code:

```
def PRINTME(me):print(me)
import tkinter
x=y=z=1
PRINTME(z)
from tkinter import *
```

The following is an example of good code:

```
#=======================
# imports
#=======================
import tkinter as tk
from tkinter import ttk
```

It has a natural flow that follows how the widgets get laid out in the main GUI form.

In the spaghetti code, the bottom `LabelFrame` gets created before the top `LabelFrame`, and it is intermixed with an `import` statement and some widget creation.

Consider the following example of spaghetti code:

```
import tkinter.scrolledtext
outputFrame=tkinter.ttk.LabelFrame(win,text=' Type into the scrolled text
                                   control: ')
scr=tkinter.scrolledtext.ScrolledText(outputFrame,width=scrolW,height=scrol
H,wrap=tkinter.WORD)
e='E'
scr.grid(column=1,row=1,sticky=WE)
```

```
outputFrame.grid(column=0,row=2,sticky=e,padx=8)
lFrame=None
if y:chck2=tkinter.Checkbutton(lFrame,text="Enabled",variable=chVarUn)
wE='WE'
if y==x:PRINTME(x)
lFrame=tkinter.ttk.LabelFrame(win,text="Spaghetti")
```

Consider the following example of good code::

```
#==============================================================
# Adding a LabelFrame, Textbox (Entry) and Combobox
#==============================================================
lFrame = ttk.LabelFrame(win, text="Python GUI Programming Cookbook")
lFrame.grid(column=0, row=0, sticky='WE', padx=10, pady=10)


#==============================================================
# Using a scrolled Text control
#==============================================================
outputFrame = ttk.LabelFrame(win, text=' Type into the scrolled text
                               control: ')
outputFrame.grid(column=0, row=2, sticky='E', padx=8)
```

It does not contain unnecessary variable assignments and neither does it have a print function that does not do the debugging one might expect it to when reading the code.

For example, consider the following spaghetti code:

```
def PRINTME(me):print(me)
x=y=z=1
e='E'
WE='WE'
scr.grid(column=1,row=1,sticky=WE)
wE='WE'
if y==x:PRINTME(x)
lFrame.grid(column=0,row=0,sticky=wE,padx=10,pady=10)
PRINTME(z)
try: win.mainloop()
except:PRINTME(x)
chck2.deselect()
if y==x:PRINTME(x)
```

Good code has none of the instances mentioned for the spaghetti code.

The import statements only import the required modules. They are not cluttered throughout the code. There are no duplicate import statements. There is no import * statement.

Again, let's have a look at another instance of spaghetti code:

```
import tkinter
x=y=z=1
PRINTME(z)
from tkinter import *
scrolW=30;scrolH=6
win=tkinter.Tk()
if x:chVarUn=tkinter.IntVar()
from tkinter import ttk
WE='WE'
import tkinter.scrolledtext
```

Now, take a look at good code:

```
import tkinter as tk
from tkinter import ttk
from tkinter import scrolledtext
```

The chosen variable names are quite meaningful. There are no unnecessary if statements that use the number 1 instead of True.

The following shows spaghetti code:

```
x=y=z=1
if x:chVarUn=tkinter.IntVar()
wE='WE'
```

The following shows good code:

```
#===========================================================
# Using a scrolled Text control
#===========================================================
outputFrame = ttk.LabelFrame(win, text=' Type into the scrolled text
                             control: ')
outputFrame.grid(column=0, row=2, sticky='E', padx=8)
scrolW = 30
scrolH =  6
scr = scrolledtext.ScrolledText(outputFrame, width=scrolW,
                                height=scrolH, wrap=tk.WORD)
scr.grid(column=1, row=0, sticky='WE')
```

We did not lose the intended window title and our check button ended up in the correct position. We also made the LabelFrame surrounding the check button visible.

Spaghetti code: GUI_Spaghetti.py

We lost both the window title and did not display the top `LabelFrame`. The Check button ended up in the wrong place.

Good code: `GUI_NOT_Spaghetti.py`

```
#=======================
# Create instance
#=======================
win = tk.Tk()

#=======================
# Add a title
#=======================
win.title("Python GUI")

#=============================================================
# Adding a LabelFrame, Textbox (Entry) and Combobox
#=============================================================
lFrame = ttk.LabelFrame(win, text="Python GUI Programming Cookbook")
lFrame.grid(column=0, row=0, sticky='WE', padx=10, pady=10)

#=============================================================
# Creating a checkbutton
#=============================================================
chVarUn = tk.IntVar()
check2 = tk.Checkbutton(lFrame, text="Enabled", variable=chVarUn)
check2.deselect()
check2.grid(column=1, row=4, sticky=tk.W, columnspan=3)

#=======================
# Start GUI
#=======================
win.mainloop()
```

Using __init__ to connect modules

When we create a new Python package using the PyDev plugin for the Eclipse IDE, it automatically creates an __init__.py module. We can also create it ourselves manually, when not using Eclipse.

 The __init__.py module is usually empty and, then, has a size of 0 kilobytes.

We can use this usually empty module to connect different Python modules by entering code into it. This recipe will show how to do this.

Getting ready

We will create a new GUI similar to the one we created in the previous recipe, *Avoiding spaghetti code*.

How to do it...

As our project becomes larger and larger, we naturally break it out into several Python modules. Sometimes it can be a little bit complicated to find modules that are located in different subfolders, either above or below the code that needs to import it.

One practical way to get around this limitation is to use the __init__.py module.

In Eclipse, we can set the Eclipse internal project PyDev **PYTHONPATH** to certain folders and our Python code will find it. But outside Eclipse, for example, when running from a command window, there is sometimes a mismatch in the Python module import mechanism, and the code will not run.

Here is a screenshot of the empty __init__.py module which appears not with the name __init__ but with the name of the PyDev package it belongs to when opened in the Eclipse code editor. The **1** on the left-hand side of the code editor is the line number and not any code written in this module. There is absolutely no code in this empty __init__.py module:

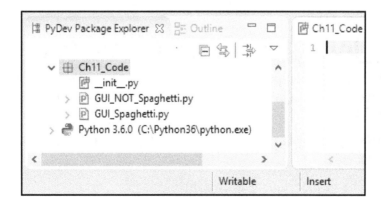

This file is empty but it does exist:

When we run the following code and click the **clickMe** button, we get the result shown post the code. This is a regular Python module that does not yet use the __init__.py module code:

The __init__.py module is not the same as the __init__(self): method of a Python class.

```
# GUI__init.py
#=======================
# imports
#=======================
import tkinter as tk
from tkinter import ttk

#=======================
# Create instance
#=======================
win = tk.Tk()

#=======================
# Add a title
#=======================
win.title("Python GUI")

#================================================================
# Adding a LabelFrame and a Button
#================================================================
lFrame = ttk.LabelFrame(win, text="Python GUI Programming Cookbook")
lFrame.grid(column=0, row=0, sticky='WE', padx=10, pady=10)

def clickMe():
    from tkinter import messagebox
```

```
    messagebox.showinfo('Message Box', 'Hi from same Level.')

button = ttk.Button(lFrame, text="Click Me ", command=clickMe)
button.grid(column=1, row=0, sticky=tk.S)

#=======================
# Start GUI
#=======================
win.mainloop()
```

Running the preceding code named GUI__init.py, we get the following output:

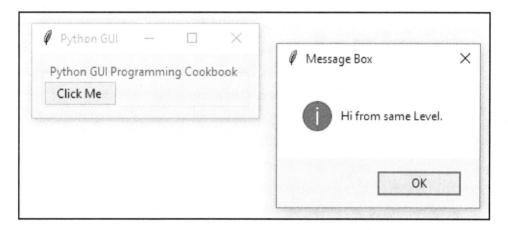

In the preceding code, we created the following function, which imports Python's message box and then uses it to display the message box dialog window:

```
def clickMe():
    from tkinter import messagebox
    messagebox.showinfo('Message Box', 'Hi from same Level.')
```

When we move the clickMe() message box code into a nested directory folder and try to import it into our GUI module, we might run into some challenges.

We have created three subfolders below where our Python module lives. We have then placed the clickMe() message box code into a new Python module, which we named MessageBox.py. This module lives in Folder3, three levels below where our Python module lives.

We need to import this MessageBox.py module in order to use the clickMe() function that this module contains.

We use Python's relative import syntax:

```
from Ch11_Code.Folder1.Folder2.Folder3.MessageBox import clickme
```

The import statement and folder structure can be seen in the following screenshot:

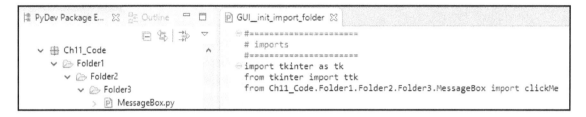

We have deleted the local `clickMe()` function and now our callback is expected to use the imported `clickMe()` function. This works from within Eclipse.

Running the code file `GUI__init_import_folder.py` with the preceding changes gives the following result:

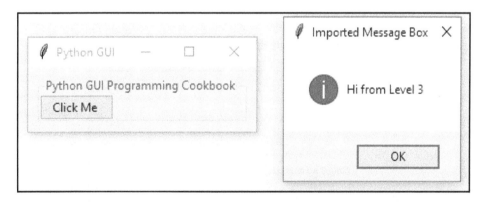

When we run it from a command prompt, we get an error:

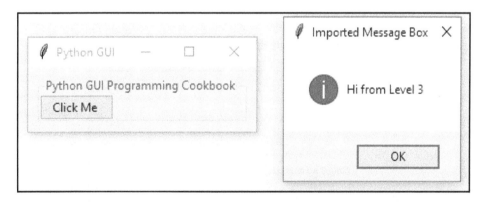

In order to solve this error, we can initialize our Python search path from within the __init__.py module by adding the following code to the __init__.py module:

```
print('hi from GUI init\n')
from sys import path
from pprint import pprint
#=========================================================================
# Required setup for the PYTONPATH in order to find all package folders
#=========================================================================
from site import addsitedir
from os import getcwd, chdir, pardir
while True:
    curFull = getcwd()
    curDir = curFull.split('\\')[-1]
    if 'Ch11_Code' == curDir:
        addsitedir(curFull)
        addsitedir(curFull + 'Folder1\Folder2\Folder3')
        break
    chdir(pardir)
pprint(path)
```

In the module where we import the clickMe function, we no longer have to specify the full folder path. We can import the module and its function directly:

 We have to explicitly import __init__ for this code to work.

When we now run our GUI code, we get the same windows as before, but we have removed our dependency on the Eclipse PYTHONPATH variable.

Now, we can successfully run the same code outside the Eclipse `PyDev` plugin:

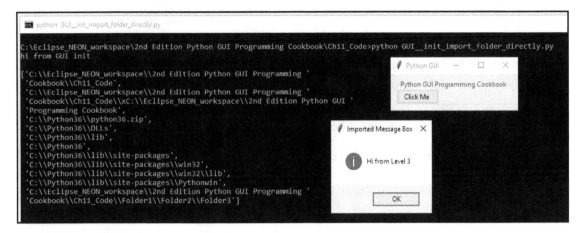

Our code has become more Pythonic.

How it works...

In this recipe, we imported a function from a module that is nested in a folder structure.

We saw that we can use the `__init__.py` module to add the folder structure to the Python search path. We did this by first adding code to, and then explicitly importing, the `__init__.py` module.

In a loop, we search the directory structure until we find the root folder we are looking for.

We then get the full path to this folder and append the three folders. We are not hardcoding the entire search path. We only append the known folders to wherever our module is located.

Using the code we added to the `__init__.py` module enabled us to run the code successfully both from within Eclipse as well as from a command prompt.

Using pure Python is usually the best way to go.

Mixing fall-down and OOP coding

Python is an object-oriented programming language, yet it does not always make sense to use OOP. For simple scripting tasks, the legacy waterfall coding style is still appropriate.

In this recipe, we will create a new GUI that mixes both the fall-down coding style with the more modern OOP coding style.

We will create an OOP-style class that will display a tooltip when we hover the mouse over a widget in a Python GUI that we will create using the waterfall style.

 Fall-down and waterfall coding styles are the same. It means that we have to physically place code above code before we can call it from the code below. In this paradigm, the code literally falls down from the top of our program to the bottom of our program when we execute the code.

Getting ready

In this recipe, we will create a GUI using `tkinter`, which is similar to the GUI we created in the first chapter of this book.

How to do it...

In Python, we can bind functions to classes by turning them into methods using the `self` naming convention. This is a truly wonderful capability of Python, and it allows us to create large systems that are understandable and maintainable.

Sometimes, when we only write short scripts, OOP does not make sense because we find ourselves prepending a lot of variables with the `self` naming convention and the code gets unnecessarily large when it does not need to be.

Let's first create a Python GUI using `tkinter` and code it in the waterfall style.

The following code `GUI_FallDown.py` creates the GUI:

```
#=======================
# imports
#=======================
import tkinter as tk
from tkinter import ttk
from tkinter import messagebox
```

```
#=======================
# Create instance
#=======================
win = tk.Tk()

#=======================
# Add a title
#=======================
win.title("Python GUI")

#=========================
# Disable resizing the GUI
#=========================
win.resizable(0,0)

#============================================================
# Adding a LabelFrame, Textbox (Entry) and Combobox
#============================================================
lFrame = ttk.LabelFrame(win, text="Python GUI Programming Cookbook")
lFrame.grid(column=0, row=0, sticky='WE', padx=10, pady=10)

#============================================================
# Labels
#============================================================
ttk.Label(lFrame, text="Enter a name:").grid(column=0, row=0)
ttk.Label(lFrame, text="Choose a number:").grid(column=1, row=0,
sticky=tk.W)

#============================================================
# Buttons click command
#============================================================
def clickMe(name, number):
    messagebox.showinfo('Information Message Box', 'Hello '+name+
                        ', your number is: ' + number)

#============================================================
# Creating several controls in a loop
#============================================================
names         = ['name0', 'name1', 'name2']
nameEntries   = ['nameEntry0', 'nameEntry1', 'nameEntry2']

numbers       = ['number0', 'number1', 'number2']
numberEntries = ['numberEntry0', 'numberEntry1', 'numberEntry2']

buttons = []

for idx in range(3):
    names[idx] = tk.StringVar()
```

```
        nameEntries[idx] = ttk.Entry(lFrame, width=12, textvariable=names[idx])
        nameEntries[idx].grid(column=0, row=idx+1)
        nameEntries[idx].delete(0, tk.END)
        nameEntries[idx].insert(0, '<name>')

        numbers[idx] = tk.StringVar()
        numberEntries[idx] = ttk.Combobox(lFrame, width=14,
                                       textvariable=numbers[idx])
        numberEntries[idx]['values'] = (1+idx, 2+idx, 4+idx, 42+idx, 100+idx)
        numberEntries[idx].grid(column=1, row=idx+1)
        numberEntries[idx].current(0)

        button = ttk.Button(lFrame, text="Click Me "+str(idx+1),
                        command=lambda idx=idx: clickMe(names[idx].get(),
                        numbers[idx].get()))
        button.grid(column=2, row=idx+1, sticky=tk.W)
        buttons.append(button)
#========================
# Start GUI
#========================
win.mainloop()
```

When we run the code, we get the GUI and it looks like this:

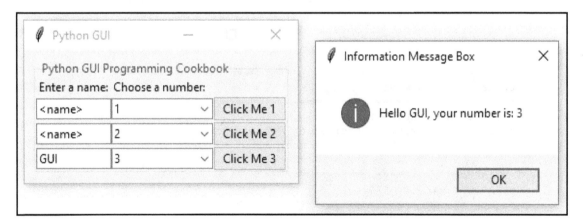

We can improve our Python GUI by adding tooltips. The best way to do this is to isolate the code that creates the tooltip functionality from our GUI.

We do this by creating a separate class, which has the tooltip functionality, and then we create an instance of this class in the same Python module that creates our GUI.

Using Python, there is no need to place our `ToolTip` class into a separate module. We can place it just above the procedural code and then call it from below the class code.

The code will look as follows:

```
#========================
# imports
#========================
import tkinter as tk
from tkinter import ttk
from tkinter import messagebox


#-----------------------------------------------
class ToolTip(object):
    def __init__(self, widget):
        self.widget = widget
        self.tipwindow = None
        self.id = None
        self.x = self.y = 0


#-----------------------------------------------
def createToolTip(widget, text):
    toolTip = ToolTip(widget)
    def enter(event): toolTip.showtip(text)
    def leave(event): toolTip.hidetip()
    widget.bind('<Enter>', enter)
    widget.bind('<Leave>', leave)


#-----------------------------------------------
# further down the module we call the createToolTip function
#-----------------------------------------------

for idx in range(3):
    names[idx] = tk.StringVar()
    nameEntries[idx] = ttk.Entry(lFrame, width=12, textvariable=names[idx])
    nameEntries[idx].grid(column=0, row=idx+1)
    nameEntries[idx].delete(0, tk.END)
    nameEntries[idx].insert(0, '<name>')

    numbers[idx] = tk.StringVar()
    numberEntries[idx] = ttk.Combobox(lFrame, width=14,
                                      textvariable=numbers[idx])
    numberEntries[idx]['values'] = (1+idx, 2+idx, 4+idx, 42+idx, 100+idx)
    numberEntries[idx].grid(column=1, row=idx+1)
    numberEntries[idx].current(0)

    button = ttk.Button(lFrame, text="Click Me "+str(idx+1),
                        command=lambda idx=idx: clickMe(names[idx].get(),
```

```
                            numbers[idx].get()))
        button.grid(column=2, row=idx+1, sticky=tk.W)
        buttons.append(button)

    #-------------------------------------------------
        # Add Tooltips to more widgets
        createToolTip(nameEntries[idx], 'This is an Entry widget.')
        createToolTip(numberEntries[idx], 'This is a DropDown widget.')
        createToolTip(buttons[idx], 'This is a Button widget.')
    #-------------------------------------------------
```

Running the code creates tooltips for our widgets when we hover the mouse over them:

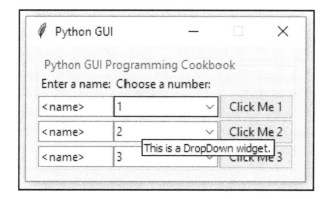

How it works...

In this recipe, we created a Python GUI in a procedural way and later added a class to the top of the module.

We can very easily mix and match both procedural and OOP programming in the same Python module.

Using a code naming convention

The first recipes in the *First Edition* of this book did not use a structured code naming convention. This recipe will show you the value of adhering to a code naming scheme because it helps us to find the code we want to extend, as well as reminding us of the design of our program.

Getting ready

In this recipe, we will look at the Python module names from the first chapter of the *First Edition* of this book and compare them with better naming conventions.

How to do it...

In the first chapter of this book, we created our first Python GUI. We improved our GUI by incrementing the different code module names via sequential numbers.

 The following screenshots are from the First Edition of this book.

It looked like this:

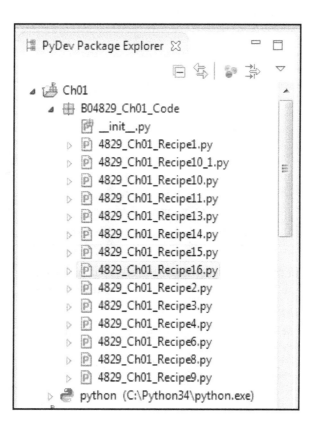

While this is a typical way to code, it does not provide much meaning. When we write our Python code during development, it is very easy to increment numbers.

Later, coming back to this code, we don't have much of an idea which Python module provides which functionality and, sometimes, our last incremented modules are not as good as the earlier versions.

A clear naming convention does help.

We can compare the module names from Chapter 1, *Creating the GUI Form and adding Widgets*, to the names from Chapter 8, *Internationalization and Testing*, which are much more meaningful:

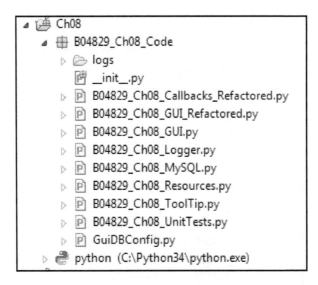

While not perfect, the names chosen for the different Python modules indicate what each module's responsibility is. When we want to add more unit tests, it is clear in which module they reside.

The following code naming convention is another example of how to use a code naming convention to create a GUI in Python:

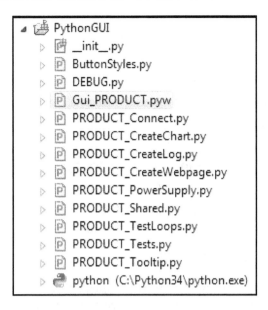

Replace the word PRODUCT with the product you are currently working on.

The entire application is a GUI. All parts are connected. The DEBUG.py module is only used for debugging our code. The main function to invoke the GUI has its name reversed when compared with all the other modules. It starts with Gui and ends with a .pyw extension.

It is the only Python module that has this extension name.

From this naming convention, if you are familiar enough with Python, it will be obvious that, in order to run this GUI, you have to double-click the Gui_PRODUCT.pyw module.

All other Python modules contain functionality to supply to the GUI as well as execute the underlying business logic to fulfill the purpose this GUI addresses.

How it works...

Naming conventions for Python code modules are a great help in keeping us efficient and helping us remember our original design. When we need to debug and fix a defect or add a new functionality, they are the first resources to look at.

Incrementing module names by numbers is not very meaningful and eventually wastes development time.

On the other hand, naming Python variables is more of a free form. Python infers types, so we do not have to specify that a variable will be of type `<list>` (it might not be, or later in the code, it might become a different type).

A good idea for naming variables is to make them descriptive and it is also a good idea not to abbreviate too much.

If we wish to point out that a certain variable is designed to be of the `<list>` type, then it is much more intuitive to use the full word `list` instead of `lst`.

It is similar for `number` instead of `num`.

While it is a good idea to have very descriptive names for variables, sometimes that can get too long. In Apple's Objective-C language, some variable and function names are extreme: `thisIsAMethodThatDoesThisAndThatAndAlsoThatIfYouPassInNIntegers:1:2:3`

Use common sense when naming variables, methods, and functions.

When not to use OOP

Python comes builtin with object-oriented programming capabilities, but at the same time, we can write scripts that do not need to use OOP. For some tasks, OOP does not make sense.

This recipe will show us when not to use OOP.

Getting ready

In this recipe, we will create a Python GUI similar to the previous recipes. We will compare the OOP code to the non-OOP alternative way of programming.

How to do it...

Let's first create a new GUI using OOP methodology. The following code will create the GUI displayed, succeeding the code:

GUI_Not_OOP.py

```python
import tkinter as tk
from tkinter import ttk
from tkinter import scrolledtext
from tkinter import Menu

class OOP():
    def __init__(self):
        self.win = tk.Tk()
        self.win.title("Python GUI")
        self.createWidgets()

    def createWidgets(self):
        tabControl = ttk.Notebook(self.win)
        tab1 = ttk.Frame(tabControl)
        tabControl.add(tab1, text='Tab 1')
        tabControl.pack(expand=1, fill="both")
        self.monty = ttk.LabelFrame(tab1, text=' Mighty Python ')
        self.monty.grid(column=0, row=0, padx=8, pady=4)

        ttk.Label(self.monty, text="Enter a name:").grid(column=0,
                                                      row=0, sticky='W')
        self.name = tk.StringVar()
        nameEntered = ttk.Entry(self.monty, width=12,
                                  textvariable=self.name)
        nameEntered.grid(column=0, row=1, sticky='W')

        self.action = ttk.Button(self.monty, text="Click Me!")
        self.action.grid(column=2, row=1)

        ttk.Label(self.monty, text="Choose a number:")
                .grid(column=1, row=0)
        number = tk.StringVar()
        numberChosen = ttk.Combobox(self.monty, width=12,
                                      textvariable=number)
        numberChosen['values'] = (42)
        numberChosen.grid(column=1, row=1)
        numberChosen.current(0)

        scrolW = 30; scrolH = 3
        self.scr = scrolledtext.ScrolledText(self.monty, width=scrolW,
                                                height=scrolH, wrap=tk.WORD)
```

```
            self.scr.grid(column=0, row=3, sticky='WE', columnspan=3)

            menuBar = Menu(tab1)
            self.win.config(menu=menuBar)
            fileMenu = Menu(menuBar, tearoff=0)
            menuBar.add_cascade(label="File", menu=fileMenu)
            helpMenu = Menu(menuBar, tearoff=0)
            menuBar.add_cascade(label="Help", menu=helpMenu)

            nameEntered.focus()
#=============================
oop = OOP()
oop.win.mainloop()
```

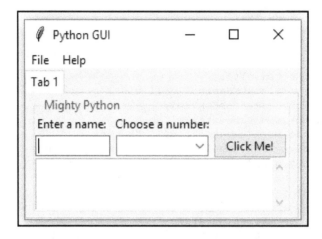

We can achieve the same GUI without using an OOP approach by restructuring our code slightly. First, we remove the OOP class and its __init__ method.

Next, we move all the methods to the left and remove the self class reference, which turns them into unbound functions.

We also remove any other self references our previous code had. Then, we move the createWidgets function call below the point of the function's declaration. We place it just above the mainloop call.

In the end, we achieve the same GUI but without using OOP.

The refactored code is shown as follows:

```
import tkinter as tk
from tkinter import ttk
from tkinter import scrolledtext
```

```
from tkinter import Menu

def createWidgets():
    tabControl = ttk.Notebook(win)
    tab1 = ttk.Frame(tabControl)
    tabControl.add(tab1, text='Tab 1')
    tabControl.pack(expand=1, fill="both")
    monty = ttk.LabelFrame(tab1, text=' Mighty Python ')
    monty.grid(column=0, row=0, padx=8, pady=4)

    ttk.Label(monty, text="Enter a name:").grid(column=0, row=0,
                                                sticky='W')
    name = tk.StringVar()
    nameEntered = ttk.Entry(monty, width=12, textvariable=name)
    nameEntered.grid(column=0, row=1, sticky='W')

    action = ttk.Button(monty, text="Click Me!")
    action.grid(column=2, row=1)

    ttk.Label(monty, text="Choose a number:").grid(column=1, row=0)
    number = tk.StringVar()
    numberChosen = ttk.Combobox(monty, width=12, textvariable=number)
    numberChosen['values'] = (42)
    numberChosen.grid(column=1, row=1)
    numberChosen.current(0)

    scrolW = 30; scrolH = 3
    scr = scrolledtext.ScrolledText(monty, width=scrolW,
                                    height=scrolH, wrap=tk.WORD)
    scr.grid(column=0, row=3, sticky='WE', columnspan=3)

    menuBar = Menu(tab1)
    win.config(menu=menuBar)
    fileMenu = Menu(menuBar, tearoff=0)
    menuBar.add_cascade(label="File", menu=fileMenu)
    helpMenu = Menu(menuBar, tearoff=0)
    menuBar.add_cascade(label="Help", menu=helpMenu)

    nameEntered.focus()
#=======================
win = tk.Tk()
win.title("Python GUI")
createWidgets()
win.mainloop()
```

How it works...

Python enables us to use OOP when it makes sense. Other languages like Java and C# force us to always use the OOP approach to coding. In this recipe, we explored a situation when it did not make sense to use OOP.

 The OOP approach will be more extendible if the codebase grows, but if it's certain that it is the only code that's needed, then there's no need to go through OOP.

How to use design patterns successfully

In this recipe, we will create widgets for our Python GUI by using the factory design pattern. In the previous recipes, we created our widgets either manually one at a time or dynamically in a loop. Using the factory design pattern, we will use the factory to create our widgets.

Getting ready

We will create a Python GUI that has three buttons, each having different styles.

How to do it...

Towards the top of our Python GUI module, just below the import statements, we create several classes:

```
import tkinter as tk
from tkinter import ttk
from tkinter import scrolledtext
from tkinter import Menu

class ButtonFactory():
    def createButton(self, type_):
        return buttonTypes[type_]()

class ButtonBase():
    relief     ='flat'
    foreground ='white'
    def getButtonConfig(self):
        return self.relief, self.foreground
```

```
class ButtonRidge(ButtonBase):
    relief      ='ridge'
    foreground ='red'

class ButtonSunken(ButtonBase):
    relief      ='sunken'
    foreground ='blue'

class ButtonGroove(ButtonBase):
    relief      ='groove'
    foreground ='green'

buttonTypes = [ButtonRidge, ButtonSunken, ButtonGroove]

class OOP():
    def __init__(self):
        self.win = tk.Tk()
        self.win.title("Python GUI")
        self.createWidgets()
```

We create a base class that our different button style classes inherit from and in which each of them overrides the `relief` and `foreground` configuration properties. All subclasses inherit the `getButtonConfig` method from this base class. This method returns a tuple.

We also create a button factory class and a list that holds the names of our button subclasses. We name the list `buttonTypes`, as our factory will create different types of buttons.

Further down in the module, we create the button widgets, using the same `buttonTypes` list:

```
def createButtons(self):

    factory = ButtonFactory()

    # Button 1
    rel = factory.createButton(0).getButtonConfig()[0]
    fg  = factory.createButton(0).getButtonConfig()[1]
    action = tk.Button(self.monty, text="Button "+str(0+1),
                    relief=rel, foreground=fg)
    action.grid(column=0, row=1)

    # Button 2
    rel = factory.createButton(1).getButtonConfig()[0]
    fg  = factory.createButton(1).getButtonConfig()[1]
    action = tk.Button(self.monty, text="Button "+str(1+1),
                    relief=rel, foreground=fg)
```

```
action.grid(column=1, row=1)

# Button 3
rel = factory.createButton(2).getButtonConfig()[0]
fg  = factory.createButton(2).getButtonConfig()[1]
action = tk.Button(self.monty, text="Button "+str(2+1),
                       relief=rel, foreground=fg)
action.grid(column=2, row=1)
```

First, we create an instance of the button factory and then we use our factory to create our buttons.

The items in the `buttonTypes` list are the names of our subclasses.

We invoke the `createButton` method and then immediately call the `getButtonConfig` method of the base class and retrieve the configuration properties using dot notation.

When we run the entire code, we get the following Python `tkinter` GUI:

GUI_DesignPattern.py

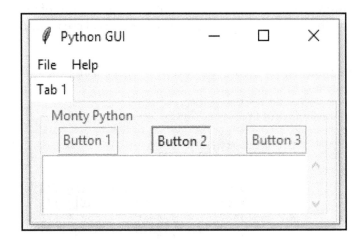

We can see that our Python GUI factory did indeed create different buttons, each having a different style. They differ in the color of their text and in their `relief` property.

How it works...

In this recipe, we used the factory design pattern to create several widgets that have different styles. We can easily use this design pattern to create entire GUIs.

Design patterns are a very exciting tool in our software development toolbox.

Avoiding complexity

In this recipe, we will extend our Python GUI and learn ways to handle the ever-increasing complexity of our software development efforts.

Our co-workers and clients love the GUIs we create in Python and ask for more and more features to add to our GUI.

This increases complexity and can easily ruin our original nice design.

Getting ready

We will create a new Python GUI similar to those in the previous recipes and will add many features to it in the form of widgets.

How to do it...

We will start with a Python GUI that has two tabs and which looks as follows. Running `GUI_Complexity_start.py` results in the following:

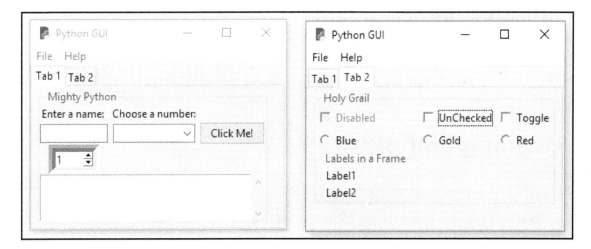

The first new feature request we receive is to add functionality to **Tab 1**, which clears the `scrolledtext` widget.

Easy enough. We just add another button to **Tab 1**:

```
# Adding another Button
self.action = ttk.Button(self.monty, text="Clear Text",
command=self.clearScrol)
self.action.grid(column=2, row=2)
```

We also have to create the callback method to add the desired functionality, which we define towards the top of our class and outside the method that creates our widgets:

```
# Button callback
def clickMe(self):
    self.action.configure(text='Hello ' + self.name.get())

# Button callback Clear Text
def clearScrol(self):
    self.scr.delete('1.0', tk.END)
```

Now, our GUI has a new button and, when we click it, we clear the text of the
ScrolledText widget. Running GUI_Complexity_start_add_button.py gives us that
new button:

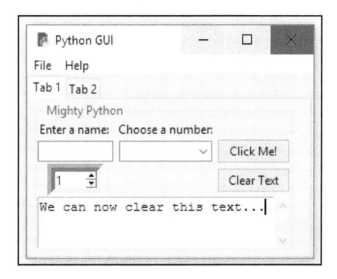

In order to add this functionality, we had to add code in two places in the same Python
module.

We inserted the new button in the createWidgets method (not shown) and then we
created a new callback method, which our new button calls when it is clicked. We placed
this code just below the callback of our first button.

Our next feature request is to add more functionality. The business logic is encapsulated in
another Python module. We invoke this new functionality by adding three more buttons to
Tab 1. We use a loop to do this:

```
# Adding more Feature Buttons
for idx in range(3):
    b = ttk.Button(self.monty, text="Feature" + str(idx+1))
    b.grid(column=idx, row=4)
```

Our GUI now looks like this, post running
`GUI_Complexity_start_add_three_more_buttons.py`:

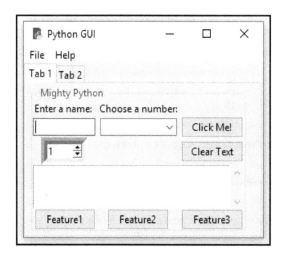

Next, our customers ask for more features and we use the same approach. Our GUI now looks as follows:

`GUI_Complexity_start_add_three_more_buttons_add_more.py`

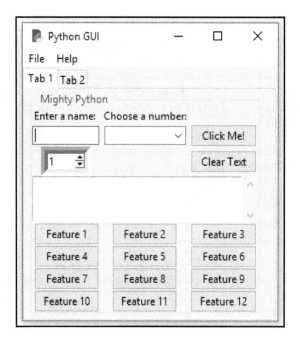

This is not too bad. When we get new feature requests for another 50 new features, we start to wonder if our approach is still the best approach to use...

One way to manage the ever-increasing complexity our GUI has to handle is by adding tabs. By adding more tabs and placing related features into their own tab, we get control of the complexity and make our GUI more intuitive.

Here is the code, `GUI_Complexity_end_tab3.py`, which creates our new **Tab 3**:

```
# Tab Control 3   -----------------------------------------
        tab3 = ttk.Frame(tabControl)           # Add a tab
        tabControl.add(tab3, text='Tab 3')     # Make tab visible

        monty3 = ttk.LabelFrame(tab3, text=' New Features ')
        monty3.grid(column=0, row=0, padx=8, pady=4)

        # Adding more Feature Buttons
        startRow = 4
        for idx in range(24):
            if idx < 2:
                colIdx = idx
                col = colIdx
            else:
                col += 1
            if not idx % 3:
                startRow += 1
                col = 0

            b = ttk.Button(monty3, text="Feature " + str(idx+1))
            b.grid(column=col, row=startRow)

        # Add some space around each label
        for child in monty3.winfo_children():
            child.grid_configure(padx=8)
```

Running the preceding code gives the following new Python GUI:

How it works...

In this recipe, we added several new widgets to our GUI in order to add more functionality to our Python GUI. We saw how more and more new feature requests easily got our nice GUI design into a state where it became less clear how to use the GUI.

 Suddenly, widgets took over the world...

We saw how to handle complexity by modularizing our GUI by breaking large features into smaller pieces and arranging them in functionally related areas using tabs.

While complexity has many aspects, modularizing and refactoring the code is usually a very good approach to handling software code complexity.

GUI design using multiple notebooks

In this recipe, we will create our GUI using multiple notebooks. Surprisingly, `tkinter` does not ship out of the box with this functionality, but we can easily design such a widget.

Using multiple notebooks will further reduce the complexity discussed in the previous recipe.

Getting ready

We will create a new Python GUI similar to the one in the previous recipe. This time, however, we will design our GUI with two notebooks. In order to focus on this feature, we will use functions instead of class methods.
Reading the previous recipe will be a good introduction to this recipe.

How to do it...

In order to use multiple notebooks within the same GUI, we start by creating two frames. The first frame will hold the notebooks and their tabs, while the second frame will serve as the display area for the widgets each tab is designed to display.
We use the grid layout manager to arrange the two frames, placing one above the other. Then, we create two notebooks and arrange them within the first frame:

```
#-------------------------------------------------------
# Create GUI
#-------------------------------------------------------
win = tk.Tk()                 # Create instance
win.title("Python GUI")    # Add title
#-------------------------------------------------------


win_frame_multi_row_tabs = ttk.Frame(win)
win_frame_multi_row_tabs.grid(column=0, row=0, sticky='W')

display_area = ttk.Labelframe(win, text=' Tab Display Area ')
display_area.grid(column=0, row=1, sticky='WE')

note1 = ttk.Notebook(win_frame_multi_row_tabs)
note1.grid(column=0, row=0)

note2 = ttk.Notebook(win_frame_multi_row_tabs)
note2.grid(column=0, row=1)
```

Next, we use a loop to create five tabs and add them to each notebook:

```
# create and add tabs to Notebooks
for tab_no in range(5):
    tab1 = ttk.Frame(note1, width=0, height=0)          # Create a tab for notebook 1
    tab2 = ttk.Frame(note2, width=0, height=0)          # Create a tab for notebook 2
    note1.add(tab1, text=' Tab {} '.format(tab_no + 1)) # Add tab notebook 1
    note2.add(tab2, text=' Tab {} '.format(tab_no + 1)) # Add tab notebook 2
```

We create a callback function and bind the click event of the two notebooks to this callback function. Now, when the user clicks on any tab belonging to the two notebooks, this callback function will be called:

```
# bind click-events to Notebooks
note1.bind("<ButtonRelease-1>", notebook_callback)
note2.bind("<ButtonRelease-1>", notebook_callback)
```

In the callback function, we add logic that decides which widgets get displayed after clicking a tab:

```
#-------------------------------------------------
def notebook_callback(event):
    clear_display_area()

    current_notebook = str(event.widget)
    tab_no = str(event.widget.index("current") + 1)

    if current_notebook.endswith('notebook'):
        active_notebook = 'Notebook 1'
    elif current_notebook.endswith('notebook2'):
        active_notebook = 'Notebook 2'
    else:
        active_notebook = ''

    if active_notebook is 'Notebook 1':
        if   tab_no == '1': display_tab1()
        elif tab_no == '2': display_tab2()
        elif tab_no == '3': display_tab3()
        else: display_button(active_notebook, tab_no)
    else:
        display_button(active_notebook, tab_no)
```

We add a function that creates a display area and another function that clears the area:

 Note how the callback function calls the `clear_display_area()` function.

```
    #------------------------------------------------
def create_display_area():
        # add empty label for spacing
        display_area_label = tk.Label(display_area, text="", height=2)
        display_area_label.grid(column=0, row=0)


    #------------------------------------------------
def clear_display_area():
        # remove previous widget(s) from display_area:
        for widget in display_area.grid_slaves():
            if int(widget.grid_info()["row"]) == 0:
                widget.grid_forget()
```

The `clear_display_area()` function knows both the row and column in which the widgets of tabs are being created, and by finding row zero, we can then use `grid_forget()` to clear the display.

For Tabs 1 to 3 of the first notebook, we create new frames to hold more widgets. Clicking any of those three tabs then results in a GUI very similar to the one we created in the previous recipe.

These first three tabs are being invoked in the callback function as `display_tab1()`, `display_tab2()`, and `display_tab3()` when those tabs are being clicked.

Here is the code that runs when clicking on **Tab 3** of the first notebook:

```
#--------------------------------------------------
def display_tab3():
    monty3 = ttk.LabelFrame(display_area, text=' New Features ')
    monty3.grid(column=0, row=0, padx=8, pady=4)

    # Adding more Feature Buttons
    startRow = 4
    for idx in range(24):
        if idx < 2:
            colIdx = idx
            col = colIdx
        else:
            col += 1
        if not idx % 3:
            startRow += 1
            col = 0

        b = ttk.Button(monty3, text="Feature " + str(idx + 1))
        b.grid(column=col, row=startRow)

    # Add some space around each label
    for child in monty3.winfo_children():
        child.grid_configure(padx=8)
```

Clicking any tab other than the first three tabs of notebook one calls the same function, `display_button()`, which results in a button being displayed whose text property is being set to show the notebook and tab number:

```
#--------------------------------------------------
def display_button(active_notebook, tab_no):
    btn = ttk.Button(display_area, text=active_notebook +' - Tab '+ tab_no, \
                     command= lambda: showinfo("Tab Display", "Tab: " + tab_no) )
    btn.grid(column=0, row=0, padx=8, pady=8)
```

Clicking any of these buttons results in a Message box.

At the end of the code, we invoke the `display_tab1()` function. When the GUI first starts up, the widgets of this tab are what get displayed in the display area:

```
# bind click-events to Notebooks
note1.bind("<ButtonRelease-1>", notebook_callback)
note2.bind("<ButtonRelease-1>", notebook_callback)

create_display_area()

create_menu()

display_tab1()

#-------------
win.mainloop()
#-------------
```

How it works...

Running the `GUI_Complexity_end_tab3_multiple_notebooks.py` code of this recipe creates the following GUI:

Clicking on **Tab 2** of the first notebook clears the tab display area and then displays the widgets created in the `display_tab2()` function:

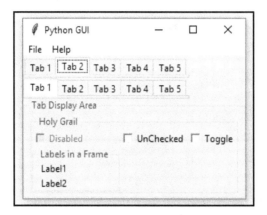

 Note how the tab display area automatically adjusts to the sizes of the widgets being created.

Clicking **Tab 3** results in the following GUI display:

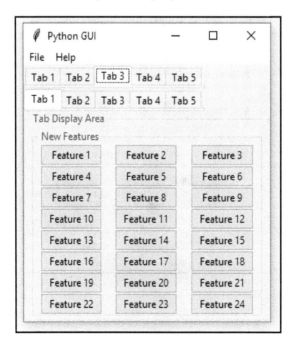

Clicking any other tab in either the first or the second notebook results in a button being displayed in the tab display area:

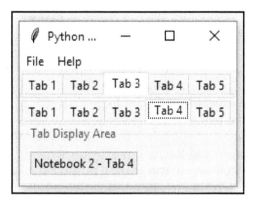

Clicking any of those buttons results in a Message Box:

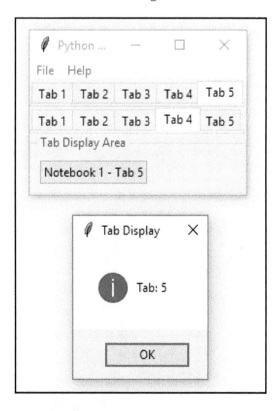

In this recipe, you learned how to create more than one notebook within the same GUI design.

There is no limit to creating notebooks. We can create as many notebooks as our design requires.

In programming, at certain times, we run into a wall and get stuck. We keep banging our head against this wall but nothing happens.
Sometimes, we feel like we want to give up.
Miracles do happen...
By keeping on banging against this wall, at a certain moment in time, the wall will collapse and the road will be open.
At that point in time, we can make a positive dent in the software universe...

Index